The religion of the poor is an ambitious survey of Catholic missions into the European countryside from 1500 to 1800. In it the distinguished French historian of religion Louis Châtellier, author of the acclaimed *Europe of the devout* (Cambridge, 1989), analyses the impulses to missionary activity at the end of the Middle Ages, and the specific conception of Ignatius Loyola. The author then outlines the development of missionary activity after the Council of Trent, particularly that of the Jesuits and the Capuchins: he details how these missions provided both a propagandistic counter to Protestantism in areas where the Reformation was a threat and also a revival of piety and doctrine in those areas not under such a threat.

In the second part Professor Châtellier discusses the type of religion proffered by the missionaries, examining a variety of key themes in Catholic belief, including the roles of the deity, of the cross and of Satan. The book contains a concluding summary of the impact of these rural missions up to the French Revolution, and documents the way in which they changed in reaction to external social and political circumstance.

Now available in English for the first time, *The religion of the poor* is an accessible insight into the rural religion of 1500–1800, and is suitable for students and scholars of European religious, social and cultural history at all levels.

The religion of the poor

The religion of the poor

Rural missions in Europe and the formation
of modern Catholicism, *c*.1500–*c*.1800

Louis Châtellier
Translated by Brian Pearce

CAMBRIDGE
UNIVERSITY PRESS

Maison des Sciences de l'Homme

PUBLISHED BY THE PRESS SYNDICATE OF THE UNIVERSITY OF CAMBRIDGE
The Pitt Building, Trumpington Street, Cambridge CB2 1RP, United Kingdom

CAMBRIDGE UNIVERSITY PRESS
The Edinburgh Building, Cambridge CB2 2RU, United Kingdom
40 West 20th Street, New York, NY 10011–4211, USA
10 Stamford Road, Oakleigh, Melbourne 3166, Australia

Originally published in French by Aubier as *La religion des pauvres: les missions rurales en Europe et la formation du catholicisme moderne xvième-xixème siècles*
© 1993, Aubier, Paris
First published in English by Cambridge University Press and Editions de la Maison des Sciences de l'Homme 1997 as *The religion of the poor: rural missions in Europe and the formation of modern catholicism, c. 1500–1800*
© in the English translation Cambridge University Press and Editions de la Maison des Sciences de l'Homme 1997

First published 1997

Printed in the United Kingdom at the University Press, Cambridge

Typeset in Plantin

A catalogue record for this book is available from the British Library

Library of Congress cataloguing in publication data

Châtellier, Louis.
[Religion des pauvres. English]
The religion of the poor: rural missions in Europe and the formation of modern Catholicism, c.1500 – c.1800 / Louis Châtellier; translated by Brian Pearce.
    p.   cm.
Includes bibliographical references and index.
ISBN 0 521 56201 5
1. Catholic Church – Missions – Europe – History. 2. Church work with the poor – Catholic Church – History. 3. Church work with the poor – Europe – History. 4. Catholic Church – Europe – History – Modern period, 1500–   .
5. Europe – Church history. 6. Europe – Religious life and customs.
I. Title.
BV2900.C4313   1997
266'.24–dc21   96-45552 CIP

ISBN 0 521 56201 5 hardback
ISBN 2–7351–0758–2 French only

CE

Contents

Illustrations

Figures

Preface

When we read the great writers we sometimes wonder if, in the seventeenth and eighteenth centuries, religion was a privilege of the rich. What, in the sermons, the pastoral letters and, still more, the works of spirituality by Bossuet, Fénelon and Massillon – who yet were bishops – could have been understood by the humble countryfolk of their dioceses? The Council of Trent (1545–63), which regulated religious life in Catholic countries for almost three centuries, made it an obligation for prelates to instruct the faithful. In every village there was a church and, almost everywhere, there was a priest responsible, under the guidance of his bishop, for instructing his parishioners and serving them the sacraments. What he said and what he thought of them is practically unknown to us. It may be that, before the beginning of the eighteenth century – meaning, until priests were trained in diocesan seminaries – their sermons and instructions, indeed their entire pastoral work, were in many cases confined to essentials. That was why the Popes and the bishops considered it useful to make up for this lack of zeal by sending missionaries into the towns and, especially, into the country districts. These missionaries stayed for eight days, fifteen days or a month in a certain place, where they instructed the people, prepared them for confession and communion, and tried to pacify quarrels and establish peace in the village before leaving for other places where they would perform the same task.

In Early Modern times (sixteenth to eighteenth centuries) those missionaries travelled around Europe while others were taking the Gospel to Asia or America. Both groups compiled reports for their superiors in which they described the regions and the people assigned to their care, the instruction they imparted and the sermons they delivered to them, the ceremonies they organised and, sometimes, the unusual events which they had had the opportunity to observe. These documents have been for several years objects of interest to historians and ethnologists specialising in the study of extra-European societies, and have provided them with very valuable information in all branches of knowledge. (See on this subject the works of Serge Gruzinski and his team about the American field of operations.)

As regards Europe it must be admitted that the documents in question are not interesting to ethnologists to the same extent as the others. The missionaries who wrote them were little concerned to describe a landscape that was familiar to them, or customs which often seemed similar to those they knew already. It is on how the Church's teachings were diffused among the poor, and also on how the latter received them, that the European missionaries' reports furnish information. Thanks to what they tell us, we can attempt our analysis of rural Christianity in the epoch of Baroque civilisation and in the age of Enlightenment.

A choice had to be made in carrying out this investigation. If I have dealt mostly with the eighteenth century this is, in the first place, because good studies on the previous period, especially in France, are already available (for example those of Alain Croix and Fanch Roudaut on Brittany and of Bernard Dompnier on Dauphiné). But it also seemed to me that an approach, by way of the missions, to the Catholic religion as it was on the eve of a crisis – that of the Enlightenment and the French Revolution – from which it was to emerge quite transformed might be a way of understanding, through its origins, the nature of present-day Catholicism.

This study covers a wide area of Western, Southern and Central Europe because it seemed to me hard to understand the history of Catholicism after the Council of Trent, and especially, perhaps, in the eighteenth century, without situating this history in a sufficiently extensive setting. There could be no question of covering all the European missions, even if this were possible, and still less of examining all the mission reports that still exist. What was essential was to work on a group of reports, all drawn from the same period (1700–70), but from different regions.

My search for mission reports took me from Naples to Rome, from Rome to Madrid, from Madrid to Paris, from Paris to Brussels, from Brussels to Zurich, from Zurich to Munich and Regensburg. I was excellently received in all these places, especially by the archivists of the various religious orders, both central and regional. Nor was that all: I shall always remember the fruitful discussions, about the past or the present, which accompanied me as I was writing these pages. Great institutions such as the French School in Rome, the Casa de Velazquez in Madrid and the Deutscher Akademischer Austauschdienst helped me at various stages of my research. To all I express my deepest thanks. As for my wife, who has been so closely associated with this protracted task, this book of mine is hers as well.

Abbreviations

ACJM Paris	Archives of the Congregation of Jesus and Mary (Eudists), Paris
AC, Paris	Archives of the Capuchin Fathers, Paris
ADMM	Departmental Archives of Meurthe-et-Moselle, Nancy
AHN, Madrid	Archivo Historico Nacional, Madrid
AJF, Vanves	Archives of the French Jesuits, Vanves
AN, Luxemburg	National Archives, Luxemburg
AN, Paris	National Archives, Paris
AOF	Archives de l'Oratoire de France
APM, Paris	Archives of the Missionary Fathers, Paris
ARB, Brussels	Belgian Royal Archives, Brussels
ARSI	Archivum Romanum Societatis Jesu, Rome
ASJ, Cologne	Archives of the Society of Jesus, Cologne
ASJ, Zurich	Archives of the Society of Jesus, Zurich
ASS, Paris	Archives of the Company of Priests of Saint-Sulpice, Paris
BH, Munich	Bayerisches Hauptstaatsarchiv, Munich
BM, Nancy	Municipal Library, Nancy
BN, Madrid	Biblioteca nacional, Madrid
BN, Paris	Bibliothèque Nationale, Paris
BSJ, Chantilly	Library of the Society of Jesus, Chantilly
BZAR	Bischöfliches Zentralarchiv Regensburg
CPF, Rome	Congregatio de Propaganda Fide, Rome
OP, Munich	Oberdeutsche Provinz SJ, Munich
SA, Mainz	Stadtarchiv, Mainz

Dictionaries

Catho.	*Catholicisme hier, aujourd'hui, demain*
DHGE	*Dictionnaire d'histoire et de géographie ecclésiastique*
DTC	*Dictionnaire de théologie catholique*
Dict.spir.	*Dictionnaire de spiritualité*
LTK	*Lexikon für Theologie und Kirche*

Part 1

The extent of the missions in Europe

In a famous book which influenced an entire generation, *La France, pays de mission?*, Henri Godin and Yves Daniel contrasted 'the lands of Christendom with the missionary lands'.[1] The former are those where the Gospel has already been fully preached and whose inhabitants have been instructed therein, even if they have subsequently forgotten it. The latter, in the authors' words, are those 'where there has so far been nothing'.[2] Such were most of the countries of Europe at the beginning of the Middle Ages, when Boniface and Columbanus undertook their great journeys. The situation was similar at the end of the nineteenth century in the new towns created by the Industrial Revolution, in which uprooted and huddled masses had forgotten their Christian traditions. Between these two phases Europe could be seen as being, on the whole, a Christian continent. However, this Christianity was for a long time in a fragile condition. Held in a pincer-grip, from the west and the south, and especially from the east, by conquering Islam, it felt, until the seventeenth century at least, that it was under threat. Torn apart within by the rival churches, their mutual excommunications and the wars they waged against each other, Christian Europe was never able, after the thirteenth century, to recover its lost unity. In the sixteenth century this division was intensified by the Reformation and the Council of Trent. Protestants and Catholics were thenceforth absolutely separate and very often in conflict. The situation was all the worse because, in those days, it was hard to distinguish between temporal and spiritual matters. Rulers looked on those of their subjects who did not practise the same religion as they did as being potential rebels. In many countries the rule laid down, or tacitly recognised, was: *cuius regio eius religio* (the religion of a country shall be that of its ruler). These principles also led rulers to intervene constantly in the management of their church. On their part, the spiritual authorities sought the rulers' support and themselves in some cases exercised actual power over

[1] Godin, Henri and Daniel, Yves, *La France, pays de mission?*, Lyons, L'Abeille, 1943.
[2] *Ibid.*, p. 20.

populations and over entire territories. The Pope was the head of a state, bishops were princes, and it could happen that a mere preacher, such as Savonarola in late-fifteenth-century Florence, became the master of a whole country.[3]

Consequently, there was always scope for missions in Europe. Their function was no longer to implant Christianity but to renew it in spirit and effects, to re-awaken Christians by recalling to their minds the teachings of Christ and his commandments. Only priests who were completely free (preferably, members of religious orders) and who were convinced of the need to resume unceasingly this work of evangelisation in town and country, without feeling bound to any parish or diocese, could be in a position to take upon themselves this apostolic activity.

[3] Antonetti, Pierre, *Savonarole, le prophète désarmé*, Paris, Perrin, 1990, p. 127.

I   From the Middle Ages to modern times

Itinerant preachers had long been traversing Europe in the task of reviving the faith of the inhabitants and reminding them of the penitence they needed. In the thirteenth century the Mendicant Orders had been founded with this as their main purpose, and in subsequent centuries they had undergone considerable development.[1] In France alone 800 friaries subject to the rule of St Francis of Assisi or of St Dominic had been established between 1250 and 1550.[2] Only at the end of the Middle Ages, however, did the type of great missionary able to gather crowds gain recognition in the Church, and only at the beginning of modern times was a precise method established for this form of apostleship.

The first great missionaries of modern Europe

As with the various reform movements that the Church had experienced, since the early Middle Ages, the initiative again came from the South. Italy and Spain provided the example. In Tuscany at the beginning of the fourteenth century the Franciscans had systematically established centres in the small towns from which they sent forth friars into the villages.[3] Later they were to install themselves in Southern Italy and proceed in the same way.[4] Much more spectacular, though, were the missions of Thomas Cornette, Vincent Ferrer or Bernardin of Siena.[5]

---

[1] Rapp, Francis, *L'Eglise et la vie religieuse en Occident à la fin du Moyen Age*, Paris, PUF (coll. 'Nouvelle Clio'), 1971, p. 126.

[2] Martin, Hervé, *Le Métier de prédicateur en France septentrionale à la fin du Moyen Age (1350–1520)*, Paris, Cerf, 1988, p. 146.

[3] La Roncière, Charles M. de, 'L'influence des Franciscains dans la campagne de Florence au XIVe siècle (1280–1360)', in *Mélanges de l'Ecole française de Rome, Moyen Age, Temps modernes*, 87, 1975/1, pp. 27–103.

[4] Cestaro, Antonio, 'Le structure ecclesiastiche del Mezzogiorno dal cinquecento all'eta contemporanea', in *Società et religione in Basilicata, Atti del convegno di Potenza-Matera* (1975), 2 vols., *Collana di studi storici*, s.l., D'Elia Editori spa., 1977, vol. I, pp. 179–219. See p. 200.

[5] On Thomas Cornette in northern France, see Martin, *Le Métier de prédicateur*, pp. 54–7 and 173–4.

In less than 20 years (1399–1419) the Dominican Vincent Ferrer travelled through Castile, Aragon and Catalonia, southern and central France and the eastern borderlands of that realm, from Lorraine to the southern Alps, northern Italy from Genoa to Bologna, western France from Caen to Angers, and Brittany, where he died. In this long apostolic march across Europe there is something reminiscent of the immense enterprises of men like Columbanus and Boniface at the beginning of the Middle Ages, though with more feverish haste, since everywhere he went the missionary stayed for only one or two weeks in the more important places, and usually for only a few days. He presented himself, moreover, in the guise of a mere pilgrim travelling on foot, with capacious cloak over his shoulders and staff in his hand. But he was not looking for holy relics. It was the faithful who came to meet him and who obtained miracles from him. Like Christ he preached as he walked, or settled cases of conscience that were put to him. As he drew near a village a long procession of flagellants took form, crying 'Mercy!' as they thrashed themselves with whips that they flung over their shoulders as hard as they could.[6] 'Since the outpouring of Our Saviour's blood', it was said of the flagellants in Tournai in 1349, 'there has been no such notable shedding of blood as they produced'.[7] The villagers, impelled to leave their houses, first saw a cloud of dust, then heard the cries and weeping, saw the cross that headed the procession, and trembled at the dull and rhythmic sound of the scourges as they beat the bloody backs. Soon the first groups were entering the village. The master followed, making his way to the church. When the crowd was too great it was led to a field where a platform had been hastily erected so that the missionary could be seen and heard by all.[8] The mournful procession was naturally followed by a sermon on the last things and the need for penitence.

The words of Vincent Ferrer, however, were more terrible still. What he proclaimed was nothing less than the end of time and the imminent arrival of the Antichrist who 'will come soon, very soon, quite soon'.[9] In Murcia his prophecy was still more precise: God's wrath was such, he declared, that within 'forty-five days' we shall all perish in fire from heaven.[10] It is easy to imagine the wave of panic that swept over the

---

[6] Gorce, Matthieu-Maxime, *Saint Vincent Ferrier (1350–1419)*, Paris, Plon, 1923, pp. 81–117 and 183–6.

[7] Martin, *Le Métier de prédicateur*, pp. 32–3.   [8] *Ibid.*, p. 55.

[9] Gorce, *Saint Vincent Ferrier*, p. 142. On preaching about the end of the world in the Christian West during the Middle Ages and the Early Modern period, see the classical work of Jean Delumeau, *Le Péché et la peur: la culpabilisation en Occident XIIIe–XVIIIe siècle*, Paris, Fayard, 1983.

[10] Gorce, *Saint Vincent Ferrier*, p. 144.

town – especially as this preacher who had come as a pilgrim from a faraway land often seemed, when out of his native region, Valencia, like a stranger unknown to anyone. Was this not the Angel of the Apocalypse come to announce, as was said in Scripture, the imminent end of the world? 'And so now', he added, 'you have only to reconcile yourselves and cleanse your consciences so as to receive at Easter the body of Our Lord.'[11] Imminent punishment and necessary penitence were the two parts of a sermon that aimed at immediate conversion of sinners. Once the shock effect had been produced, the penitent needed to be guided in examining, one by one, his various sins. Lust and quarrelling were the first to be nailed to the pillory. 'Make faggots for me of these weeds and cast them into the fire – one faggot for each of the seven deadly sins. Oh! Oh! With all these fine faggots, what a bonfire for the eternal brazier. There! Plop! Into the pan.'[12] Then, since, eventually, the goodwill shown by the population might well restrain the vengeful arm of the Almighty and the 'forty-five days' might turn into forty-five years, or even more, it was necessary to teach the people to live as Christians. On Sunday, he went on, do not be like those men sitting at table in the tavern who wait for the bell to ring for the elevation before hurrying to the church, 'like a mob of pigs in a sty'.[13] Be present, rather, throughout Mass, 'and when hearing it do not be idle, but have faith in God, saying to yourselves: my God whom we are now adoring, thou art the one God in three persons who has created all things'.[14] One should also say one's prayers every day. This is what a man from Limoges remembered from Brother Vincent's teaching: kneel when you get out of bed and say the *Pater*, the *Ave* and the *Credo*, cross yourself in the proper manner, and hear Mass, from beginning to end.[15] There could be added: flee from sin, from shameful distractions, from disguises 'in which human nature is distorted', from intemperance and from exaggerated fashions in women's dress.[16] Above all, in order to be saved, one must banish from one's mind all superstitions, one of the commonest of which consisted in deifying the stars, especially the sun, and worshipping them. In one of his sermons the preacher imagined the ascent of the elect into Paradise and made them converse with God. ' "What, Lord, is this the moon, then? How foolish were they who worshipped it, saying: moon, moon, my protectress . . ." Then they will rise into the other heavens, wondering at their beauty. And when they reach the fourth heaven, which is the sun, they will say: "What, Lord, hasn't the sun eyes? It's nothing but a stone that shines: how crazy were

---

[11] *Ibid.*, p. 144.   [12] *Ibid.*, pp. 162–8.   [13] *Ibid.*, p. 154.
[14] Martin, *Le Métier de prédicateur*, p. 357.   [15] *Ibid.*, pp. 607–8.
[16] *Ibid.*, p. 379; Gorce, *Saint Vincent Ferrier*, p. 154.

they who worshipped it." [17] Being well-informed as to the weakness of human nature, Vincent Ferrer cherished no illusions concerning the lasting conversion of his listeners after they had heard a few sermons. Accordingly he encouraged the creation, in the larger towns at least, of confraternities of flagellants who would maintain the spirit of penitence, if only among a few. [18]

Vincent Ferrer was not the only one to think about the consequences of his apostolic activity. One of his fellows in the Dominican order, Alain de La Roche, inspired a form of devotion that was destined to enjoy a great future in Christian Europe: telling, in honour of the fifteen joyful, sorrowful and glorious mysteries of the life of the Virgin, the same number of decades of one's beads. The rosary, as it was called, would become a fresh link between fervent souls who themselves were not slow to form themselves into confraternities. [19]

The fame of the missions of Vincent Ferrer, who left so great a memory, and who in many ways was the inspirer of a number of similar undertakings in the Baroque age, should not cause us to overlook the work of many religious who were his contemporaries or immediate successors. The Franciscan Bernardin of Siena (1380–1444) seems to have enjoyed in Italy a prestige comparable to that of Brother Vincent. While also arousing immense popular fervour, he nevertheless did not preach in the apocalyptic style that was often characteristic of the famous Dominican missionary. In the steps of Francis of Assisi, he was concerned to establish the reign of Christ here below, in an Italy torn apart by struggles between rival factions. The partisan 'dead with weapons in his hands must not expect any mercy in the after-life', he declared. [20] In order to prepare the future by changing men's hearts he caused the name of Jesus to be inscribed everywhere (and particularly wherever Guelph or Ghibelline symbols were to be seen) in the form of a monogram destined for great success: IHS, surrounded with golden rays. [21] In this way there developed another great devotion of modern times, that of the Holy Name of Jesus. His disciples were to carry on in the same direction and to emphasise still further some features of his teaching. A certain Brother Didier, in Picardy, urged his hearers, during

---

[17] Gorce, *Saint Vincent Ferrier*, pp. 130 and 181.

[18] *Ibid.*, pp. 184–6.

[19] *Ibid.*; Martin, *Le Métier de prédicateur*, pp. 606–7; *Dict. spir.*, vol. XIII, cols. 937–80 (art. 'Rosaire'); on the functioning of the confraternity, Jean-Claude Schmitt, 'Apostolat mendiant et société. Une confrérie dominicaine à la veille de la Réforme', *Annales ESC*, 1971/2, pp. 83–104.

[20] Thureau-Dangin, Paul, *Un Prédicateur populaire dans l'Italie de la Renaissance: Saint Bernardin de Sienne 1380–1444*, Paris, Plon, 1897, p. 213.

[21] *Ibid.*, p. 79; *Dict. spir.*, vol. VIII, cols. 1109–26.

Lent in 1455, to forgive each other's trespasses and become publicly reconciled.[22] Devotion to the Virgin was vigorously encouraged by Brother Bernardin. It was promoted no less at the end of the fifteenth century, by the Franciscans and Observants, who developed, in Spain, Italy and France, a new devotion: that of the Immaculate Conception of the Virgin.[23]

Matteo da Bascio and Ignatius Loyola: two conceptions of mission at the dawn of the sixteenth century

When in 1525 a Friar Minor Observant, Matteo da Bascio, decided, being equipped with an authorisation from Pope Clement VII, to preach freely all over the Papal States, he was continuing a Franciscan tradition made famous in the previous century by Bernardin of Siena.[24] However, this reformer who was to launch the Capuchins linked with his vocation a concern to go back as faithfully as possible to what the founder, Francis of Assisi, had wanted. Hence the rules adopted at the first chapter-general in 1536, 'to the end that [our congregation] may, like the impregnable Tower of David, have ramparts by means of which we can defend ourselves against all foes of the life-giving spirit of Our Lord Jesus Christ and all laxities contrary to the most fervent and seraphic zeal of our Father St Francis'.[25] Now, the 'spirit' of St Francis, wrote the Capuchins of the Marais convent in Paris at the beginning of their Annals, 'was none other than the conversion of sinners and the salvation of souls, so that his life was simply a continual mission'.[26] Yet a mission as understood by Matteo da Bascio, following the sainted founder of the Franciscans, could not consist of a continual apostolic pilgrimage. It had to take its place in a life divided between preaching among the people and austere retreats in places remote from them. The first Capuchins wrote:

And so that they [the preachers], in preaching to others, may not themselves become reprobate, let them from time to time cease to frequent the people and return to solitude, ascending, after the most sweet Saviour, the mountain of sacred prayer and contemplation, and remaining there until, filled with God, they are driven by the impetuosity of the Spirit once more to spread its divine

[22] Martin, *Le Métier de prédicateur*, pp. 78–9.
[23] *Ibid.*, p. 607; Thureau-Dangin, *Un Prédicateur populaire*, p. 213; *DTC*, vol. VII, 1, cols. 845–1218.
[24] *Catho.*, vol. I, cols. 1278–79; *LTK*, vol. VII, col. 173.
[25] *La Reigle et Constitutions des frères mineurs cappucins de S.François, reveües et de nouveau corrigées*, Arras, 1592, pp. 25–6.
[26] BN, Paris, MSS, Nouvelles acquisitions françaises 4135, fo. 61; *Recueil de ce qui s'est passé de plus notable en ce couvent du Marais, depuis son establissement en l'année 1622*.

mercies about the world, striving to blaze like Seraphim of divine love, so that they, being so hot, may bring warmth to others. And so doing, sometimes serving in Martha's ministry and sometimes in Mary's silence, they will follow, in a varied life, the example of Jesus Christ, who, after praying on the mountain, came down to the Temple to preach, just as he came down from Heaven to Earth in order to save souls.[27]

This passage shows how the work of mission was conceived, on the eve of the Council of Trent, by religious who were regarded as exemplary. Preaching to the people was doing the work of Martha – useful, indispensable, but by its nature inferior in value to listening to the Truth, the choice made by Mary.[28] According to the Capuchins' rule, the true missionary thus had to devote the greater part of his time to meditation, in silence, retreat and privation, and then, when impelled once more by the Spirit, to descend from 'the mountain' to address the people. His sermons would thus have meaning and would not risk betraying 'the naked and humble Crucified'.[29] It was to satisfy this requirement as much as out of fidelity to 'holy humility' that the rule ordered missionaries to take with them nothing but the Holy Scriptures, and especially the New Testament, 'because in Jesus Christ are all the treasures of divine wisdom and knowledge'.[30] The preacher thus inspired became truly an emissary of God, almost a prophet. Was it not natural to expect from him surprising revelations about the future and miraculous cures, as so many signs proving that he had been sent from God?

The life of Ignatius Loyola, the founder of the Society of Jesus, was likewise a 'continual mission'. But it became so through a decision carefully thought-out, the stages of which were reproduced in that guide to the inner life and perfect conversion, the *Spiritual Exercises*. After a first week devoted to acquiring self-knowledge, awareness of his faults and confession of them, comes the moment when the retreatant is brought to make his choice. At the very heart of the *Exercises*, on the fourth day of the second week, we find the meditation on the two standards, that of Christ and that of Lucifer, when the Christian is called on 'to see how the Lord of the whole world Himself sends forth throughout the Earth the apostles He has chosen, His disciples and other ministers, so that they may spread among men of every kind, estate and condition His sacred and saving doctrine'.[31] Carrying out a mission meant fulfilling the expressed will of Christ who, when he

---

[27] *La Reigle*, pp. 101–2.   [28] Luke, X, 38–42.
[29] *La Reigle*, p. 97.   [30] *Ibid.*, p. 100.
[31] Ignace de Loyola, *Ecrits*, translated and presented under the direction of Maurice Giuliani, SJ, by a group of Jesuit Fathers, with the collaboration of Pierre-Antoine Fabre and Luce Giard, Paris, Desclée de Brouwer, 1991, p. 127, *Exercices spirituels*.

appeared to the Apostles for the last time, in Galilee, repeated his wish: 'Go ye therefore and teach all nations . . . ' (Matthew, XXVIII, 19). For a Society that was to bear the name of Jesus there could be no holier activity than fulfilling the last order given by Christ.

Ignatius consecrated himself very early to his mission. In 1535, at Azpeitia in Guipúzcoa, on returning to his native land after his studies in Paris, he refused to lodge with his brother and went to live in the poorhouse. There he led the life of the poor, begging alms around the country. He instructed the unfortunates who were with him and went out regularly to teach the catechism to the village children. On Sundays and feast-days he preached to audiences that rapidly increased to thousands of persons. He also attacked abuses and sought aid from the civil power in suppressing them – gambling and concubinage of girls with priests in particular. He caused measures to be taken to renew the religious life of the village, such as those relating to the maintenance of the poor or the ringing of church bells three times a day, in the morning, at noon and in the evening, so as to accustom the people to say the *Ave Maria*.[32] In the years that followed, Ignatius, together with his first comrades Laynez, Favre and Jaÿ, undertook missions on a larger scale, in Italy. In Venice and Rome he preached and held catechism sessions. He began conducting the *Spiritual Exercises* with priests. In small towns and big villages he combined, as he had in Guipúzcoa, assistance to the poor with public reconciliations between hostile families, and endeavoured to bring as many persons as possible to confession.

Thus, the mission as Ignatius and his comrades understood it was, in contrast to the concept of the first Capuchins, the holy work *par excellence* to which the members of the Society of Jesus were to devote themselves exclusively. In order to be effective, however, it had to be conducted in accordance with precise rules.

How Ignatius Loyola thought missions should be carried out

One of the reasons for the power that the Society of Jesus acquired very soon was the capacity which its founder possessed, to a high degree, for translating ideas into instructions, instructions into rules, and rules into concerted actions upon people and institutions. This was what Ignatius called 'reforming the world'. The first stage was 'discovery' of the sacredness and primacy of missions. The second stage was reached with the *Spiritual Exercises*: what was a mission according to Christ? To this

[32] *Ibid.*, pp. 1064–5, *Récit*, 8.

he replied by grouping into three points the contents of chapter X of St Matthew's Gospel. First, Jesus conferred on his disciples the power to drive out devils and cure the sick, then he taught them prudence and patience ('Be ye therefore wise as serpents and harmless as doves'), and, finally, he told them how to go about their work: 'Provide neither gold nor silver . . . Freely ye have received, freely give . . . ', and what they were to preach: 'And as ye go, preach, saying, "The Kingdom of heaven is at hand." '[33]

But how were they to proceed in practice? (Ignatius wrote *El modo de proceder*) The *Constitutiones circa missiones*, one of the first drafts, composed by Ignatius in 1544–5, of the future Constitutions, gave the necessary instructions. Pilgrims wandering as their inspiration might lead them were not to Ignatius' taste. The head of the Society alone was empowered to send forth missionaries, and it was for him to decide their destination. 'And because what is good is more divine the more universal it is', we read in the *Constitutions*, 'we must give preference to persons and places that, after having benefited from it themselves, will cause what is good to be extended to many others who are under their authority or take them as their model.'[34] Preference is therefore to be given to 'persons of high rank', such as princes or prelates, and, for the same reason, 'great nations' like India, or important towns, are to have priority.[35] An entire strategy was thus revealed, requiring of the missionary an apostleship conducted with discernment and political sense.[36] Moreover, these rules allowed of no exceptions and were applicable equally to Christian Europe and to the 'infidel' Indies. This is why Francis Xavier can be regarded as the first Jesuit who applied them on a large scale and whose reports sent to Rome served as instructions for all who went on mission.[37] Ignatius and his first comrades who remained in Italy conformed to them no less closely. After the Guipúzcoa episode it was substantial cities like Venice and Rome that benefited from the preaching of the Society's founder.[38] He chose with care the places and persons whither and to whom he sent his religious. The Viceroy of Naples and the Republic of Genoa were chosen because

[33] *Ibid.*, pp. 198–201, *Exercices spirituels*, para. 218.
[34] *Ibid.*, p. 548, *Constitutions*, 622.
[35] *Ibid.*, pp. 548–9.
[36] Durand, Dominique, *La Politique de Saint Ignace de Loyola*, Paris, Cerf, 1985.
[37] François Xavier, St, *Correspondance 1535–1552, lettres et documents*, translated and presented by Hugues Didier, Paris, Desclée de Brouwer, 1987. See his 'Instruction pour les catéchistes de la Compagnie' (in the Indies), dated from Molucca, 10 November 1545, pp. 168–71.
[38] Ignace de Loyola, *Ecrits*, pp. 1067–73, *Récit*, 9 and 10; Ravier, André, SJ, *La Compagnie de Jésus sous le gouvernement d'Ignace de Loyola (1541–1556): d'après les chroniques de J. A. de Polanco*, Paris, Desclée de Brouwer, 1991, pp. 22 and 32.

much support and the greatest advantage for future establishments could be expected from them.[39] However, Ignatius did not forget the rebel lands, those in which 'the enemy of Christ Our Lord has sown tares'. It was appropriate to send to them the best men available, 'especially where an important place was in question'.[40] That was how Peter Canisius came to be sent to the Emperor and the Duke of Bavaria, with a field of activity covering all the German-speaking lands of Central and Eastern Europe.[41]

Nothing was left to chance. The way the religious sent on campaign were to use their time was determined with the greatest care. At first, mention was made only of the three functions practised by Ignatius himself in his first missions, namely, the catechism, preaching and assistance to the poor. In 1540, however, a fourth activity appeared which was destined to become central: preparing the faithful as a whole for examination of conscience with a view to confession and communion.[42] Thereafter the *Spiritual Exercises* for the first week, which culminate precisely in reconciliation with God, were to serve as a pillar of the Jesuit missions. The meditations on sin, hell and penitence which constituted their main points were used as themes for different sermons.[43]

Thus, a concept of the mission, modern in its spirit, objective and methods, had already been fully worked out and put into practice even before the Council of Trent opened. What remained was to spread it about the world and adapt it to circumstances.

[39] Ravier, *La Compagnie de Jésus*, pp. 143 (1551) and 239 (1554).
[40] Ignace de Loyola, *Ecrits*, p. 548, *Constitutions*, 622.
[41] Ravier, *La Compagnie de Jésus*, pp. 109–10 (1549); Brodrick, J., SJ, *Saint Peter Canisius*, Baltimore, The Carroll Press, 1950.
[42] Ravier, *La Compagnie de Jésus*, pp. 23–6 ('Premières missions en Italie des pères Laynez, Favre et Jaÿ, SJ').
[43] *Ibid.*, pp. 133–4 (1556).

2   The spirit of the Council

Study of the work of Ignatius Loyola leads us naturally to the Catholic Reformation. This was, in fact, no new construction emerging from the insight of a few exceptional men. It meant above all the organising and harmonising of a number of initiatives which had appeared, in some cases several centuries earlier, in a disconnected way in various parts of Europe, in the apostolic and pastoral sphere. This rationalisation – which was doubtless not unrelated to the birth of modern thought – appeared at a time when a need for it was especially strongly felt. The Church could no longer rely on the inspiration of this or that missionary when its field of operation had expanded so considerably, both westward and eastward, as a result of the great geographical discoveries. Threatened in its European homeland by the advance of Islam on the borders of the Holy Roman Empire, and in its very heart by the Lutheran and Calvinist 'Reformation', it had with all urgency to take the measures necessary to confront this new situation. The Council of Trent (1545–63) was convened for that purpose. Then it still remained to put into practice the decisions adopted by the Council and, what was doubtless more important still, the spirit that had inspired them. The missions, remodelled and adapted to the new circumstances, served as the instrument for that task.

Reformation and Counter-Reformation

The great importance of the Council of Trent in the history of modern Catholicism is due to its twofold character as an operation of combat against the Protestants and an enterprise for renovating the Roman Church.[1] Accordingly, it is conventional nowadays to describe this dual function by the terms 'Counter-Reformation' and 'Catholic Reformation'. The first of these terms relates essentially to matters of doctrine. After firmly denouncing Luther and Calvin, for whom the sources of the faith were to be found exclusively in the Scriptures, the bishops

[1] Héfelé, Charles-Joseph, and Leclerc, Dom H., *Histoire des conciles*, vol. X: *Les Décrets du concile de Trente*, ed. A. Michel, Paris, Letouzey et Ané, 1938.

assembled at the Council affirmed the eminent position, alongside Holy Writ, due to tradition, meaning the teaching of the Fathers of the Church and of the bishops themselves. They especially attacked the Reformers' doctrine according to which man is saved by faith. To this they counterposed salvation by grace, a gift from God which man comes to deserve through his works. Among the latter were not only the traditional works of mercy directed towards one's neighbour but also the practice of the seven sacraments (baptism, confession, eucharist, confirmation, marriage or, for priests, ordination, and extreme unction), whereas the Protestants retained only two of these: baptism and eucharist. The power of the intercessors – the Virgin and the Saints, venerated in the form of their images or relics – was confirmed, whereas this was formally rejected by the Protestants. The latter conceived the Church only in its invisible form of the assembly of the elect, whereas for Catholics it was quite visible, with a well-defined hierarchy (Pope, bishops, priests). And the priesthood of all men proclaimed by Luther and the reformers horrified the participants in the Council.

At the same time, the Council was unwilling to leave to the Lutherans and Calvinists alone the privilege of standing for reform. That, too, should be a matter of concern for Catholics, provided it was effected within the Church. Bishops were reminded of their principal duties. They were required to reside in their dioceses so that, in particular, they could regularly visit all the parishes in their charge, in order to restore discipline and check on the orthodoxy of what was being taught there. To this end a measure of great importance had been taken. It consisted in obliging every bishop to found an establishment wherein future priests would be prepared for the tasks before them. These were the seminaries. Even more important was the obligation imposed on every believer to know his religion. This was a major turning-point in the history of Christianity (already announced by the Protestant reformers): henceforth, in order to be saved, one had to know. The catechism, at least in its essential articles, as brought together in Pius IV's Profession of Faith (1564), must be known by all.[2] Furthermore, all must be instructed in it and be able to draw the conclusions from it in everyday life. During three centuries, at least, this was the task performed by the missionaries in town and country. This was why, at first, they made no great difference between regions affected by Protestantism and regions unaffected thereby. All had need of instruction. Perhaps they also thought that, given instruction, persons who had gone astray would immediately be undeceived and converted.

[2] *Ibid.*, pp. 638–41; Dhotel, Jean-Claude, SJ, *Les Origines du catéchisme moderne*, Paris, Aubier, 1967.

The first Jesuits followed the example of their founder. They lived 'like the Apostles' and preached the points for meditation offered in the first week of the *Spiritual Exercises*. In Calabria Father Alfonso Bobadilla went from village to village, followed, like Vincent Ferrer before him, by those who wanted to profit by his words.[3] His colleague Andrea Oviedo, who was sent by Ignatius in 1552 to Rome and Naples, preached at each stage of his journey in the main square. He began by accosting people in the street, inviting them to follow him. Then he addressed the crowd he had got together. Some people often followed him to the hostelry where he continued his sermon. After that he heard confessions until late into the night.[4] Father Silvestro Landini, who won a great reputation all over Italy during his brief ministry (1547–54), worked in the same way, traversing entire dioceses (e.g., Modena). But he had a predilection for the islands, which had frequently been neglected by their natural pastors. He spent more than a month on Capri and nearly two years in Corsica (1552–4), when he visited most of that island.[5] On the other side of Europe Father Bernard Olivier was doing the same thing in the dioceses of Tournai and Cambrai in 1554. He wrote to Ignatius about himself and his partner: 'We have instructed many people whom we met on the road, in inns and elsewhere, especially in the monasteries where we have often preached. Everywhere crowds gathered to hear our sermons, even on working days.'[6] When he went from one village to another 'the crowd followed, as in times past the Jews followed Our Lord', a witness recorded, 'and as he walked along he heard confessions, settled doubts, gave decisions and comforted souls'.[7] When they put up somewhere it was usually, as with Ignatius, the poorhouse that they chose for their lodging, or else a hermitage. That was the case with Francis Borgia, preaching in Guipúzcoa in 1552 around the hermitage of the Magdalene near Oñate, where he had hidden himself. He lived like one of the poor, begging alms – 'which', wrote the Society's chronicler, 'was preaching by deed'.[8]

The 'apostolic' life, though edifying, was not enough. In the deed of foundation of the college which he caused to be established at Murcia in 1557, the Bishop of Cartagena, Estevan de Almeida, specified that certain Jesuit fathers 'will have to leave the see in order to preach the Gospel and teach Christian doctrine to the faithful, performing all the works of charity that their rules require of them'.[9] Preaching, the

---

[3] Guidetti, Armando, SJ, *Le missioni popolari: i grandi Gesuiti italiani*, Milan, Rusconi, 1988, p. 14; Ravier, *La Compagnie de Jésus*.

[4] Guidetti, *Le missioni popolari*, p. 36.   [5] *Ibid.*, pp. 21–9.

[6] Poncelet, Alfred, *Histoire de la Compagnie de Jésus dans les anciens Pays-Bas*, Publications de l'Académie royale de Belgique, vol. XXI, in 2 parts, Brussels, 1927, part 1, p. 65.

[7] *Ibid.*, pp. 71–2.   [8] Ravier, *La Compagnie de Jésus*, p. 186.

[9] AHN, Madrid, *Jesuitas*, 124, p. 557.

catechism and charity were already the three basic functions of a mission, as Ignatius himself had practised them in Guipúzcoa. The information we have on the activity of Father Landini, when he was sent, some years earlier, to Corsica, is more precise. His preaching dealt first and foremost with the 'three sins' described in the *Spiritual Exercises*. The first was that of the angels who, out of pride, revolted against their creator. The second was original sin, and the third 'the particular sin of each individual'.[10] From this theme he passed to death, judgment and hell, with descriptions that made his listeners tremble. These sermons were delivered in the morning and the evening, framing the lesson in Christian doctrine, aimed at everyone, young and old, which took place in the afternoon. At a time when there could be no question of the Council of Trent's catechism, which had not yet been completed, or even of Peter Canisius' manual, this teaching was conducted in accordance with a method laid down by Ignatius himself. It began by starting from what should be known by any Christian – the Ten Commandments. The preacher took the first commandment, explained what it orders and what it forbids, how one keeps it and how one disobeys it, and made his listeners ask forgiveness for their violations of this commandment and pray for grace to obey it in future. He did the same with the other commandments and then with the articles of the *Credo* and the requests in the *Pater*.[11] In this manner were bound together in the same instruction an introduction to the fundamental prayers and knowledge of Christian doctrine with the basic elements of a Christian life. The intended conclusion was confession by the entire community. Olivier was acting similarly at Tournai in the same period. 'In his sermons', a contemporary wrote, 'he dealt with matters neither high-flown nor curious, but what served his purpose, which was to implant in his listeners' hearts the fear and love of God . . . The fruit of his preaching was confessions by all sorts of people, from morning till evening and often into part of the night.'[12] The sacrament of penitence was, of course, not entirely unfamiliar to these populations, but, as the same observer remarked, 'most of those who come to us have never before confessed fully, either from false shame or from ignorance'.[13]

Instructing and causing the sacraments to be practised – these were the guiding principles of the missionaries in South and North alike. In Tournai and its neighbourhood, however, Lutheranism was seriously

[10] Ignace de Loyola, *Ecrits*, pp. 80–5, *Exercices spirituels*, 80–2.
[11] Guidetti, *Le missioni popolari*, pp. 25–7.
[12] Poncelet, *Histoire*, part 1, p. 67.
[13] *Ibid.*, p. 72.

present in the middle of the sixteenth century.[14] But this did not lead Father Olivier to modify the themes of his sermons. His chief concern, according to one of his colleagues, was 'to stir up Catholics to show themselves frankly to be such'.[15] This consideration took precedence over everything else, including desire to engage in controversy. It revealed clearly what the principal objective of missionaries was in the period of the Council.

Already, however, an evolution could be observed. This was shown in the activity and works of Peter Canisius.[16] Sent by Ignatius into Germany to defend there Roman orthodoxy against the infiltrations of heresy among clergy and laity alike, he came to the conclusion that preaching was not enough, even with backing from the princes and bishops. What was needed was to supervise the formation of priests and of secular elites. To this end the University of Dillingen was founded and that of Ingolstadt transformed in accordance with the Tridentine spirit (1556). It was necessary also to check on the religious instruction being given to schoolchildren and students, and to Christians generally. With this intention he compiled his famous catechism, the different versions of which ('small', 'medium', 'large') were aimed at adapting the content to the varying capacities of children and adults. This very soon became the favourite tool of missionaries who wanted both to instruct the people and to warn them against Protestantism.[17] One of the first to use it was Father Antonio Possevino, SJ, who launched in Piedmont, with the aid of the bishops and of the clergy both secular and regular, a veritable crusade against the Calvinism which was spreading among the Vaudois and other subjects of the Duke of Savoy (1560).[18] In Alsace a few years later the first representatives of the Society of Jesus called in by the bishop undertook a similar task.[19] Thousands of copies of Canisius' catechism were distributed in the villages to all who could read – priests, schoolmasters, notables.

Soon, however, it was not enough to spread the 'pure' doctrine and preserve the faithful from anything that might shake their beliefs. When

[14] Halkin, Léon-E., *La Réforme en Belgique sous Charles-Quint*, Brussels, La Renaissance du Livre, 1957.
[15] Poncelet, *Histoire*, part 1, p. 72 (1556).
[16] Brodrick, *Saint Peter Canisius*.
[17] Bellinger, G., *Der Catechismus Romanus und die Reformation*, Paderborn, Bonifacius, 1970, pp. 48–53.
[18] Guidetti, *Le missioni popolari*, p. 45; Scaduto, Mario, 'Le missioni di A. Possovino in Piemonte. Propaganda calvinista e Restaurazione cattolica 1560–1563', *Archivum Historicum Societatis Jesu*, 1959/1, pp. 51–191.
[19] Barth, Medard, 'Die Seelsorgetätigkeit der Molsheimer Jesuiten von 1580 bis 1765', *Archiv für elsässische Kirchengeschichte*, 1931, pp. 325–400. See p. 336, note 4 (1582 and subsequent years, distribution of 17,000 volumes in the diocese of Strasburg).

the adversary, having become powerful, seemed likely to carry all before him, he had to be attacked directly. In 1566–7 the wave of iconoclasm swept over the Low Countries. This immense popular and religious movement targeted the monasteries, but also the traditional faith in its attachment to sacred things present in this world – images of saints, relics, processions or pilgrimages to a venerated place.[20] In Antwerp Father François Coster, known as 'the hammer of the heretics' (just as, a little earlier, there had been talk of a 'hammer of the witches'), publicised his sermons by means of posters in all public places – markets, churches, the Stock Exchange.[21] In Maastricht Father Henri Denis, SJ, guarded by armed co-religionists, preached three times a day 'until he could no longer speak a single word', as he wrote. In January 1567 he uttered a cry of triumph: 'I have already deprived them of over a thousand of their followers!'[22]

A comparable offensive policy was adopted in France during the Wars of Religion. In 1570, by order of King Charles IX and his adviser the Cardinal of Lorraine, a group of Jesuits which included the well-known scholar Jean Maldonat was sent to Poitiers and its neighbourhood. They were concerned 'to root out the impressions that the people had received from the new religion', wrote the author of an account of this mission.

> They preached there without respite, engaged in controversy and taught the catechism, so that all the sectaries were convinced and hardly one was left who did not think of abandoning his errors, which they would willingly have done if the King's authority had compelled them . . . After accomplishing this fine work they then took steps to ensure that divine service was performed with decorum and ceremony. That was why they caused the churches to be decorated. They strengthened the old Catholics, supporting them in their piety. Then they spoke of setting up a Jesuit college in the town.[23]

The construction of this passage is informative. Controversy with the heretics and their instruction is followed by a mission among the 'old Catholics', the results of which need to be consolidated by a permanent institution, the college. Here we perceive an entire strategy which shows that the college was the culmination of a short apostolic action, lasting no more than three or four weeks.

This process was, perhaps, not exceptional. It shows the relation that existed between the Society's houses, including those intended for

[20] Deyon, Solange, and Lottin, Alain, *Les 'Casseurs de l'été 1566': l'iconoclasme dans le Nord*, Paris, Hachette, 1981; for France, Christin, Olivier, *Une Révolution symbolique: l'iconoclasme huguenot et la reconstruction catholique*, Paris, Minuit, 1991.
[21] Poncelet, *Histoire*, part 1, p. 272 (1556).
[22] *Ibid.*, pp. 249–50.
[23] BM, Nancy, MS 40 (P. Abram, SJ), *Histoire manuscrite de l'université de Pont-à-Mousson*, translation and notes by Murigothus, 1756, 8 vols., vol. II, pp. 172–4.

teaching, and the missions. Although the University of Pont-à-Mousson, in Lorraine (another of the Cardinal of Lorraine's foundations), was established in 1572 to form a Francophone Catholic elite, just as Ingolstadt was to perform the corresponding task in the German-speaking lands, it also had the function, from the outset, to instruct townspeople who had abjured Calvinism 'out of fear of the laws' issued by the Duke, but who in the depths of their hearts were still remote from what they were being taught. 'For heresy', wrote one of the Fathers of Pont-à-Mousson, 'had struck such strong roots in their hearts, especially because of the proximity of the town of Metz, which was almost wholly infected with the errors of the time.'[24] The Jesuits therefore employed themselves in multiplying sermons and catechism sessions in the town and its neighbourhood. In 1581 the Duke entrusted them with a still larger task. This was to 'uproot error' in all parts of the Duchy, including the remotest towns where it might be hiding. Two missionaries set out, staff in hand, and began with Sainte-Marie-aux-Mines, a town which the Duke of Lorraine shared with the Lutheran Counts of Ribeaupierre, and where there were numerous miners who had come from eastern Germany and Bohemia. 'The inhabitants of these two towns [the two parts of Sainte-Marie-aux-Mines] whom neither laws nor writings had been able to restrain were infected with the errors of the time and lived in great licentiousness.'[25] From there they moved to Saint-Dié and then to Nancy, where they presided over the initiation of a confraternity of the Holy Sacrament. At Saint-Nicolas-de-Port, famous as a place of pilgrimage and also for its fairs, which Protestant merchants attended in great numbers, they busied themselves with persuading these visitors that 'the new religion which they had embraced was a manifest heresy'. From there they went to Remiremont, to preach in Advent, and crossed the whole width of the Duchy to Gondrecourt in the far west, 'a small town into which heresy had insinuated itself little by little'. It is worthy of remark that the method used in Lorraine was in no way different from that already described for Poitou: 'They converted many souls to God', writes the annalist, 'and strengthened in their piety those who had not yet renounced the true religion, while causing to be proscribed and expelled those who were most stubborn in their errors and did not wish to receive their wise instruction.'[26] The need to distinguish between 'old Catholics' and Christians who were more or less affected by 'the new religion', or had been converted to a wavering faith, was something new. This was one of the immediate consequences of the Council of Trent.

[24] *Ibid.*, vol. III, pp. 12–13.   [25] *Ibid.*, vol. III, p. 59.

[26] *Ibid.*; on Protestantism in Lorraine, Châtellier, Louis, ed., *Les Réformes en Lorraine 1520–1620*, Nancy, PUN, 1986.

The missionaries on the ground soon became aware of the abyss that separated Protestants from Catholics. They formed two distinct communities to whom one could no longer speak the same language. Those loyal to the Church needed to be 'strengthened', 'fortified': that is to say, instructed. They had to be taught to know a religion whose rituals should now be performed with 'decorum' and 'ceremony'. As for the other Christians who were disinclined to listen to preachers for whom they felt no need, they would be brought to conversion only by the order and authority of the prince.

The will to conquer

In its closing decree the Council of Trent expressly asked for the support of the temporal power in disposing of irreconcilables. It was a Christian prince's duty to go to the aid of the Church in order to put into effect, *manu militari* if necessary, the decrees promulgated by its supreme assembly.[27]

When Charles III of Lorraine ordered the mission of 1581 he had acted in that spirit.[28] This was the case, too, with Archduke Ferdinand when he established Jesuit missionaries throughout Tyrol by his licence of 22 January 1591.[29] But when the clergy took up the Council's decree they demanded more than that. They desired that the prince show clearly his will to make all his subjects good Catholics and that he accompany his order, where necessary, with measures of constraint.

During the entire period of his mission in Chablais (1595–8) François de Sales, like Jean Maldonat in Poitou twenty years earlier, kept coming back to this question. In the first months of the mission he regretted strongly the reserve shown by Charles-Emmanuel, the Duke of Savoy, who failed to support the preachers' efforts with a solemn gesture. If the Duke were firmly to invite his subjects to come and hear the sermons of François and his companions, the latter would no longer find themselves speaking, François hoped, in empty churches. The villagers, indeed, 'usually protest that they have no other rule for their religion than the will of the Prince who, as they say, is better listened to than they are'.[30] When, at last, the duke did adopt rigorous measures forbidding the

---

27 Héfelé and Leclerc, *Histoire*, vol. X, pp. 630–1: 'That the Council's decrees are to be received and observed'.
28 Cf. above p. 18.
29 OP, Munich, *Germania Sup.*, II, 11.
30 Kleinemann, Ruth, *Saint François de Sales et les protestants*, trans. Fr. Delteil, Collection 'Parole et tradition', Lyons, 1967, p. 136. The text is taken from François de Sales, *Œuvres*, vol. XXII, p. 143, 'Mémoire à Charles-Emmanuel', May–June 1595.

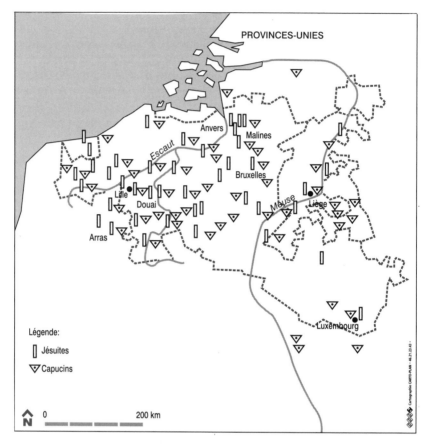

Map 1   The mission centres of the Jesuits and the Capuchins in the southern Netherlands, *c.* 1640.

exercise of Protestant worship and banishing inveterate heretics from his realm (1598), François de Sales approved, saying that 'by this means many will avoid suffering banishment from Paradise so as not to incur banishment from their homeland'. As for those who, in spite of everything, refused to abjure, he explained to the Duke that they were 'persons whose loyalty has already been perverted and who follow Huguenotism more as a party than as a religion'.[31] The meaning was clear and comprehensible by reference to the French wars of religion which had only just ended. The Huguenots obeyed their leader rather

[31] *Ibid.*, p. 141.

than their prince. As subjects who were unreliable, if not disloyal, they no longer had a place in the realm.

Spain set the example, by not only supporting the missionaries in the Low Countries but also giving them powerful encouragement in their work of reconquest. In 1583 four Capuchins (three Flemings and an Italian) were sent northward by the Provincial of Paris in order to implant their Order. After being welcomed at Saint-Omer they soon pushed on to Antwerp, which had long been the chief centre of the Protestant revolt but had just been reconquered by the King of Spain's troops.[32] 'Prince Alexander Farnese, Duke of Parma and Governor-General of the Low Countries, received them with all signs of goodwill, promised them his protection, and gave them for residence in Antwerp a small house near Saint-Julien's hospital, where they could reside until they obtained a more extensive piece of ground on which to build a convent.'[33]

What was accomplished so easily in Antwerp was reproduced elsewhere as the rebels were overcome. Each town taken was at once provided with a Capuchin convent and a college or residence of the Society of Jesus, which in 1598 possessed seventeen such houses. In 1640 the Society had 43 in the Southern Netherlands as a whole and the Principality of Liège. There was a considerable increase in the number of religious in the early 1600s. The Jesuits, who numbered 420 in 1596, had 730 members in 1609.[34] As for the Capuchins, of whom there were four when they arrived in 1583, they had nearly a thousand around 1620, since the Walloon province alone numbered 450 in 1623 (and 639 in 1631). They had fifty-five houses in the Low Countries as a whole by the middle of the seventeenth century. Thus, the establishments of the Society of Jesus and the Seraphical Order formed a network which literally enclosed those provinces (see Map 1). If we realise that these centres were all destined to extend their influence over the neighbouring country areas, it is hard to suppose that any village of importance remained unaffected by them.

These serried ranks of convents and colleges, inserted as a wedge between the heretical United Provinces and a Kingdom of France that was highly suspect since it came under a king who was a former Protestant, were so many spiritual fortresses. Were not the enemies of the Catholic religion and those of the prince one and the same? That was

---

[32] 17 August 1585, Van Acker, Jan, *Anvers d'escale romaine à port mondial*, Antwerp and Brussels, Mercurius, 1975, pp. 201–13.

[33] AN, Luxemburg, *Abteilung* 15/39, 'Mémoires pour les annales des Capucins de la province wallonne dans les Pays-Bas espagnols depuis l'an 1586 jusqu'à 1704', vol. I, fo. 4 vo.

[34] Poncelet, *Histoire*, part 1, pp. 415–28.

certainly why Governor-General Alexander Farnese, 'after numerous talks with Father Foelix conceived such veneration for him that he made him his confessor, doing nothing without his advice, receiving cheerfully his warnings or corrections, and setting forth on no warlike expedition without obtaining his blessing, even upon his arms'.[35]

Here, then, were missionaries whose duties included interceding with God for victory for the Church's defender. Often they did more than that. At the battle of Nieuport (2 July 1600) three Jesuit chaplains who were addressing the combatants were killed in the fray.[36] Ten others suffered the same fate at the siege of Ostend. The slaughter was such that their Provincial thought it his duty to remind these enthusiastic preachers that it was 'for the commanders, not for us, to lead the troops in action. Before the battle begins the priest can be the voice *clamans in deserto*, but during action his role is that of Moses praying on the mountain.'[37] This 'voice crying in the wilderness' before the battle was that, twenty years later, on the slopes of the White Mountain, of Father Dominic of Jesus Mary, who on the morning of 8 November 1620 prepared the troops of Maximilian I, Elector of Bavaria, for their attack on the Protestants who were defending Prague. 'Render unto Caesar that which is Caesar's, and to God that which is God's', he cried, quoting the Gospel for the day and identifying the standards of the Catholic League with those of Christ. The password was a real war-cry of holy war, shouted to the heavens: 'Sancta Maria'.[38] This religious enthusiasm which seized the army helped to adorn the battle of the White Mountain with an aura of the providential. These missionaries summoning the troops to a holy war against the heretics recalled memories of the long struggle, still unfinished, against the Crescent. They were messengers from heaven inspiring the fighters with conviction that they were instruments of divine wrath.

In Rome the will to conquer was omnipresent. In 1590 the General of the Jesuits, Acquaviva, considering the substantial importance 'and urgent necessity' of the ministry of mission in Europe, decided that in each of the Society's provinces twelve Fathers (or six, at least) should be assigned each year to perform this function, at times judged favourable by their superiors. They were to go two by two, on foot, 'as is appropriate to real poor men', to the rescue of the most deprived villages and small towns. In 1599 the General made his intentions still clearer by imposing on all the Fathers, turn and turn about, the work of apostleship, even if only in the mitigated form of teaching the catechism and

[35] AN, Luxemburg, *Abteilung* 15/39, 'Mémoires', vol. I, fo. 4 vo–5.
[36] Poncelet, *Histoire*, part 1, pp. 415–16.   [37] *Ibid.*
[38] Tapié, Victor-Lucien, *La Guerre de Trente Ans*, Paris, SEDES, 1989, p. 107.

preaching in the neighbourhood of their residence. He especially called on each Provincial to establish in his area of responsibility two or three houses which should serve as bases for a group of six specialist missionaries who were to pay systematic visits to neighbouring places. When their superiors considered the work sufficiently advanced, they could move the residence to another location. Thus an entire region would in a few years benefit from this form of apostleship. Within the Society these houses were called 'missions'.[39] The Capuchins evidently acted similarly, since it was reported that those who had participated in the expedition in Chablais along with François de Sales, established in 1602 at Thonon 'a dwelling in the form of a mission and hospice for the great results to be achieved there, being close to Geneva, in a region infected with heresy'.[40] This was the origin of new foundations.

Eventually the Popes applied their minds, after the Council, to the means needful if the world was to be effectively Christianised. After the organs of repression, such as the Holy Office (1543), came the German College (1555), intended for the training of a new body of clergy in the regions most affected by heresy, and, above all, in 1622, the creation of the congregation for propagating the faith, De Propaganda Fide.[41] The purpose of this institution was to co-ordinate the undertakings begun up to that time, in a scattered way, by religious in regions that were heathen or affected by Protestantism. It was intended to give them a fresh impetus, but also aimed to bring under exclusive control by the Roman Curia what had been the responsibility either of a Catholic prince, of an enterprising prelate or of a missionary order. Henceforth it was the Propaganda, in principle, which sent out teams of preachers, gave them their instructions and told them whose orders they were to obey. It was to the Propaganda that reports on activity were to be sent, together with requests for advice on ticklish matters and appeals for subsidies. Missionary activity throughout the world had its centre, as is still the

---

[39] Guidetti, Le missioni popolari, pp. 52–5; Delattre, Pierre, SJ, Les Etablissements des Jésuites en France depuis quatre siècles, 5 vols., Enghien and Wetteren, 1949–55, vol. I, p. xii.

[40] Dompnier, Bernard, 'Le premier apostolat des Capucins de la province de Lyon (1575–1618)', Revue de l'histoire de l'Eglise de France, 75, no. 194, 1989, transactions of the colloquium 'Les débuts de la Réforme catholique dans les pays de langue française', Nancy, May 1988, p. 131.

[41] On the German College, see Schmidt, Peter, Das Collegium Germanicum in Rom und die Germaniker, Bibliothek des deutschen historischen Instituts in Rom, 56, Tübingen, Niemeyer, 1984. On the congregation De Propaganda Fide, a collective work published in connection with the 350th anniversary of its creation presents a vast panorama of the institution and of its world-wide activity: Sacrae Congregationis de Propaganda Fide Memoria Rerum, 1622–1972, ed. J. Metzler, Rome and Vienna, 5 vols. in 7, 1972–3.

case today, in a Roman palace where, under direction by a congregation of cardinals, a prefect and a secretary, with their staff, are at work.[42]

One of the first enterprises sponsored by the *Propaganda* in Europe was what was called 'the Poitou mission'. This had, in fact, been in progress for several years, since the Capuchins, who began it, founded their first convent in Poitiers in 1609.[43] Within eleven years nine more followed. This dynamism was doubtless to be put to the credit of the sons of St Francis, but also to the man who guided them and inspired the undertaking, the famous Father Joseph du Tremblay. In 1616 he had explained his plan to the Pope, who had declared the region a mission territory, directly attached to the Holy See. Naturally, therefore, in 1623 Poitou was subject to the *Propaganda*. Meanwhile, the Capuchins had practised their apostleship on a wide scale, 'going through cities and towns . . . preaching controversially and working at the instruction of heretics'.[44] They attacked directly the Huguenots' Bible, striving to show that it could only lead one into heresy. They revived the faith of the Catholics, and of those whose Protestant convictions were still uncertain, by means of grand ceremonies in honour of the Holy Sacrament, or on the occasion of the Forty Hours. The latter devotion, something quite new, was spread by the Capuchins, and later by the Jesuits, from the middle of the sixteenth century onward. It consisted of three days of penitence and instruction, intended to prepare believers for Lent and also to obtain forgiveness for excesses committed during Carnival.[45] Bringing the participants to confession was, indeed, the dominant preoccupation of the religious, who did not hesitate to remind their listeners, in the oppressive setting of a cemetery, of their future condition as corpses. 'Fleshless skeletons', cried the preacher at Saint Jean-d'Angély, 'hear the word of the Lord!' At the same moment, as though the entire world of the dead was joining in this appeal, the tomb on which the Capuchin was standing slowly began to sink. Everyone cried out in fear. Was this enough, though, to bring about the thousands of conversions which the chroniclers of the time mention so smugly? The advance of the king's forces, taking stronghold

[42] Metzler, Josef, 'Foundation of the Congregation *de propaganda fide* by Gregory XV', in *Sacrae Congregationis*, vol. I, pp. 79–111; Metzler, 'Die Kongregation im Zeitalter des Aufklärung. Struktur, Missionspläne und Massnahmen allgemeiner Art (1700–1795)', in *Sacrae Congregationis*, vol. I, part 2, pp. 23–83.

[43] Pérouas, Louis, 'La mission de Poitou des Capucins pendant le premier quart du XVIIe siècle', *Bulletin de la Société des antiquaires de l'Ouest et des musées de Poitiers*, 1964/1, pp. 349–62.

[44] *Ibid.*, p. 353.

[45] Dompnier, Bernard, 'Un aspect de la dévotion eucharistique dans la France du XVIIe siècle: les prières des Quarante Heures', *Revue d'histoire de l'Eglise de France*, 67, no.178, 1981, pp. 5–31.

after stronghold and laying siege to La Rochelle, was doubtless an argument even weightier than the rhetoric of the Capuchins.[46] At the other end of Europe, in Bohemia, Moravia and Silesia, the use of missionaries and troops in combined operations began to become current practice. It went along with an express order from the sovereign for the Protestants to submit, something which had often previously been missing, to the great regret of the religious. When, after the battle of the White Mountain (8 November 1620), the Emperor was in a position to impose his will on all Bohemia, pressure was strongly exerted on him, while prelates and pious princes appealed to missionaries, to banish all the Protestant clergy. When the Nuncio was able to announce that the Emperor's representative in Prague, Prince Liechtenstein, had not only taken action against the pastors but had forbidden 'heretics' to remain in Bohemia and confiscated their property, there was an explosion of enthusiasm in the *Propaganda*.[47] 'All the Cardinals who were present at this meeting were filled with such joy when they heard this news that they praised the Emperor as another Constantine or Theodosius.'[48] Similar satisfaction was shown in 1627 when news was received of the Imperial edict expelling the Protestant princes and barons and establishing Catholic schools everywhere, and in 1629, when the Edict of Restitution was published.[49]

Nevertheless it was clear that, on the spot, the initiative belonged to the Emperor and his representatives. The Pope merely associated himself with the work undertaken, by giving it his support. The reports written by Cardinal Dietrichstein, the Bishop of Olmütz, by the Nuncio or by the missionaries spoke of the conversion of entire regions. After Moravia, Silesia went over to Catholicism almost in its entirety. In January 1629 it was learnt in Rome that the town of Glogau, situated north-west of Breslau in an area where the Lutherans formed the majority, had become Catholic, and four other towns with it.[50] This gave cause for rejoicing and a proposal to send a letter of congratulation to the chief agent of so massive a conversion, Colonel Count Karl Hannibal von Dohna.[51] In Glogau, however, the event did not arouse

---

[46] Pérouas, 'La mission de Poitou', p. 360 (the example of the small town of Maillezais in 1621).
[47] *Acta S.C. de Propaganda Fide Germaniam Spectantia: Die Protokolle der Propagandakongregation zu deutschen Angelegenheiten 1622–1649*, ed. Hermann Tüchle, Paderborn, Bonifacius, 1962, pp. 34–5 and 65; Tüchle, Hermann, 'Im Spannungsfeld des lutherischen Christentum (Böhmen, Deutschland und Skandinavien)', in *Sacrae Congregationis*, vol. I, part 2, pp. 26–63.
[48] *Acta S.C.*, p. 65 (August 1624).   [49] *Ibid.* pp. 164–5 and 235.
[50] *Ibid.*, pp. 214–15.   [51] *Ibid.*, p. 235.

such euphoria. The account left by the chronicler of the Society of Jesus reveals, unintentionally, a different reality.[52]

The Jesuits of Breslau had, since 1582, busied themselves now and again with the small Catholic community in Glogau (see Map 2). Suddenly, in 1625, the effects of the advance of the Imperial Army made themselves felt. The Emperor's representative for the region, Count von Oppersdorf, summoned two Fathers whom, at first, he installed in his own house. Then came the Imperial decree of 20 May 1626 which assigned to the Church's institutions the confiscated property and the fines paid by the Protestant gentry. Thereby the Glogau Jesuits received 70,000 thalers, paid by Count Schönaich. A college could be founded. They also needed a church. By imperial decree of 1628 they obtained the parish church, which until then had been a Protestant temple. That was too much. As the Lutheran festival of 31 October drew near (the anniversary of Luther's protest against the preaching of indulgences), the Protestant population of the town rose in revolt. But Colonel von Dohna, who had been warned, was on the alert. During the night of 30 October he surrounded the town with his dragoons. The town militia was disarmed and the soldiers billeted on the inhabitants, with complete licence to behave as they wished, short of violence to persons. Amid the general disarray and plundering some news was spread: those persons who became Catholics and presented the colonel with a certificate bearing the seal of the Society of Jesus, testifying to their profession of faith, would at once be freed of the soldiers. People rushed to the Jesuits. In a few hours their house, their chapel, their school and even the cemetery were filled with poor panic-stricken people who were ready to promise anything in order to regain their freedom. This went on for six days without a break. After that, von Dohna regarded his mission as accomplished. For greater security, he had the town magistrates decree that henceforth only Catholics would be allowed citizenship, that they would have exclusive access to municipal posts, and that the Protestant schools would be closed. Then he set off for other places, accompanied by his faithful helpers, three Jesuit Fathers. The author of the annual *Letter* artlessly concludes his report for 1628 with a victory bulletin. Twenty thousand persons, he wrote, had been brought to abjuration in the Principality of Glogau by the Society of Jesus, 'without anyone's backing' (*nemine cogente*).[53]

To be sure, the Society did not confine itself to mere registration. During four days the Fathers followed each other in the pulpit to instruct

---

[52] Hoffmann, Hermann, 'Die Jesuiten in Glogau', *Zur schlesischen Kirchengeschichte*, 1, Breslau, 1926.
[53] *Ibid.*, p. 16.

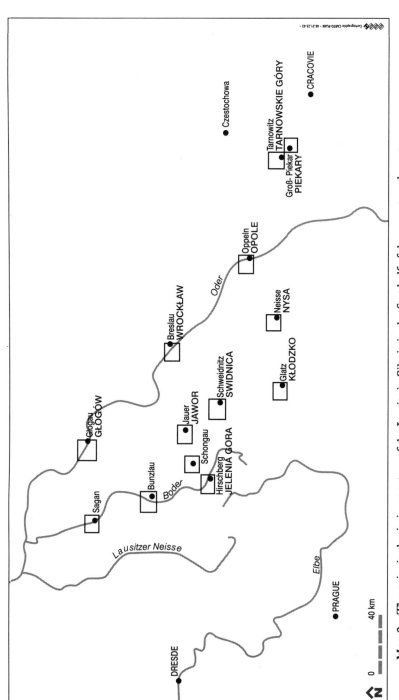

Map 2   The principal mission centres of the Jesuits in Silesia in the first half of the seventeenth century.

the candidates for conversion in the rudiments of the Catholic faith. They completed this rapid education by discussions with individuals. Like the Capuchins of Poitou they counted also on impressive ceremonies to strike imaginations and arouse respect. On 31 October old Catholics and new converts were invited to enter in procession into God's house. Armed soldiers formed a guard on either side of the procession and the Emperor's representative, Count von Oppersdorf, occupied the place of honour. Gorgeous banners were unfurled, while numerous musicians heightened the brilliance of the ceremony and supported the hymns sung by the crowd. The people sang the litanies of the saints, ending with the invocation, thrice repeated: 'Saint Nicholas, pray for us'. This ceremony, in the form of a *Te Deum*, to the glory of the Imperial Army and of the Church triumphant, celebrated grandly, on 31 October, the substitution of the victorious Catholic cult for the defeated heresy. The invocations to the saints and, especially, to the patron saint Nicholas, were not only a manifestation of Catholic piety in what, in the eyes of most, was its specific character, but also a wish to emphasise the link with a past which had been obliterated by the Reformation. Perhaps also it was a way, through ascribing the triumph of the day to the almighty host of heaven's saints, of causing their power of intercession to be better appreciated. Not long afterward the suffragan Bishop of Breslau arrived to rededicate the church. While he was giving his blessing and the people were singing and processing, executions were taking place. The pastor, banished, had to go off into exile, the Protestant schools were closed, and, as we have mentioned, only Catholics were henceforth to be admitted to citizenship. That was how all Glogau was converted.[54]

A few weeks later it was the turn of Schweidnitz (Swidnica), southwest of Breslau, to suffer the rigours of Von Dohna's dragoons. The procedure followed was the same, and the high point was again the restoration of Catholic worship in the parish church. That day an old Protestant woman, heartbroken, cried out: 'O merciful God, say that we mustn't see such abominations in this town (*Lass dichs Gott erbarmen, dass wir in dieser Stadt solchen Greuel müssen sehen!*).' Hardly had she uttered those words when she fell down in the snow, smitten by an apoplexy. Heaven's justice for some, excess of sorrow for others.[55] This incident reported by the chronicler showed clearly that the Jesuits themselves had no illusions about the sudden change of convictions which had, in appearance, been achieved by their efforts. In a level tone,

[54] *Ibid.*, pp. 16–17.
[55] Hoffmann, 'Die Jesuiten in Schweidnitz', *Zur schlesischen Kirchengeschichte*, Breslau, 1930, pp. 7–8.

without showing the slightest surprise, the author of the annals of the Jesuit house recorded that when the troops of Saxony and Brandenburg arrived, in September 1632, the Jesuits were obliged, along with the other religious, to leave the town, while the former pastor was re-established in triumph in his church.[56] A year earlier the same thing had happened at Glogau – said at the end of 1628 to have become entirely Catholic, as though by a miracle.[57] In Rome the officials of the *Propaganda* were soon informed of the real situation. In 1629 they learnt that the Jesuits had shared in the violence committed against the heretics in Silesia and that those heretics had been so embittered thereby that they had sent the Elector of Saxony an appeal to come to their rescue. In this letter they confirmed to him that 'they remained inwardly faithful' to their religion.[58]

It was the same in a small region which was intensely disputed between the great powers from 1620 onwards – the Swiss canton of Grisons. In this strategic sector which allowed communication between the Milanese, which belonged to the Spanish Habsburgs, and Tyrol, one of the patrimonial possessions of the Austrian branch of the family, the population had long since gone over to the Reformation. The Arch-bishop of Milan, Federigo Borromeo, whose archdiocese was directly adjacent, and the Pope, through the Nuncio in Lucerne, had undertaken a major missionary action, conducted by the Capuchins. It was during this implantation in these high valleys and these villages hard of access in the Engadine and the Prätigau that the Order acquired its first martyr, soon to be beatified, Brother Fidel of Sigmaringen (at Seewiss in April 1622).[59] Very soon, however, thanks to support from the Habsburgs, who were keen to extend, from Innsbruck, their protectorate over this passageway, the Catholic cause gained successes. Father Ignatius of Bergamo, an active missionary of the time, sent to the *Propaganda* victory bulletins announcing the conversion of whole villages. From 1623, though, matters became complicated in the Upper Engadine owing to the presence of French troops. At the end of 1624 the Capuchins and the Catholic communities were on the defensive. In 1625 the advance of the king of France's armies in this region was accompanied by amends of a religious nature made to the inhabitants and expulsion of everything that might recall the presence of the

[56] *Ibid.*, p. 20.
[57] Hoffmann, 'Die Jesuiten in Glogau', 1926, p. 18.
[58] *Acta S.C.*, p. 247.
[59] Metzler, Joseph, 'Religiöse Interessen in den Westalpen, Schweiz, Savoyen-Piemont', in *Sacrae Congregationis*, pp. 64–92 and 79–80; Father Daniel de Paris, *Vie du B.P. Fidel de Sigmaringa, capucin, missionnaire et premier martyr de la mission apostolique établie par la Sacrée Congregation de Propaganda Fide, chez les Grisons*, Paris, 1745 (2nd edition).

Habsburgs either of Spain or of Austria. The Capuchins from the Milanese were strictly watched or sent away. By the middle of 1625 all the converts of the preceding years had apostasised and followed once more with zeal the teaching of their pastors.[60] The expression 'apostasised' is perhaps excessive since one may wonder whether the population had perceived the change otherwise than as the departure of the pastors and the arrival of the Capuchins. The latter, in fact, while waiting for an edition of the New Testament authorised by Rome, had allowed the inhabitants to use their old Bibles. Baptisms took place in the presence of Protestant godfathers and godmothers. Apparently, the religious had not shown eagerness to demand from the villagers any solemn acts of abjuration, but had been content to make them attend, for many weeks, perhaps longer, their lessons on the catechism.[61]

Much has been said of *cuius regio eius religio*, the principle of partition between the religious denominations agreed under the Peace of Augsburg in 1555, according to which subjects had to follow their ruler's religion. Actually, although during the great upheavals that accompanied the Thirty Years War (1618–48) the application of that principle doubtless entailed great suffering among the people, it rarely brought about, on its own, any lasting changes in religious allegiance. In 1620–30 there were still in Europe immense areas wherein adherence to a particular religion continued to be uncertain, fragile and constantly under threat, along with the territorial ascendancy of a given ruler. Were the inhabitants Catholics? Or were they Protestants? It was still hard to decide. Only with time could the pastors, on the one hand, and the missionaries, on the other, succeed in making them Christians with clearly defined convictions.

'The poor people in the fields'

It is true that missionaries did not always show much enthusiasm for the task they were called upon to perform among the Protestants. In the Grisons the Capuchins eventually refused to preach, on the pretext that they were there only to say Mass and instruct the people in accordance with Bellarmine's catechism.[62] In 1641 they were unwilling to go to Saxony, declaring that this mission (in the form intended by the *Propaganda*) was incompatible with their institution and their profession.[63] Nor were they alone in that opinion. When Vincent de Paul founded in Paris in 1625 the Order of the Mission, he made it clear to his companions that he did not destine it for systematic conversion of

[60] *Acta S.C.*, pp. 99–100.   [61] *Ibid.*, pp. 45–7.
[62] *Ibid.*, p. 443 (1638).   [63] *Ibid.*, p. 492 (1641).

Protestants. He was equally opposed to discussions with pastors and to controversial sermons.[64] In his view, clearly, priests should devote their activity to Catholics, whether 'old' or 'new'. It was from concern about the latter that he had been led to interest himself in Lorraine and Guyenne.[65] This prudence was shared by other founders of apostolic orders such as Pierre de Bérulle, for the Oratory, or Jean Eudes, for the Congregation of Jesus and Mary. Jean Eudes considered that controversy should be restricted to relations with 'Catholics doubtful and wavering in their faith'.[66]

In practice the famous Jesuit missionary Jean-François Régis acted on the same principle. It is quite remarkable that, at Sommières, at the edge of the Cévennes, a town regarded as the centre of a Huguenot area, 'the holy man', so we are told by his biographer, did not see as useful any change in the method he employed with Catholic audiences, but delivered his habitual sermons on death, the Last Judgment, Hell and the danger entailed in putting off confession. 'He made peace in all the families by settling disputes between individuals, he established the practice of evening and morning prayer in all households, and regulated the procedure for helping the poor in each parish.' Finally, he 'instituted the confraternity of the Holy Sacrament in Sommières and in all the small towns and villages of the Lavouage.'[67] Rather than controversy with pastors, it was for the formation of a Catholic community that he worked. The establishment of a confraternity of the Holy Sacrament, as both a sign and a school of Catholicism, was, from his point of view, the best guarantee that the work undertaken would be consolidated.

This conduct of his was similar to that of Monsieur Vincent, of whom it was said that 'God had made him aware of . . . the need for this means [missions] in order to remedy the ignorance and dissoluteness of the poor people in the fields, and especially the great faults that most of them had committed, up to that time, in their customary confessions.'[68] In the contract that he signed in 1625 with Monsieur and Madame de Gondi, for instructing their peasants in the Paris region, it was laid down that 'since the towns are, by God's mercy, furnished with good ministers

[64] Abelly, Louis, *La Vie du vénérable serviteur de Dieu Vincent de Paul, instituteur et premier supérieur général de la Congrégation de la mission,* Paris, 1684 (3rd edition), p. 155.
[65] Coste, Pierre, *Le Grand Saint du grand siècle: Monsieur Vincent,* 3 vols., Paris, Desclée de Brouwer, 1934, vol. II, pp. 75–162.
[66] Berthelot du Chesnay, Charles, *Les Missions de saint Jean Eudes: contributions à l'histoire des missions en France au XVIIe siècle,* Paris, Procure des Eudistes, 1967, p. 80. See also Milcent, Paul, *Un Artisan du renouveau chrétien au XVIIe siècle, saint Jean Eudes,* Paris, Cerf, 1983.
[67] Daubenton, Father Guillaume, *La Vie du bienheureux J.Fr. Régis,* Paris, Nicolas Le Clère, 1716, pp. 43–50.
[68] Abelly, *Vincent de Paul,* p. 146.

and ardent religious', there were only 'the poor people of the countryside who seem to be deprived of any spiritual aid'. So Monsieur Vincent 'will have to select a certain number of priests . . . whose duty it will be to devote themselves wholly to the care of the poor countryfolk and, consequently, will undertake not to preach or administer any of the sacraments in any town where there is an archbishopric, a bishopric or a presidial, except in cases of notable necessity, but instead to carry out, from one five-year period to another, a mission in all the lands belonging to the said lord and lady'.[69] The Oratorians were guided by the same spirit, since, according to their founder's intention, they 'apply themselves to teaching the catechism and instructing families, or go out into the countryside, and, by missions both humble and charitable, rescue the poor peasants from ignorance and sin'.[70] Here we meet again the purposes of the post-Tridentine missions: to instruct in Christianity and cause it to be put into practice. However, an additional concern now appears. Priority was to be given to the poorest, the most neglected and the most numerous. Apostleship of the masses thus became, at the beginning of the seventeenth century, a project of wide interest among those men and women who were most advanced in devotion. They took it upon themselves to put this apostleship into action with extensive means and a new concern for effectiveness.

As in the previous century, the example came from both South and North. Traversing indefatigably the poor dioceses of Catanzaro, Cosenza and Castellamare, the Jesuit Paolo Principe (who died in 1613) was the educator of the poorest and most neglected of Italy's peasants. He did not preach but was content tirelessly to teach the catechism. At the end of his life, having been summoned to Naples, he had the idea of presenting, for the benefit of the humble folk of that city, the truths of Christianity in the form of stage-plays. He thus became known everywhere as the Father of Christian Doctrine.[71] That epithet would have fitted perfectly another Jesuit, Nicolas Leyen, who was born at Cues, near Trier, and therefore called Cusanus. For more than thirty years (1603–36) he moved around the Eifel district and the Duchy of Luxemburg, sometimes on his own and sometimes in the train of the Vicar-General when the latter was performing his pastoral visitation on behalf of the Archbishop of Trier. His aim was not merely to teach the catechism but, more broadly, to teach piety in the form conceived by the

[69] Quoted by Father Louis Batterel, *Mémoires domestiques pour servir à l'histoire de l'Oratoire*, ed. A. M. P. Ingold and E. Bonnardet, Paris, Picard, 1903–5, vol. I, pp. 332–4.

[70] [R. P. Senault], *La Vie du réverendissime Jean-Baptiste Gault de la congrégation de l'Oratoire de Jésus-Christ – Notre-Seigneur évesque de Marseille* . . . , Paris, 1647, p. 39.

[71] Guidetti, *Le missioni popolari*, p. 43.

Council of Trent. Hence the title of his manual, which enjoyed considerable success in all the lands along the Rhine and in Germany: the *Christliche Zuchtschul*, translated into French as *Eschole chrestienne*.[72] Cusanus was far from being alone in the Low Countries. Mission activity was on the agenda in those regions, since in 1609 a Twelve-Years Truce had been signed with the Protestant provinces of the north. Fear of contamination was stronger than ever, and the General of the Society of Jesus wrote to the Provincial: 'We must increase the number of apostolic expeditions, so as to protect the faith of the rural populations.'[73] From the colleges there set out, consequently, every Sunday, groups of catechists accompanied by laymen, enthusiastic adult pupils or dynamic young confraternity members. Such were the Sunday expeditions organised round Antwerp by Father De Pretere or by Father van Lutzenkercke round Alost.[74] Similar activity went on in the Rhine valley. The Jesuits of Molsheim in Lower Alsace and of Ensisheim in Upper Alsace went out every Sunday to teach Christian doctrine in the surrounding villages.[75]

It often happened, though, that in order to reach a largely illiterate population recourse was had to a more elaborate method. In his *Guidance for Missions* the third superior of the Oratory, Father Bourgoing, stressed that, at the end of every sermon, the preacher should recite from the pulpit a 'summary of Christian doctrine' which must be known by all.[76] The most famous missionary of this congregation, Father Jean Lejeune, referred to this practice late in his life, justifying it from his personal experience. 'For forty years', he wrote, for the benefit of his successors, 'everywhere that I preached in Advent and in Lent, on almost all the Sundays and feast-days, I spoke at the end of my sermon explicitly about the mysteries of the faith, namely, the Holy Trinity, the Incarnation, the Passion, the Death, Resurrection and Ascension of Our Saviour, and about what is essential in the Sacraments of Baptism, Eucharist and Penitence. This has always been well received . . . You should do likewise, else the people will remain in frightful ignorance of

---

[72] Birsens, Josy, *Manuels de catéchisme, missions de campagnes et mentalités populaires dans le duché de Luxembourg aux XVIIe et XVIIIe siècles*, Publications de la section historique de l'Institut G.-D. de Luxembourg, vol. CV, Luxembourg, 1990, pp. 45–68.

[73] Poncelet, *Histoire*, part 2, p. 391.

[74] Châtellier, Louis, *L'Europe des dévots*, Paris, Flammarion, 1987, pp. 36–7 (Antwerp) (Eng. trans., *The Europe of the Devout*, Cambridge, Cambridge University Press, 1989, p. 22). Poncelet, *Histoire*, part 2, p. 393 (Alost).

[75] Barth, 'Die Seelsorgetätigkeit', pp. 328–42 (Lower Alsace); BH, Munich, *Jesuiten*, 107, p. 59 (Upper Alsace, mission by the Jesuits of Ensisheim to Riquewihr in 1648).

[76] [Bourgoing, R. P.], *Direction pour les missions qui se font par la Congrégation de l'Oratoire de Jésus-Christ N.S. contenant les advis nécessaires, afin de les rendre fructueuses*, Paris, 1646, p. 42.

these mysteries that are so necessary for salvation.'[77] He hoped that in this way the message would eventually be heard by the most stubborn.

Others counted less on the passage of time than on the emotion produced by an image or a cleverly contrived spectacle. Among these was the missionary of Lower Brittany, Dom Jean Le Nobletz, who reproduced the essentials of the Church's teaching in large pictures which he displayed before the public and commented on from the pulpit.[78] The testimony of Pierre Jakez Hélias reveals how, in the twentieth century still, these pictures hung up in a church long struck the imaginations of those who took part in a mission.[79] In Sicily the Jesuit Father Luigi La Nuza resorted to another method no less spectacular. He moved from village to village accompanied by young men whom he had trained. Having arrived, he walked around the village holding a crucifix and followed by a group full of fervour. All sang the litanies of the Virgin and then, from time to time, came to a halt. A voice rang out: 'In whose hands is the soul that is in mortal sin?' 'In the Devil's hands', responded the youths. A little later the same voice was heard: 'What punishment awaits the one who dies in a state of mortal sin?' 'Hell', came the response. 'How long does one suffer in Hell?' Response: 'For all eternity'. When the litanies were ended the conclusion came: 'What is the remedy that relieves from sin?' 'Penitence, penitence!' sounded the chorus. And that was to be the leitmotiv of the whole mission.[80]

As the missionaries advanced they found new fields for activity. There were regions even more deprived than the ones where stood those poor churches of Eifel or of Sicily. Such was the Camargue, with which Adrien Bourdoise, founder of the Community of Priests of Saint-Nicolas-du-Chardonnet, began to concern himself in 1635. He wrote:

There were only a few chapels, such as that of Saint Cecilia, where Mass was said on Sundays and feast-days throughout the year, and that of Saint Michael, where it was said during six months only. The only instruction given there was to announce the feast-days and fast-days for the week . . . so that there are persons on the Island who have not seen a priest for ten or a dozen years and who, consequently, have not been able to hear Mass, confess and communicate during all that time. If some servant falls ill, he is sent to the hospital in the town [Arles]. If his illness is acute and he cannot go there, they lay him on some straw

[77] Lejeune, Father Jean, priest of the Oratory, *Le Missionnaire de l'Oratoire ou sermons pour les Advents, Caresmes et Dimanches de l'Année, dans lesquels sont expliquées les principales Vérités Chrestiennes que l'on enseigne es missions*, 10 vols, Toulouse, 1662–76, vol. I, 'Avis aux jeunes prédicateurs', n.p.

[78] Croix, Alain, and Roudaut, Fanch, *Les Bretons, la mort et Dieu de 1600 à nos jours*, Paris, Messidor, 'Temps actuels', 1984.

[79] Hélias, Pierre Jakez, *Le Cheval d'orgueil*, Paris, France Loisirs, 1975, pp. 143–6.

[80] Guidetti, *Le missioni popolari*, pp. 93–5.

near a wall, far from the house, and bring him a piece of bread and a little water, as one would do for a dog. If he dies and is found to have had some money, they take him to a place where there is a cross and bury him there. Otherwise, some one of his comrades who is charitable digs a ditch in the same place where he died and puts him in it.

That was what, before the embellishments brought by the Romantic age, the life and death of a *gardian* was like at the beginning of the seventeenth century. Carried away by his zeal, Monsieur Bourdoise decided to do what he could to remedy this sad situation. He traversed most of the Island

catechising and instructing all whom he encountered: and since the servants were the ones who were in greatest need, he went out to look for them in the fields and woods, among their herds. He showed great friendliness, adapting himself to their weaknesses and rough ways, even going so far as to play with them, without (he says) losing anything of his priestly gravity. These poor men, charmed by so much goodness, listened to him with pleasure and entered willingly into the sentiments with which he sought to inspire them, showing clearly that their ignorance was due only to the fact that they had found nobody ready to take the trouble to instruct them.

The missionary at once conceived the idea of a pastoral organisation with a parish church in the middle, five or six chapels of ease in various parts of the Island, separate schools for boys and girls, and a community of eight or ten priests to serve all this. First of all, though, it was necessary to conduct a mission that was adapted to the lie of the land and to the spiritual state of the population. 'It would not be enough', he thought, 'to preach in the churches, because those who have most need of instruction will not be able to go there, being either too far away or too busy. Two priests must proceed from house to house in the districts assigned to them and remain in each place as long as they think necessary for instructing the rough people and teaching them to receive properly the Sacraments of Penitence, Eucharist and Confirmation.'[81] Bourdoise discovered in the Camargue the problems involved in catechising the poor, the illiterate, the rejects of Christian civilisation. He thought of solutions for the future, showing thereby how far Vincent de Paul's ideal of pastoral activity focused on the humblest folk was beginning to be accepted among the French clergy at the beginning of the seventeenth century.

The same desire was present in the Jesuit Julien Maunoir, who succeeded Dom Le Nobletz in Lower Brittany. One of his first expeditions, undertaken in 1641, was to the island of Ushant – another

[81] Descourveaux, Philibert, *La Vie de Monsieur Bourdoise, premier prestre de la communauté de S. Nicolas du Chardonnet*, Paris, 1714, pp. 308–13.

'world's end' – which he described in his *Diary* as a regular fragment of Canada, as much remote from Christianity as it was from any land. 'The approach to this island is so dangerous', he observed, 'that nobody remembers a visit by a bishop. No priest taught there. So great an ignorance reigned in that island . . . that one could barely find a dozen persons with knowledge of the mysteries of the Trinity and of man saved by God, or of the Ten Commandments.'[82] In this abandoned country the missionaries began their teaching. As it was hard for them, in a few days, to get into heads so unprepared for theology all of the Council's catechism, they put the latter into 'Breton verses'. 'Everyone comes running, attracted by the novelty, and they sing our hymns even when out at sea.' The sermons, also delivered in Breton, dealt with 'the torments of Hell and the sins that bring men to that place'. The crowd which had gathered outside, because the church was now too small, began to be gripped by fear. 'Alas', they moaned, 'we have been living like beasts! Most good God, how grateful must we be to the Fathers who have rescued us from this wretched state.' The priests were indeed messengers from Heaven. Their most holy life was adequate proof of that. They were therefore called *tadou santel*, meaning 'holy fathers', and the sick were brought to them to be cured by their blessings.[83] By a miracle this almost heathen place was suddenly covered with a supernatural aura and its inhabitants entered almost at once into Paradise. But, for all that, were they actually converted?

The missionaries of the sixteenth and the beginning of the seventeenth centuries strove to put into effect the decisions of the Council of Trent everywhere, and especially in those places where they came up against the biggest obstacles – countries won for the Protestant Reformation and thankless rural areas with priests either few or incompetent. For carrying out this considerable task, support from the Catholic rulers, which the Council had prescribed, seemed very soon to be indispensable. But this support was rarely disinterested. It could become also utilisation of the missionaries by a ruler for the purposes of his own policy. In Catholic territory the preachers found themselves facing other difficulties. A message had to be conveyed to persons who mostly were unready to hear it. An entire scheme of pedagogy was called for – but this entailed a risk that, through adaptation to the needs of the pupils, the teaching itself might be transformed. The Baroque Age which opened about 1650, after the Thirty Years War, was thus also an age of great uncertainties.

[82] Croix and Roudaut, *Les Bretons*, pp. 227–8.
[83] *Ibid.*

3 From the missionary impulse to the impossible mission

The years that followed the end of the Thirty Years War (1648) were marked by a missionary impulse that was quite stupendous. Groups of secular priests and religious set to work, or expanded their activity, in every part of Europe. From Scandinavia to Andalusia, from Brittany to Bulgaria, they were everywhere. Moreover, they were led in many cases by distinguished men who made this apostolic undertaking successful wherever they went. Paolo Segneri, SJ, in Central Italy, Tirso Gonzalez, SJ, a future General of the Society of Jesus, in northern Spain, Julien Maunoir, SJ, and Honoré de Cannes, Capuchin, in France, and Philipp Jeningen, SJ, in central Germany were all contemporaries, known to everyone, and able to draw crowds in any place where they appeared. The scope of this movement and the successes obtained by its illustrious leaders may have given some the idea that this method, seemingly so effective, could be used to bring about mass conversion of the Protestants. But did this not amount, in the age of the French School and of the circulation of great works on spiritual themes, to diverting missions from their purpose?

The triumph of rhetoric

This vast movement found expression first of all in the establishment of foundations. In Paris, Caen or Madrid pious circles set the example by associating themselves with the initiatives of the Jesuits and the Lazarists, or of Father Jean Eudes in Normandy, through guaranteeing the continuity of their work by means of contracts signed in due and proper form before a notary.[1] The bishops followed suit: Monsignor François de Harlay, Archbishop of Paris, in 1672, Monsignor Ferdinand von

---

[1] AN, Paris, M 211, Congrégation de la Mission (fondations dont celle de Marie Camus, veuve de Michel Particelli d'Emery en 1656); on the missions in the Paris regions and their founders, Ferté, Jeanne, *La Vie religieuse dans les campagnes parisiennes (1622–1695)*, Paris, Vrin, 1962, pp. 196–230; on the founders and benefactors of the missions of Jean Eudes in Normandy, Berthelot du Chesnay, *Jean Eudes*, pp. 45–55 and 135–7.

Fürstenberg, Bishop of Paderborn and Münster, in 1682.[2] The princes did not lag behind. In 1682 Maximilian-Emmanuel of Bavaria urgently called upon the Bishop of Passau to combat the ignorance of religion prevalent among 'the peasant folk as a whole' by supporting religious who would go out every year, when Lent came, to remind the inhabitants of village after village about the rudiments of their faith.[3] Seven years later the Countess Palatine, Emperor Leopold's own sister, granted the Jesuits a capital sum of one thousand florins towards the establishment of a residence for two missionaries in the lands of Jülich and Berg.[4] In Modena in 1683 the Barberina Foundation created by Duchess Lucrezia Barberini was to serve the same purpose for all the parishes of the diocese and adjacent districts.[5] This awareness of the importance of missions, restricted as yet to a few pious individuals, arose at a time when the brilliance of the apostolic activities began to make an impression on everybody.

Never, doubtless, had there been among the missionaries so many highly talented preachers. 'These times', wrote the compiler of the *Annals* of the Capuchins of the Marais, 'are like the time of the Apostles, when everyone hastened to hear them.'[6] Indeed, the preachers in question included Bossuet, Bourdaloue and Fénelon.[7] Their participation, even though temporary, testified to the importance accorded by the Church and by the Most Christian King to the work of teaching the masses. Other orators who were famous at that time devoted themselves wholly to this work. Abbé La Pérouse, of Saint-Sulpice, was in great demand in all parts of France.[8] There were always crowds at the exercises of Father Honoré de Cannes, probably the most celebrated of

---

[2] Order by François de Harlay de Champvallon, Archbishop of Paris, for the establishment of missions in his diocese (1672), quoted by Jean Mauzaize, *Le Rôle et l'action des capucins de la province de Paris dans la France religieuse du XVIIe siècle*, 3 vols., Lille, Atelier de reproduction des thèses, 1978, vol. II, p. 1008; Duhr, Bernhard, SJ, *Geschichte der Jesuiten in den Ländern deutscher Zunge*, 4 vols in 5, Freiburg-im-Breisgau, 1913–21, vol. III, p. 683 (foundation of fifteen missions, of which fourteen in Germany, particularly in the Protestant regions of Hanover, Lower Saxony and, especially, the North).

[3] Baumgartner, Konrad, *Die Seelsorge in Bistum Passau zwischen Barocker Tradition, Aufklärung und Restauration*, Passau, St Ottilien, Münchener Theologische Studien, I, Historische Abteilung, vol. XIX, 1975, p. 313.

[4] Duhr, *Geschichte der Jesuiten*, vol. III, p. 682.

[5] Orlandi, Giuseppe, 'L. A. Muratori e le missioni di P. Segneri Jr', *Spicilegium Historicum Congregationis SSmi Redemptoris*, 1972, pp. 158–294. See p. 164.

[6] BN, Paris, MSS, Nouvelles acquisitions françaises, 4135, 'Recueil de ce qui s'est passé de plus notable en ce couvent du Marais, depuis son establissement en l'année 1622', fos. 63–4.

[7] Cf. pp. 52–5.

[8] ASS, Paris, Correspondence of M. Tronson, Superior of Saint-Sulpice. Numerous mentions, e.g. in MSS 33, 35.

French popular preachers at the end of the seventeenth century.[9] He was asked for in the chief towns, where, at the head of a group of several dozen Capuchins, he organised large-scale missions which were much like those taking place at the same time in Italy. One such was the Toulouse mission of 1678, which began at the end of Lent and lasted for three months. 'He caused his mission to be proclaimed', wrote the compiler of the *Annals* of the Capuchins' Toulouse province, 'from the pulpits of all the parish churches of the town, and himself took the pulpit, on the afternoon of the day he had indicated, in the Church of La Dalbade, which has the biggest nave in the town.' There he preached for a month, then 'being requested by the chapter of St Etienne, he moved his mission to their church and a month after that to the church of St Sernin'.[10] It was said that, so as more certainly to lead everyone to penitence, Father Honoré did not shrink from showing to his audience, from the height of the pulpit, a skull on which he placed, successively, a magistrate's cap, a fashionable lady's ribboned hat and a doctor's wig, in order to illustrate what he had to say about death and judgment.[11] Preaching formed, of course, only part of his activity. He also, helped by his thirty companions, heard confessions. For general communion he organised a great street procession. The mission was completed by the 'planting of a great cross' which he set up at the end of the avenue which ran to the Muret gate. For the ceremony he needed the collaboration of the Confraternity of Black Penitents, to which 'the greatest men of the Parlement belonged'. When the cross had been erected, a hut was built beside it, to shelter a priest who would receive offerings and also, no doubt, would keep an eye on the pious persons who arrived in great numbers, in the following days, to venerate the cross. It was reported that miracles occurred there. 'What is true is that, out of devotion, people cut bits of wood from this cross, either to use in curing illnesses or to carry as relics.' To prevent the cross falling down it had to be strengthened with planks as high as a man.[12]

This procedure was not peculiar to the Capuchins. To consolidate the conversion of the inhabitants of a market town in Brittany Father Maunoir had the idea of organising, at the end of his mission, a theatrical performance the scenario of which was constituted by the hymn he had himself composed on 'the torments of Hell'. The procession was to end at a stage set up in the middle of a field, on which children, properly

---

[9] Raoul de Sceaux, Father, OFM Cap., 'Le père Honoré de Cannes, capucin missionnaire au XVIIe siècle', *XVIIe siècle*, 1958/4, pp. 349–74.
[10] AC, Paris, MS 553, 6, 'Annales des Capucins de la province de Toulouse', p. 1060.
[11] Mauzaize, *Le Rôle et les actions*, vol. II, p. 1020.
[12] AC, Paris, MS 553, 6, pp. 1062–4.

rehearsed, would put questions to 'the dead' (other actors, doubtless from an older age-group) who were hidden under the stage.

When the procession arrived at that place the living began to question the damned. The whole audience was moved by their questions, which interested all. But the gloomy voices, expressing the tortures of the damned, which emerged from under the stage, as though from the bottom of the abyss, frightened this great crowd of more than four thousand persons so much that everyone beat his breast and made new resolutions to repent and avoid sin.[13]

At this time when, in France, religious were constructing, each according to his own sensibility, these great spectacles intended to touch the people's emotions, Father Paolo Segneri, in Italy, was giving the Baroque mission its definitive form. Paolo Segneri the Elder (to distinguish him from his nephew who continued his work) was certainly the most famous European missionary of the second half of the seventeenth century. He owed his prestige to the extent of his activity, since in twenty-seven years, between 1665 and 1692, he travelled through sixteen dioceses completely and seven others in part, all in the Papal States and northern Italy, making a total of 540 missions at the rate of twenty a year. Even more than his activity it was the method he employed, the 'Segnerian' method, that ensured his success. Paolo Segneri did not conceive missionary work otherwise than as performed 'in the manner of the Apostles'. Accordingly, he was seen making his way across country, barefoot, carrying a staff, and dressed in a poor, ragged habit on which he wore a crucifix. 'Father Segneri's dominant virtue', wrote one of his biographers, 'was mortification.' He always slept on planks. He mixed ashes with his food and always wore either a hair-shirt or else an iron belt with long sharp projections.[14] A single companion, Father Giovanni Pietro Pinamonti, accompanied him. 'A multiplicity of missionaries', he said, 'results in diversity of views and is detrimental to the service of God.'[15] In any case, it was him alone that people were waiting for. 'As soon as it became known that he was about to arrive at a certain place', wrote his old historian, 'people flocked to meet him, decorating the road with flowers, and, sometimes, bringing him a canopy. The moment he appeared they prostrated themselves before him. They competed in getting nearer to him, in kissing the hem of his robe and in striving to be closest to him when he blessed them.'[16] In their turn the clergy of the

[13] Boschet, R. P., *Le Parfait Missionnaire ou la vie du R. P. Julien Maunoir de la Compagnie de Jésus, missionnaire en Bretagne*, Paris, 1697, pp. 164–6.
[14] Segneri, Father, of the Society of Jesus, *Méditations sur des passages choisis de l'Ecriture Sainte, pour tous les jours de l'année*, 5 vols., Paris, 1755, vol. I, preface, p. xvii.
[15] Guidetti, *Le missioni popolari*, p. 115.
[16] Segneri, *Méditations*, vol. I, preface, p. viii.

Fig. 1   Welcoming the missionaries. (Missions of the Jesuit Fathers, seventeenth-century engraving, Library of the Society of Jesus, Chantilly, Cliché Flammarion.)

town or village turned out to meet him, offering a cross before which he and his companion prostrated themselves. Then, in procession, all made their way to the parish church, where a *Veni creator* was sung (see Fig. 1).

During the previous days a platform had been set up in some clear area, a square or crossroads. On leaving the church the missionary proceeded thither to deliver his opening sermon, on the theme of II Corinthians, V, 20: 'Now then we are ambassadors of Christ.' His companion stood beside him, holding up the crucifix so that all could see it. The mission usually lasted eight days, except in big towns, where it might go on for longer. The time-table was strict, in order to ensure the complete performance of all the 'actions'. As soon as he arrived the missionary had given instructions as to the hymns to be learnt, the programmes to be kept to, and the places to be occupied by men and by women in front of the platform or during the processions. Each day began, at dawn, with a lesson on the catechism, taken by Father Pinamonti. Then everyone went to the church to tell their beads. After that they came out in procession, led by Father Segneri, who conducted the crowd as they sang the *Miserere*, and went to the spot where the trestles had been set up. All took their places to hear the sermon, which, as was the Jesuits' custom, was inspired by a meditation taken from the first week of the *Spiritual Exercises*. On Monday the preacher's theme was the need to respond to God's call. Tuesday's theme was the price of the soul. On Wednesday the audience learnt how mortal sin makes one God's enemy; on Thursday, that the dishonest sinner is a great sinner; on Friday, that trespasses should be forgiven; and on Sunday, about the eternity of hell-fire. After the solemn sermon came counsels adapted to particular categories among the listeners. Parents were reminded of their duty to give their children a Christian education, while children were ordered to obey their parents.

The Segnerian mission took place at a centre – some large market-town visited by the inhabitants of three or four neighbouring villages. The latter were not, however, to suppose that the Father had come chiefly for the benefit of the faithful of the central parish. Accordingly, once the sermon was over, a procession was organised to go to one of the neighbouring villages, where another sermon was delivered. On the first day this dealt with death, on the second with sin and its unhappy consequences, on the third with the terrible death of the hardened sinner, and on the fourth with sacrilegious confession. There followed the same counsels that had been given in the principal parish, to which all then returned, in orderly fashion, singing the litanies of the Virgin. At the church the Father again took the pulpit for an instruction which dealt, on the first day, with Jesus' journey in Palestine, on the second with the way of the Virgin looking for Jesus, on the third with the ascent of Jesus to Calvary, and on the fourth with the Apostles' expeditions to convert the world. Mass followed. For three days on end – Wednesday, Thursday and Friday – when night fell there were processions of penitents. These began with a procession, round the village, by torch-light, with singing of litanies. Then the women were asked to go back home while the men were led to the church. After a short address the missionary gave himself a vigorous flogging and called on the audience to imitate him. They sang the *Miserere* as the thongs beat down on the penitents' shoulders. From time to time they would raise their voices in some pious aspiration such as 'Die rather than sin again!'

On Friday everyone joined in preparing for the great concluding ceremony, to take place on Sunday. Women and children brought greenery and flowers and arranged them. The men's task was to build, in a clear space outside the village, a wooden chapel to house the two altars (one for the Mass, the other for communion) that were needed for open-air worship on Sunday. Saturday was entirely devoted to confessions. At last came the great Sunday procession, in which all were asked to take part dressed as penitents – crown of thorns on the head, rope around the neck, and, on the shoulder, a cross, big or small depending on the individual's strength. The parishes followed each other in order, with men, women and children clearly separated. It could happen during this final procession that a group might wish to continue doing their penance by flogging themselves thoroughly. On reaching the chapel the faithful followed the Mass and then, one after the other, received communion, before hearing the Father give them his final advice, in the form of a sermon 'on perseverance'.[17]

This description, drawn from a large number of accounts by witnesses, enables us to grasp what the Baroque mission consisted of. It was, first, a spectacle in which every Christian had his place but with the leading roles played by the two missionaries. One of these was the 'soft' one, in this case Pinamonti. Responsible for doctrine, he taught the public the principles of religion, prayer and the sacraments. He caught their attention by telling many stories, amusing ones if necessary. The other, the 'terrible' one, responsible for preaching, made his audience tremble as he dwelt upon the ultimate fate of the faithless: sin, death, Hell.[18] That concluding sermon of Segneri's was especially famous. The missionary appeared on the stage accompanied by four priests. One of these held a whip, another a skull, the third had a rope round his shoulders, and the fourth, with a crown of thorns on his head, raised a crucifix high. During his sermon Segneri spoke now to one, now to another of his assistants. So, in order to make everyone fully conscious

[17] Guidetti, *Le missioni popolari*, pp. 104–25.
[18] Orlandi, Giuseppe, 'Missioni parochiali e drammatica popolare', in *La drammatica popolare nelle valle padana*, Atti del 4o Convegno di studi sul folklore padano, Modena, 23–26 May 1974, Modena, Università del tempo libero, 1976, pp. 305–33.

that death was unavoidable, he would begin by asking of the priest who carried the skull: 'Dear brother, give me the mirror!'[19] Affecting people's emotions was not, however, the only purpose of this pious presentation. It sought to reach the intelligence even as it acted upon the will. When the spectator entered into the game, letting himself be led alternately by Segneri and by Pinamonti, he became aware of the dialogue going on between them, which developed with arguments and replies just as in any stage-play. While one described the atrocious sufferings of the damned, the other set forth the remedies thereto which were available to all. Finally, both spoke in unison, coming together to present Christ both as the model to copy in the way of penitence and as the sole salvation, through the Eucharist he instituted. The conclusion was intended to bring to all the participants that peace without which nothing can be undertaken, not even the good struggle in sight of the other world.[20]

This intellectual coherence and this concern for order – one might almost say for 'policing' – were at least as much characteristic of the Segnerian mission as were the appeal to the will through emotion, the senses and spectacle. Penitence was preached in those days in many other places, but there it remained an end in itself or the means to appease divine wrath during great calamities. Thus it was at Kaufbeuren, in Swabia, when the congregation of the Holy Name of Jesus celebrated the recruitment of its thousandth member in 1661 by impressive processions on Corpus Christi, with hundreds of flagellants and cross-bearers.[21] The sermons of the renowned Augustinian Abraham at Santa Clara, in Vienna, during the great plague of 1679 were inspired by the same spirit.[22] It was the same in Pomerania when at Walcz and Pila (Deutsch Krone and Schneidemühl), during Holy Week, the Jesuits introduced edifying dialogues in the church, followed by 'scourging' sessions for the men of the two towns.[23]

However, despite Paolo Segneri's prestige, it was far from being the case that his method was followed everywhere, even in his own order. Many distrusted its pomp and theatricality. They feared that, once the surprise-effect had passed, lassitude would take over, and even, perhaps,

[19] Guidetti, *Le missioni popolari*, p. 123.
[20] Orlandi, 'Missioni parochiali', pp. 305–33.
[21] BH, Munich, *Jesuiten*, 110, fo.112 (Kaufbeuren).
[22] P. Abraham's a Sancta Clara, *Auserlesene Werke*, 2 vols., Vienna and Leipzig, R. Sammer, 1846, vol. II, pp. 537–614. 'Mercks Wien, Das ist dess wütenden Todts ein umständige Beschreibung in der berühmten Haupt und Kayserl. Residenz Stadt in Oesterreich, im sechzehen hundert und neun und siebenzigsten Jahr.'
[23] *Historia Residentiae Walcensis Societatis Jesu ab Anno Domini 1618. Geschichte der Jesuitenresidenz in Walcz (Deutsch Krone) 1618–1773*, ed. Max Rohwerden with Annelise Triller, Cologne and Graz, Böhlau, 1967, pp. 122–4 (1688).

irony and mockery. What would be better, wrote one Provincial at the end of the seventeenth century, Father Imperiali, would be frequent missions conceived in accordance with the original spirit of the Society, rather than these grand ceremonies, costly to the people and their parish priests, and which could not be repeated.[24] Naturally, those who, like Vincent de Paul, counted above all on long weeks of religious education in order to bring a village to conversion could not be easily convinced by the startling and sudden mode of attack upon evil that was employed by the Italian Jesuit. Accordingly, the Lazarists, when they undertook in the second half of the seventeenth century to transform the parishes of the diocese of Saint-Malo, devoted an average of one month to each village or small town. There was no question of a stage or of penitents' processions by torchlight. Nor was there any impressive concluding ceremony with 'planting of a cross'. If one or two processions were organised, they took place without pomp, without special costumes and without little children got up as angels. The sole criterion was utility. Grand sermons were rejected in favour of simple instructions aimed at correcting the serious faults most common among the countryfolk: ignorance, blasphemy, hatred between neighbours, quarrelling, drunkenness. Major importance was allotted to lessons on the catechism and to confessions. To ensure a future for their work the missionaries took care to establish everywhere a charitable confraternity. They concerned themselves also, while they were carrying out their mission among the people, with assembling the priests of the deanery for an ecclesiastical conference, a real cycle of continuous training for rectors and curates not all of whom had attended a seminary. This essentially practical activity aimed at changing the countryside through a long-term operation.[25]

This was also the case in the neighbouring region of the Cotentin, where Jean Eudes and his companions carried out systematic missions covering the whole of the dioceses of Avranches and Coutances between 1632 and 1676.[26] Upper Normandy and Brittany were the next special fields of action for the Eudists, after their founder's death. Even more than the Lazarists, the Eudists believed in the efficacy of protracted activity in the same place. It was understood that a team should spend six weeks in a village and seven or eight in a town. Preaching had to be simple and practical, as advised by Vincent de Paul and Bérulle.[27] There was no question of making a shock-effect at the outset, through fear of

---

[24] Orlandi, 'L. A. Muratori', p. 167.
[25] Lebrun, François, 'Les missions des Lazaristes en haute Bretagne au XVIIe siècle', *Annales de Bretagne et des pays de l'Ouest*, 89/1, 1982, pp. 15–38.
[26] Berthelot du Chesnay, *Jean Eudes*.   [27] *Ibid.*, p. 68.

Hell, but rather of developing an entire teaching programme over a period of weeks. They began with penitence, then passed to fear of God, and dwelt in the following four weeks upon vices and virtues. These themes were taken up and developed day by day, through instruction which was adapted to different age-groups and social classes. The compiler of the order's *Annals* noted in connection with the mission to Vire in June 1682 that each day 'they gave three instructions to the people in the church, which was full, from half past four in the morning, of persons wishing to be present at the prayers and the counsels with which it was customary to accompany them, so as to instruct the simple folk and the craftsmen'.[28] The culmination of all these exercises was a thoroughgoing confession, which many admitted they had never made before, from ignorance of what their sins were.[29] They therefore had to prepare this confession with great care. Being sometimes asked to examine themselves afresh after a first confession that was considered unsatisfactory, the penitents anxiously saw the end of the mission draw near without their having been granted absolution. The crowds waiting outside the churches became more and more numerous, even though the priests of neighbouring parishes were called in to help. During the mission to Genêt, in the Bay of Mont-Saint-Michel, which took place during the 'great winter' of 1709, 'countryfolk were seen to spend the night in the cemetery, even though it was exposed to the sea winds, so that they might keep their places for the confessionals, which from five in the morning were surrounded by so many penitents that confessions could go on for the rest of the day, covering between four and five hundred persons'.[30] Already in 1659, during his mission to Vasteville, in the north of the Cotentin, Jean Eudes had written to friends in Paris to try and touch their hearts by telling of the fate of so many peasants who came to confess but had to leave without absolution, owing to the insufficient number of priests available.[31] This emphasis on the Sacrament of Penitence is connected with that reflection by the congregation's founder concerning the missionaries who formed a new 'convent' in the town.[32] The calling to apostleship had to give way to the contemplation required of priests and laymen. The spirit of the French school, of which Jean Eudes was a distinguished representative was clearly to be perceived here.

[28] ACJM, Paris, MSS, Annales de la Congrégation de Jésus et de Marie, vol. XXVII, pp. 1140–1.
[29] *Ibid.*, vol. XXVIII, p. 337 (Le Teilleul mission, 1713).
[30] *Ibid.*, vol. XXVIII, p. 241.
[31] St Jean Eudes, *Textes choisis*, presented by Father Charles Berthelot du Chesnay, Namur, Soleil Levant, 1958, pp. 47–9.
[32] Berthelot du Chesnay, *Les Missions de saint Jean Eudes*, p. 142.

It is understandable that these demands led to endeavours, besides the missions, to create institutions that would awaken, among the simplest people, a genuine spiritual life. Such were the retreats the first house for which, intended for laymen, was established at Vannes in 1660 and directed by a Jesuit, Father Huby.[33] Soon afterward a lady of the same town, Mademoiselle de Francheville, opened another, for women, and, recognising 'that peasant women are no less capable of retreats than townswomen and ladies of quality', decided that it should be open to all, without any discrimination.[34] For eight days men or women lived shut away in accordance with an almost monastic rule, concerning themselves exclusively with the spiritual life. It was no longer merely a matter of learning to practise Christianity, as was the case in the missions, but of becoming initiated into prayer. 'They are mistaken', wrote Jean Leuduger in a manual well known at the end of the seventeenth century, 'who persuade themselves that only clergy, religious or men of learning can pray. Holy Scripture teaches that countryfolk are no less capable than they, since it assures us in many places that God is pleased to communicate Himself to the simplest of souls . . . '[35] Within a few years, Jesuits, Eudists and secular priests multiplied these houses in western France, which thus became the field of experiment for a new approach to religious life of the Christian masses.

These new orders, these ever more numerous religious, and the ordinary priests who collaborated with them showed how important from now on was the work of missionaries in the country districts. But the variety of methods employed, which reflected the variety of doctrinal or spiritual schools, reflected also the differences that could exist among the rural populations. With some of these all that could be done was to attempt the conversion they needed. With others – few, to be sure – it could already be a matter of prayer and spiritual life. France was precisely the country in which there were Christians who had attained different degrees of progress in religious life thanks to missionaries who knew how to direct them and to adapt themselves to the most diverse situations. Making use of these missionaries for a new and large-scale

[33] BSJ, Chantilly, MSS in fos. 3 and 4 (nineteenth-century copy of MS 3264 in Bibl. Mazarine, Paris), 'Histoire de la première de toutes les maisons publiques de retraite fondée en l'année 1660 dans la ville de Vannes en Bretagne par monsieur Louis Eudo de Klivio'.

[34] Heduit, Jacqueline, *Initiatrice et fondatrice des retraites de femmes, Catherine de Francheville. Sa vie (1620–1689). Son œuvre: la retraite de Vannes.* Tours, Mame, 1957, p. 93.

[35] [Leuduger, Jean]. *Bouquet des retraites renfermées et autres missions, contenant les prières du matin et du soir . . . ensemble sept méditations sur les principaux mystères de la Passion, la dévotion aux cinq plaies avec les figures et méditations sur icelles pour chaque jour de la semaine, les Litanies et Chapelets . . . des Cantiques spirituels à la fin,* new edition, Rennes, n.d., p. 24.

task in the service of the state could be a very tempting prospect for politicians.

The grand design

During the evening of 18 March 1683 two Jesuits entered Deidesheim, in the Palatinate. They were no ordinary missionaries. They had a mandate from the local bishop, the Prince-Bishop of Speyer, to inspect and correct everything on his behalf, and were therefore received with great deference. The magistrate hastened to have the bell rung to summon the inhabitants, who were ordered to be present next morning at five in the parish church. Before dawn the bell rang again and the crowd gathered in the appointed place while the town's gates were shut so that nobody could yield to temptation to attend to his temporal affairs. Father Osburg said Mass, explained the reason for his coming, examined, along with his companion, the church, the schools and the hospital, and then gave a lesson on the catechism before taking post in the confessional until late in the evening. Next day, which was Saint Joseph's day, a solemn Mass with panegyric was celebrated. Then the population were invited to communicate. After that, visits to the chapels of ease began. The whole affair ended, on 23 March, with a service with a *Te Deum* held in the chapel of pilgrimage to the Holy Cross, to which the missionaries had come to bless the bells.[36]

The way these Jesuits mandated by the bishop went about their work was much cruder than the ways of Father Segneri or Father Maunoir. What mattered to them, apparently, more than rhetoric or theatricals calculated to insinuate themselves into the minds of the masses, was the number of communities they visited, which was very large. They visited 140 parishes, in 1683 alone, in the Archdiocese of Mainz.[37] They visited between 80 and 150 every year in the Luxemburg part of the Archdiocese of Trier between 1680 and 1695,[38] and 440 between 1690 and 1695 in the Duchy of Jülich, near Cologne.[39] The 230 to 250 parishes in the diocese of Strasburg were visited with care between 1684 and 1688, each receiving a mission.[40] In 1680 Monsignor d'Aubusson

[36] Duhr, *Geschichte der Jesuiten*, vol. III, p. 674; on the religious policy of the Palatinate, Stamer, L., *Kirchengeschichte der Pfalz*, vol. III, 2, *Von der Reform zur Aufklärung. Ende der mittelalterlichen Diözesen (1685–1801)*, Speyer, 1959, pp. 16–19; Schaab, Meinhard, 'Die Wiederherstellung des Katholizismus in der Kurpfalz im 17 und 18 Jahrhundert', *Zeitschrift für die Geschichte des Oberrheins*, 114, 1966, pp. 147–205.
[37] Duhr, *Geschichte der Jesuiten*, vol. III, p. 670.
[38] Birsens, *Manuels de catéchisme*, pp. 345–6.
[39] Duhr, *Geschichte der Jesuiten*, vol. III, pp. 665–6.
[40] Châtellier, Louis, *Tradition chrétienne et renouveau catholique dans l'ancien diocèse de Strasburg (1650–1770)*, Paris, Ophrys, 1981, pp. 289–94.

de la Feuillade, Bishop of Metz, undertook a systematic visitation of the Sarre region, accompanied by six Jesuits who preached and taught the catechism.[41] Under supervision by the same prelate, this enterprise was repeated five years later with considerably greater resources.[42]

This intense effort which marked the years 1680–90 was not peculiar to the Rhine area. In the *Annals* of the Languedoc Capuchins we read that between 1680 and 1683 the bishops of Montpellier, Rodez, Béziers and other places sent religious to preach systematically in all the parishes of their respective dioceses.[43] The same was done in the Archdiocese of Besançon in the time of Pierre-Antoine de Grammont. This prelate established in 1682, in his Beaupré residence, a group of missionary priests whose task at first was to act as diocesan visitors. 'They will take note of all matters [concerning the churches] that they consider ought to be reported to us', we read in the letters of institution.[44] This did not prevent them from carrying out, between 1682 and 1700, more than eighty missions, each of about four or five weeks.[45] The Jesuits of Pomerania proved able to undertake, in the year 1682 alone, sixty-eight missions from their modest residence at Wałcz (Deutsch Krone) where there were only seven religious.[46] (See Map 3.)

This was, after a forty-year lull, the first major enterprise of European dimensions aimed at challenging, from the Catholic side, the religious peace which had been secured, not without difficulty, by the Treaties of Westphalia in 1648. It was focused, for preference, on regions where the Catholic and Protestant communities lived close together and which seemed so many zones of fragility on the religious map of Europe. On the pretext of effecting a necessary consolidation of Catholics in their faith, was it not tempting to exert pressure on the Lutherans and Calvinists who lived nearby, so as to bring them to a reconciliation 'as important as it was easy, according to their own principles'?[47] For some years already controversialists had been saying that the objections presented by the non-Catholics against rejoining the Roman Church were due ultimately to mere ignorance on their part of what that church actually taught. This was the argument sustained in 1659 by Dr Thomas

---

[41] Choux, Abbé Jacques, 'Journal de la visite pastorale de Georges d'Aubusson, évêque de Metz, dans l'archidiaconé de Sarrebourg en 1680', *Le Pays lorrain*, 1980/1, pp. 13–34.

[42] ADMM, H.1959, pp. 119–20 (August 1685).

[43] AC, Paris, MS 553, 6, 'Annales des Capucins de la province de Toulouse', p. 1141.

[44] Bergier, Abbé J. B., *Histoire de la communauté des prêtres missionnaires de Beaupré et des missions faites en Franche-Comté depuis 1676 jusqu'en 1850*, Besançon, 1853, p. 47.

[45] *Ibid.*, p. 71.

[46] *Historia Residentiae*, p. 117.

[47] The phrase is from the announcement, by poster, of sermons to be given by Father Jean Dez, SJ, in Strasburg Cathedral in winter 1684–5. Archives municipales de Strasbourg, fonds Saint-Thomas, carton 88.

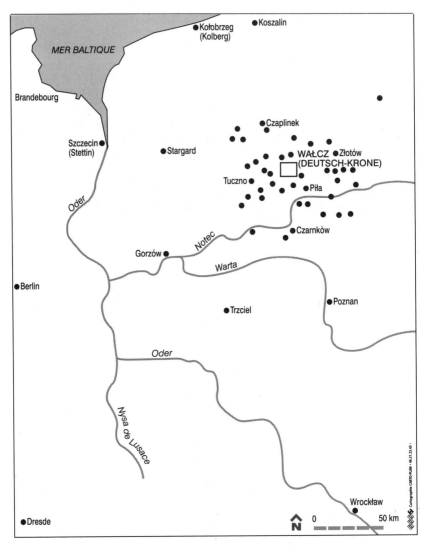

Map 3   The sphere of influence of a small Jesuit mission centre in
Pomerania (Wałcz) at the end of the seventeenth century and in the
first half of the eighteenth.

Henrici, the future suffragan Bishop of Basel, in his *Irenicum Catholicum*.[48] In Mainz the Jesuit Jakob Masen held the same opinion.[49] And Bossuet took up this argument to develop with talent in his *Exposition de la doctrine de l'Eglise catholique sur les matieres de controverse* (1671).[50] Gradually, the term 'conversion' came to be replaced by 'reunion', which seemed both more irenic and more artful.[51]

Nevertheless, this plan would have come to nothing had it not been supported by several rulers. The Catholic Duke of Neuburg, who in 1685 had just acquired the succession of the Lower Palatinate, was seen as a particularly tolerant ruler since he had granted 'free exercise of their religions in his realms' to the faithful of the three confessions. At the same time, however, he gave full support to the Jesuits of Heidelberg in their efforts to recover lost ground![52] Emperor Leopold I yielded to the arguments of a Franciscan, Spinola, whom he had made a bishop and who hoped to win over a certain number of Protestant princes to the idea of a 'reunion' with the Catholics in return for certain safeguards.[53] Parallel with this, however, the Habsburgs were intensifying their support for all Catholic missionary enterprises. Finally, Louis XIV had in 1680 charged the Jesuits to expound Catholic doctrine to the Protestants of the Sarre region and Alsace. This they did by stressing the points of similarity with Luther's teaching, whereas the minister Louvois was insistently calling on the notables to convert, and ordering troop-movements near Protestant centres which heralded what would soon become, in the west and south-west of France, the *dragonnades*.[54]

The attempt to accomplish 'reunion' of the entire city of Strasburg was perhaps the most striking manifestation of this policy, for the success of which neither Church nor king spared their efforts. Its central feature consisted of a major mission which went on all through the winter of 1684–5 and the following spring, the chief activists in it being the Jesuits of the college, led by their rector, Father Jean Dez.[55] The

---

[48] Joris, M., 'Der Basler Weihbischof Thomas Henrici (1597–1660) und sein *Irenicum Catholicum* (1659). Ein Beitrag zur Geschichte der Oekumene im Fürstbistum Basel nach dem Dreissigjährigen Krieg', *Zeitschrift fur schweizerische Kirchengeschichte*, 1978/1–2, pp. 74–107.

[49] Châtellier, *Tradition chrétienne*, p. 262.   [50] *Ibid.*

[51] This is the word used by Father Jean Dez, SJ, in his book *La Réunion des protestants de Strasbourg à l'Eglise romaine, également nécessaire pour leur salut et facile selon leurs principes*, Strasburg, 1687: see my analysis in *Tradition chrétienne*, pp. 260–2.

[52] Châtellier, Louis, 'Les catholiques rhénans et la révocation de l'édit de Nantes', *Bulletin de la Société de l'histoire du protestantisme français*, 131, 1986/2, pp. 239–55.

[53] Châtellier, *Tradition chrétienne*, pp. 260–2.

[54] Choux, 'Georges d'Aubusson'; Heck, Jacques-Henri, 'La révocation de l'édit de Nantes à Lixheim', *Les Cahiers lorrains*, 1984/1, pp. 57–66; Châtellier, *Tradition chrétienne*, pp. 266–9.

[55] Châtellier, *Tradition chrétienne*, pp. 266–80.

latter, a person respected in the Society and well connected at court (he was the Dauphin's confessor), explained point by point the articles of the Augsburg Confession, giving them a Catholic interpretation. He tried to persuade his hearers in the Cathedral that there was no longer any valid reason why they should continue to remain outside the king's own religion. In his view, the explanation he had given removed all doubts and smoothed over all objections. Enthusiastic laymen backed his teaching by circulating among the townspeople a prospectus which repeated in abridged form – with all the risks entailed in excessive simplification – the arguments expounded from the pulpit. These were the *Articles principaux de la Foy pour réunir les esprits et ramener Messieurs les Protestants de la Confession d'Augsbourg à l'église catholique romaine*, which were immediately condemned by Rome. The failure was complete and the few conversions obtained resulted more from the measures of intimidation used by Louvois, or the payments made to poor people and soldiers, than to attempts at doctrinal compromise.[56]

The missions following the Revocation of the Edict of Nantes

The failure of the grand design was, perhaps, one of the causes of the Revocation of the Edict of Nantes (18 October 1685). Yet the prohibition of Protestant worship and the forced conversions obtained by the dragoons were not enough, even in the minds of those who were most ardent advocates of violent measures to make of the kingdom an 'all-Catholic France', to use Pierre Bayle's expression. As the chronicler of the Oratory wrote, 'to make this undertaking solid and durable and cement it by methods worthier of the true religion', it was necessary to complete the effect of the law and the secular power by means of apostolic preaching.[57] Consequently, by order of the king, an immense mission was decided upon, aimed at all those who, anywhere in the kingdom, had just been obliged to change their religion[58] (see Map 4). This enterprise was very far reaching: all the religious orders and all the societies of priests were requested, and in practice compelled, to conform to the order which had been sent to them. 'So, here we are then, suddenly all become preachers', wrote the Superior of the Saint-Sulpice Seminary to one of his correspon-

[56] *Ibid.*, pp. 295–303.
[57] AOF, Paris, MSS in 4°, 5, 'Troisième partie des mémoires domestiques pour servir à l'histoire de la Congrégation de l'Oratoire . . . ', 5th period, Father de Saint-Marthe, 1672–96, fo. 244.
[58] AN, Paris, * G8 709, 'Comptes de la dépense des missions du clergé rendu en l'Assemblée de 1690', n.p.

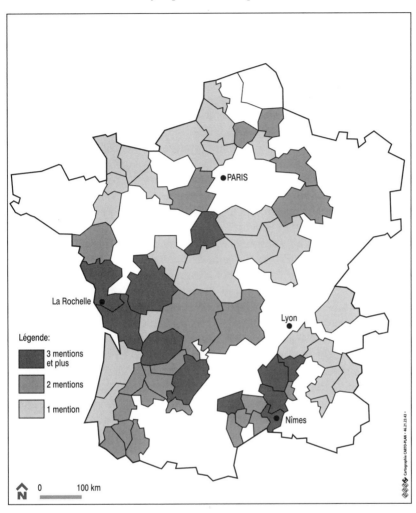

Map 4   Missions subsidised by the King and the clergy of France in the dioceses after the Revocation of the Edict of Nantes, 1685–7.

dents.[59] They had few directives beyond those to explain clearly the Catholic Church's doctrine, on the basis of the decrees of the Council of Trent or of 'the exposition of the Faith by Monseigneur the Bishop of Meaux', and to try, by their kindness and patience, to cause the cruelties of the dragoons to be forgotten.[60]

[59] ASS, Paris, Correspondence of M. Tronson, MS 43, item 101, pp. 283–4, letter of 28 December 1685.
[60] AOF, Paris, MSS in 4°, 5, 'Troisième partie', MS quoted, fos. 245–6.

It was advisable not to take literally these good words, full of unction, which had been lavished by the courtier Archbishop Harlay de Champvallon. Fénelon, having been sent to the diocese of Saintes, took it into his head to give some satisfaction to the new Catholics and thought it would facilitate a sincere change of heart on their part if they were allowed to sing psalms 'on Sundays in the church'.[61] He was soon called to order by Father de la Chaise, Louis XIV's confessor, who sharply reminded him that his task was to accustom the converts 'to the Church's practices' and not to maintain them in their old ways.[62]

Actually, apart from those who, like Bourdaloue or Abbé de la Pérouse, passed meteorically through Languedoc, preaching during Lent, most of the missionaries realised very quickly that they had been given an impossible task to perform. A certain Oratorian who had been sent, in the Montpellier diocese, to Ganges – later to be a centre of the Camisard War – was doubtless voicing a widespread opinion when he wrote to his Superior that he had met no more than 'two thousand inconvertible converts'.[63] Two of his colleagues, preachers at Mauguio, had tried to instruct five hundred Protestants, 'with much approval for the truth . . . but very little outcome'. They added that 'they would have sooner succeeded in converting five hundred ministers than in converting the women and girls of this county'.[64] The same admission recurred in most of the mission reports, whether from the west or the south of France: the people came to church only under constraint and forced by the dragoons, or as a result of a threat made by the intendant in person that their houses would be occupied.[65]

Some missionaries doubtless cherished the hope that a long-term operation would at least bring about the results that they had failed to obtain in their few weeks of missionary work. 'What is certain', wrote Fénelon to the Marquis de Seignelay, Secretary of State for the Navy, 'is that good parish priests, good schoolmasters and grey sisters will do more good in this country than we can do, especially if these helpers are accompanied by almsgiving to continue that provided by the Consistory.'[66] The view held by the Oratory was no different. Father de Chevigny regularly toured the villages around Sommières and taught the priests the art of maintaining their parishioners' fervour. He proposed

---

[61] *Correspondance de Fénelon. Lettres antérieures à l'épiscopat*, 3 vols., edited, with commentary, by Jean Orcibal, Paris, Klincksieck, 1972, vol. II, p. 21.
[62] *Ibid.*, pp. 26–7.
[63] AOF, Paris, MSS in 4°, 5, 'Troisième partie', MS quoted, fo. 262, letter of 29 November 1685.
[64] *Ibid.*, fo. 262vo.
[65] *Ibid.*, fo. 268, letter from Intendant de Baville, 3 April 1686 (Le Vigan).
[66] *Correspondance*, vol. II, p. 58.

that, every evening, they read to the latter a sermon by Father Lejeune, accompanying this with 'some other pious exercises'.[67] Everyone stressed the importance of instructing the children, 'from whom we can hope for more than from their fathers, because they have not yet been prevented by contrary impressions'. To fulfil the requirement, two establishments were needed. There had to be schools 'set up in all places, with schoolmasters whom the communities were obliged to pay'. Regular catechising was also needed. The Capuchins noted the advantage of this in respect not only of the children but also of their parents. 'For the fathers and mothers who had the pleasure of hearing their children answer publicly in the church often made them repeat before them the responses they had been taught, and so these were imprinted in the parents' minds as well as in those of the children.' Another advantage was that 'this obliged the children to be more often with the missionaries and thereby to complete their awareness of matters concerning the Catholic religion'.[68] Charity was also indispensable. Father de Chevigny, of the Oratory, furnished an example of its effectiveness which was not free from malignity towards the rival order of Jesuits. While in Montpellier, he wrote, the famous Bourdaloue 'had spoken at length and very well without winning anyone over', he, Chevigny, had gone to talk with the craftsmen and, having given them some money, had had 'the consolation of bringing them back to the faith'.[69]

But these hopes for later on which were offered to the Superiors or to the king's ministers were there, perhaps, only to mitigate the bitterness of the negative balance-sheet which, after two or three years of activity, all the missionaries who had been sent into Protestant areas were obliged to draw up. To explain this failure some wrote of the incompetence or lack of zeal of many of these improvised preachers.[70] The same ones added that the king bore some share of responsibility through having withdrawn so soon the backing he had given to the enterprise, from fear of increasing his expenses at this time when the War of the League of Augsburg was beginning.[71]

Yet these reasons did not suffice, at a time when the missionary spirit was spreading over all Europe. In the accounts of the missions to the Cévennes, whether written by Oratorians or by Capuchins, we briefly glimpse scenes that expose the alien nature of these enterprises and

[67] AOF, Paris, MSS in 4°, 5, 'Troisième partie', MS quoted, fo. 265vo, letter of spring 1686.
[68] AC, Paris, MSS, 553, 7, pp. 1202–3.
[69] AOF, Paris, MSS in 4°, 5, 'Troisième partie', MS quoted, fo. 266.
[70] AC, Paris, MSS, 553, 7, pp. 1176–7 (criticism by the Capuchins of Languedoc).
[71] AC, Paris, MSS, 553, 6, pp. 1205–6.

allow us to suspect what the future will hold. The first impression received by the Oratorians when they arrived at Genolhac, near Alès, at the end of the winter of 1686, was of men ready for combat and on their guard. 'The people of these mountains, the highest in the Cévennes', they recorded in their report, 'were like so many bandits, standing proud on their rocks which are almost inaccessible to the dragoons.' And they needed support from the latter in order to make those people come to confession a few weeks later. Very few, though, were actually converted: 'most of them doing it only outwardly, for show'.[72] To the discouragement of the missionaries was contrasted the firm resolution of the Protestant population, who could not be brought to bow the knee – and then only superficially – without the use of violence and terror. Nothing evinced the disarray of communities left leaderless after their pastors had been expelled from the kingdom under the terms of the Edict of Fontainebleau.[73] At Bolbec, in Normandy, in a region where the Protestants were far from being in the majority, the Oratorians had been reduced, in order to engage in dialogue, to going from house to house. They did not even cross the threshold of most of the houses they called at, as the occupiers took care to tell them 'that they had nothing to discuss with them, that they knew all that they needed to know about religion, and that they would continue all their lives to be what they were then'.[74] Had not the roles been reversed and the missionaries placed in the unpleasant situation of canvassers for a new religion being shown the door by believers confident that they belonged to the true Church?

The Protestants' position was indeed changing. The confusion of the time of the *dragonnades* and the Revocation had been followed by a will to resist. From 1686 onward signs seen as supernatural manifestations brought them encouragement. In Béarn the singing of psalms was heard in places where previously Protestant places of worship had stood. Soon the same thing was happening in the Cévennes, where this melodious singing was followed by beating of drums and sounding of trumpets, as though to herald a charge.[75] A prophecy circulated, to the effect that within three years – in 1689 – the true Church would be freed.[76] Next, men and women, often very young, were seized by the Holy Spirit and

[72] AOF, Paris, MSS in 4°, 5, 'Troisième partie', MS quoted, fo. 270vo, letter of 17 December 1685.
[73] Text of the edict in Isambert, *Recueil des anciennes lois françaises*, vol. XIX, Paris, 1829, pp. 530–4.
[74] AOF, Paris, MSS 4°,5, 'Troisième partie', MS quoted, fo. 248vo, letter of 14 December 1685.
[75] Douen, O., *Les Premiers Pasteurs du désert (1685–1700)*, 2 vols., Paris, Grassart, 1879, vol. II, pp. 39–43.
[76] Joutard, Philippe, *Les Camisards*, Paris, Gallimard, Coll. 'Archives', 1976, p. 60.

spoke out like Old Testament prophets. One of these, in February 1688, was Isabeau Vincent, a shepherdess at Saou, in Dauphiné, sixteen or seventeen years old. During the night, while fast asleep, she began speaking out loud, and what she said alternated between prophecies and sermons. This event did not remain a secret. Crowds gathered, coming from far off to listen to her. Excitement spread among the towns and villages round about, and affected the Catholic authorities, who considered that they must publicly denounce what the prophetess was saying nightly in her cottage. True, the impassioned speeches uttered by Isabeau, daughter of a convert, who had herself often attended Mass, included a sort of parody of the eucharist and of sermons she had heard. 'We pray to Thee for our Holy Father the Pope, for our lords and Cardinals, Archbishops and Bishops, for Monseigneur de Valence et Die, and for all the benefactors of this Church', she proclaimed, amid guffaws from those at her bedside. Then she went on, in a serious tone: 'The city has seven hills, idols, the lights of the church and, especially, the false sacrifice.' And she cried out, 'The Mass, the Mass, what, my most dear brothers, do you believe the Mass to be? I compare it to a fine silver plate, very white outside but black within.'[77] From time to time her speeches were interrupted by phrases such as this: 'It is not I who speak but the Spirit that is within me.' Then she would go on:

For when we seek the Word we are seeking God Himself. It is earthly goods that have made our purgatory and our perdition. Behold, there are but two ways, the way to Hell and the way to Paradise. The first is broad and spacious and the wicked walk along it in great numbers, but the way to Paradise is narrow. Those who are burdened with sin cannot walk along it, for it is rough and crooked. One must suffer persecution in order to reach it. But to you, believers, God will say, one day: Come, ye who are blessed by my Father, etc., and to the wicked He will say: Go, accursed ones, into eternal fire, etc.

This session ended with 'the *Pater Noster* which is said at High Mass', to which she added: 'What do you make of that? It is like everyday songs. That's how the wicked have put it into another language. But when Our Lord taught his Apostles to pray he said to them: Our Father, which art in Heaven, etc.'[78] The speeches of the young Dauphiné shepherdess were thus made up of a mixture of fragments from Protestant sermons with memories of the preaching by Catholic missionaries (the ways to Hell and to Paradise seemed to be taken straight from the panels painted by Le Nobletz, Maunoir and their colleagues), along with scraps from Calvinist worship and from High Mass.

[77] Douen, *Les Premiers Pasteurs*, vol. II, p. 51, note 1.
[78] *Ibid.*, pp. 51–8.

The case of Isabeau Vincent was not isolated. In the following year, 1689, another Dauphinois, a young farmer named Gabriel Astier, uttered similar thoughts: 'My brothers, draw near to me, reform and repent. If you do not repent you will all be doomed. Cry to God for mercy. God's judgment will come in three months' time.' He spoke thus in the Vivarais, the very region where Jean-François Régis had earlier pursued his apostleship. And so, to complete the resemblance to the Catholic missionaries who had then toured the region, he caused a 'stage' to be erected, as they had, and from it conducted the singing of psalms.[79] Later, during the Camisard War, a certain Doustin, touched by the Spirit while he was being questioned by the judge in Montpellier, exclaimed: 'Mercy! Pardon, Lord!' before adding '*Filii, Filio meo*'.[80]

Was this the outcome of the post-Revocation missions in the countryside? Had they provided a source of inspiration, a form of expression and, above all, a model of Christianity to be combated, to inspired preachers who were preparing the Protestant 'reawakening'? However, since frontiers between confessions have never been insurmountable in the history of religions, the prophets of the wilderness were also, perhaps, no less effectively, preparing new ways for future evangelisation in both Protestant and Catholic areas, if only through the role now taken by lay persons who, for the first time, emerged from anonymity and began to speak.

At the end of the seventeenth century the effects of the post-Tridentine missions were, in a way, contradictory. On the one hand were entire regions where Paolo Segneri or Julien Maunoir, Jean Eudes or Honoré de Cannes, were welcomed as true messengers from Heaven. Nothing seemed able to resist their divine fervour, their apostolic zeal and their prophetic enthusiasm. Europe, partitioned in accordance with rules accepted by all in the Treaties of Westphalia, seemed about to tip over entirely into the Catholic camp, fascinated by the words of these spiritual conquerors. But then the latter entered the Lutheran and Calvinist lands. Suddenly, what had been a source of glory for them in Catholic lands collapsed amid indifference and contempt in the Protestant territory. It even happened that their moving cries, their pressing appeals for penitence became distorted from their original sense so as to become, in the mouths of Cévenol shepherds and shepherdesses, harsh criticisms of popery or inspired words which

[79] Mours, Samuel, and Robert, Daniel, *Le Protestantisme en France du XVIIIe siècle à nos jours*, Paris, Librairie protestante, 1972, pp. 63–4.
[80] Bost, C., 'Les "Prophètes des Cévennes" au XVIIIe siècle', *Revue d'histoire et de philosophie religieuses*, 1925/5, pp. 401–30 and 419–20.

might cause the martyred community to rise up for freedom. This crude travesty was a sign. The missionaries of the Baroque age, despite all their talent and all their zeal, had not yet, perhaps, found the real language of the poor.

4 Apotheosis

Because in the eighteenth century there began to make its way into people's minds a mode of judging one's epoch by the scandals or excesses that were apparent, a tendency grew to neglect the everyday scene which offered only increasingly edifying behaviour on the part of the Christian masses. This was to a large extent the result of missionary activity carried on without respite since the end of the previous century, which in the 1720s (aided by the Enlightenment) took the form of systematic covering of entire regions, where the towns and villages, without exception, were visited one after another. Also, no doubt, some remarkable personalities influenced this persistent activity and gave it, here and there, fresh impetus. Among these were Francis of Geronimo in the Kingdom of Naples, Louis-Marie Grignion de Montfort in Lower Poitou, and also, later, Alfonso de Liguori and Pedro Calatayud. But the laity were not inactive. Just like the masses in the United Kingdom who defied their bishops by going to hear John Wesley, or like the little groups of Pietists and Moravian Brethren who avoided the vigilance of their Lutheran pastors in order to attempt, in common, a new approach to God, the Catholics of South and North felt, in an obscure way, that the missionaries who came among them had something fresh to bring them and that with them it might be possible to build a new form of Christianity.

Southern and Western Europe

The Europe of 1700–50 was one great 'missionary land'. Although Italy had been thoroughly covered in the course of two centuries, it remained the chosen territory of the principal religious orders. The Jesuits, for example, continued and even intensified their activity there.[1] Paolo Segneri the Younger carried on his uncle's work, using similar

---

[1] Faralli, Carla, 'Le missioni dei Gesuiti in Italia sec. XVI–XVII: problemi di una ricerca in corso', *Bolletino della Società di studi valdesi*, 1975, pp. 97–116, with map on p. 105, is also valuable for the first half of the eighteenth century.

methods.[2] Father Fulvio Fontana, a one-time disciple of the famous preacher, did the same for the north of Italy. Accompanied by the faithful Pinamonti, he visited in 1694 and 1695 the lands of the Duke of Tuscany, and revisited them in 1698. Between those dates he had covered the Duchy of Modena. In 1699 and 1700 came the turn of the great Archdiocese of Bologna. Then, responding to a call from Cardinal Colloredo, he concerned himself with the region of the Alpine lakes and valleys: the dioceses of Como, Lugano, Locarno and Bellinzona. In 1702 he began preaching in the Milanese, continuing, with breaks due to his long-distance journeys, until 1711.[3]

Within this vast area, however, he was not alone, but could rely on collaboration from teams of diocesan missionaries, the oblates of Saint Charles, an order founded by Charles Borromeo and renewed and reorganised by Father Martinelli at the beginning of the eighteenth century. These religious, trained in a special seminary, were employed by the bishop for particular tasks he assigned to them. They accompanied him on his pastoral visits. They applied themselves especially to working in complete co-operation with parish priests who were called upon to continue among their flocks the missionary activity begun by the oblates.[4] This situation was repeated in a number of Italian dioceses where the bishops had felt a need not to be content with the support given by itinerant religious, no matter how distinguished these might be. At the beginning of the seventeenth century Father Pavone, SJ, had founded in Naples a Marian congregation for priests, whom he prepared for helping with missions.[5] In 1693 some Neapolitan craftsmen and workers formed themselves into a congregation to act as auxiliaries to the Jesuits who were at work in the poor quarters of the city.[6] They accompanied Fathers Aloysius de Mutiis and Francis of Geronimo in their apostleship among the soap-boilers, fishermen, unemployed, prostitutes and all the poor of the outskirts and shantytowns of Naples in the 1700s.[7] The villages of southern Italy were visited, like those of the Milanese, by religious who

[2] Orlandi, 'L. A. Muratori'.
[3] Fontana, Fulvio, Quaresimale de Padre Fulvio Fontana della Compagnia di Giesù con L'Aggiunta delle serie delle Missioni da Lui fate nell'Italia e Germania, Venice, 1721, pp. 299–350.
[4] Barbieri, Gianfranco, Un prete del Settecento lombardo padre G. M. Martinelli, Milan, NED, 1982.
[5] Châtellier, L'Europe des dévots, pp. 85–90 (Eng. trans., pp. 70–3); Orlandi, Giuseppe, 'S. Alfonso Maria de Liguori e l'ambiente missionario napolitano nel settecento: la Compania di Gesu', Spicilegium historicum Congregationis SSmi Redemptoris, 1990/1, pp. 5–195. See p. 25.
[6] ARSI, Neap. 76 I, fo. 244 (1693): the confraternity members accompany the Jesuit preachers every Sunday into the most frequented parts of the town.
[7] Ibid., 76 II, fos. 424 and 580 (Aloysius de Mutiis); DHGE, vol. VXIII, cols. 719–21 (Francis of Geronimo).

specialised in this work. Such were the *Pii Operari*, the missionaries of Saint Vincent de Paul and the *Apostoliche Missioni*. By their constitutions the latter were obliged to instruct in their religion 'the poor and the ignorant'.[8] Eventually, the gradual withdrawal of the Jesuits from these obscure tasks did not matter, as others took their place, in substantial numbers.[9] In the city, too, a handing over to others began. The assemblies for prayer and catechising that Alfonso de Liguori had initiated, district by district, in 1728, and which he called the *Cappelle serotine* because they met in the evening, constituted firm bases for future missions.[10]

A similar concern to deepen and broaden apostolic work was shown in Spain at the beginning of the eighteenth century. The archives of the Jesuit colleges of Madrid and Toledo reveal how decisive were these early 1700s. In 1688 Don Alonso Sanchez Maldonado had founded two annual missions, each of thirty days, in the deprived region of the Toledo mountains. The centre of this foundation was Puertollano, south of Ciudad Real. Nineteen villages roundabout were the targets. The missionaries resided in these places during Lent and in the autumn. They had to prepare the inhabitants to perform their Easter duties and also to instruct both children and adults, as we learn from the mentions of parcels of the manual of *Christian Maxims* by Father Manni which they took with them, together with the images, medals and beads which were destined to reward the most zealous of their pupils.[11] In 1710 the Bishop of Sigüenza, north of Guadalajara, decided to get two Jesuits to travel all over his diocese: within three years they were to have carried out a mission in every one of its 450 parishes. When this work had been completed it was repeated by the same men, or their successors, starting with the first archpriestship visited, and so on.[12] Then came the identical foundations which were aimed at Casarrubios del Monte, between Madrid and Toledo (1725), at La Calera, east of Manzanares (1728), and at ninety-seven villages scattered between Toledo and Guadarrama (1738).[13] The fact that it is often hard to find on the map these places which were usually in areas difficult of access and well away from centres of population shows clearly the specific character of this new wave of missions – to reach and convert the most deprived and most neglected (see Map 5).

[8] Rienzo, Maria Gabriela, 'Il processo de Cristianizazione e le missioni popolari nel Mezzogiorno. Aspetti istituzionali e socio-religiosi', in *Per le storia sociale e religiosa del Mezzogiorno d'Italia*, 2 vols., ed. Giuseppe Galasso and Carla Russo, Naples, Guida, 1980, vol. I, pp. 439–81.

[9] Orlandi, 'S. Alfonso Maria de Liguori e l'ambiente missionario', p. 103.

[10] Orlandi, Giuseppe, 'S. Alfonso Maria de Liguori e i laici. La fondazione delle Cappelle serotine di Napoli', *Spicilegium Historicum Congregationis SSmi Redemptoris*, 1987/2, pp. 393–414, and below, part 3, chapter 11.

[11] AHN, Madrid, *Jesuitas*, Libro 70, n.p.

[12] *Ibid.*, Libro 250, fos. 93–9vo.   [13] *Ibid.*, fo. 114–114vo.

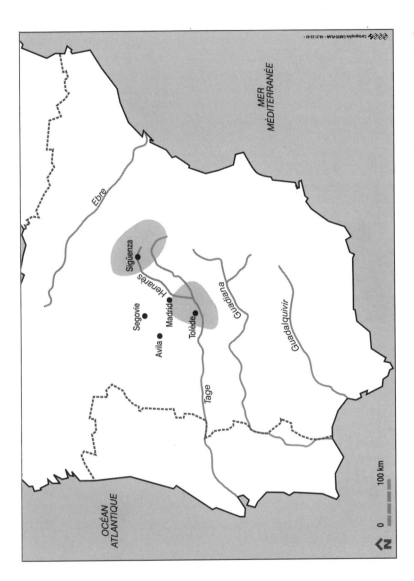

Map 5 Regions regularly visited by Jesuit missionaries from Madrid and Toledo as a result of foundations established between 1680 and 1750.

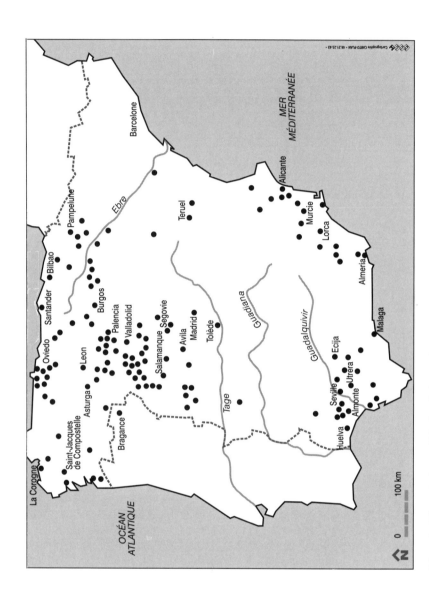

Map 6   The missions of Pedro Calatayud, 1718–60.

The journeys of one of the most famous missionaries of the time, Father Calatayud, SJ, suggest another interpretation and an even larger ambition (see Map 6). He wanted to take in the whole of Spain. Owing to his growing fame he was led to preach in the towns, but he never overlooked the larger villages, either at the beginning or at the end of his long career. One of the first expeditions assigned to him took him to Las Hurdes, that *Terre sans pain* to which Luis Buñuel devoted a great documentary. When we read the account written by the Jesuit in 1718 the film-maker's hallucinating images come to mind. 'The poverty in Las Hurdes is greater than anywhere else', noted Father Calatayud. 'When the people learnt of our arrival', he went on, 'they came in from everywhere, from the most distant parishes: not to hear preaching, though, but to ask for something to eat.'[14] In order to reach Batuecas he had to climb for hours among rocks, over burning-hot stones, with the constant fear of making a false step, of a boulder toppling over, and of the precipice. Arrived at the village, he had to put up with the uttermost destitution and the rebuffs of a hard and violent population who had many other concerns besides that of the mission he wanted to bring them. At Las Hurdes the people seemed to have been totally abandoned, even by God. Perhaps this was Hell already.

Thirteen years later Paradise had come. At Puente la Reina, south of Pamplona, the crowds who attended the Father's sermons flocked not just from the town and the adjoining villages but from afar, sometimes from very far off, after several hours of journeying through the mountains. Trailing their livestock, which they could not leave behind in the mountain pastures, the entire population of the parishes in the high valleys arrived in procession, one after another, headed by crucifixes. The men walked in front, the women followed. They all sang whatever they knew: the litanies of the Passion, those of Our Lady, or even just the *Miserere*. Some bore heavy crosses on their shoulders, while others had put on chains. Yet others gave themselves hard strokes with their scourges whenever the choirboys rang their bells. 'That was how they entered the square', wrote the preacher, 'and the audience thought they were reading a book of Christian doctrine'.[15] But the cows were lowing and had to be milked. The sad commemoration of Christ's Passion assumed the more familiar aspect of a halt on a pilgrims' road. In this Navarre, traversed through centuries by the pilgrims going to Santiago

---

[14] BN, Madrid, MSS, 5838, *Algunas noticias de mis misiones* (by Father Calatayud), fos. 5vo-6vo.

[15] *Ibid.*, fos. 41vo-42.

de Compostela, the echo of an old tradition had been awakened by the passing missionary.[16]

Enthusiasm was not confined, however, to the high mountain valleys and other remote regions. It was openly displayed in Paris, amazing the Capuchins of the Marais convent, who thought themselves back in the age of the Apostles.[17] In 1696 Father Albert de Paris preached every day of Lent in the Cemetery of the Innocents. 'It was surprising', wrote the convent's chronicler, 'to see how many people gathered there, even on Palm Sunday and on Good Friday, Easter and the two feast-days. As there was not room for everyone in the church, the Father, having obtained the parish priest's permission, preached in this cemetery, standing on a tombstone.'[18] In Normandy the Eudists methodically pursued the activity begun by the founder of their society in the Cotentin. It happened at Coutances in 1712 just as some years later at Puente la Reina: the parishes round about kept arriving in procession to join in the exercises. Some even came during the night, and by their pious singing and the steady pounding of their footsteps they awakened the townspeople and notables, who then had no choice but to join the throng in going to the Cathedral to pray.[19] Even more numerous were the crowds that gathered in Brittany and Poitou, to hear Louis-Marie Grignion de Montfort and take part in the exercises which he led – not only during the construction of the Pontchâteau calvary in 1709–10 (which occasioned, perhaps, one of the largest religious assemblies in Brittany at the beginning of the eighteenth century)[20] but also at many other times, so that people did not hesitate to recall in relation to this the most illustrious of precedents. To 'the almost incredible multitude' that came to hear him on La Ferrière heath, 'it was not difficult to declare that he was the unknown man foretold by St Vincent Ferrer'.[21] This influx of believers continued when, after Montfort's death in 1716, some of the companions he had trained took over his role (*les Montfortains*).[22]

In the Rhône valley and, soon, in the south of France, another

---

[16] Dupront, Alphonse, et al., *La Quête du sacré. Saint-Jacques-de-Compostelle*, Paris, Brepols, 1985, pp. 56–9.

[17] BN, Paris, MSS, Nouvelles acquisitions françaises, 4135, 'Recueil de ce qui s'est passé de plus notable en ce couvent du Marais, depuis son establissement en l'Année 1622', fo. 64.

[18] *Ibid.*, fo. 99.

[19] ACJM, Paris, MSS, 28, pp. 272–6 (1712).

[20] [Grandet, Joseph], *La Vie de Messire Louis-Marie Grignion de Montfort prêtre missionnaire apostolique*, Nantes, 1724, pp. 148–66, and below, chapter 6.

[21] Picot de Clorivière, P. J., *La Vie de Louis-Marie Grignion de Montfort*, Paris, 1785, pp. 154–6 (1707).

[22] Hacquet, Pierre-François, *Mémoire des missions des Montfortains dans l'Ouest (1740–1779)*, ed. Louis Pérouas, Cahiers de la Revue du bas Poitou et des provinces de l'Ouest, Fontenay-le-Comte, 1964.

missionary was drawing crowds and obtaining such successes that he became for long after the typical example of a popular preacher. Abbé Jacques Bridaine was quickly famous throughout the country. When he arrived at Tours in 1752 there were complaints that poverty increased because his charisma was such that the workers hung on his words and ceased to concern themselves with their work.[23] Like Fulvio Fontana or Pedro Calatayud he knew wonderfully well how to organise impressive missions. Thus, the mission to Marseilles, which lasted a month, from 20 January to 17 February 1732, was notable for its seven processions through the city.[24] The mission to Arles, two years later, culminated in a vigil at the cathedral, before a big catafalque lit by three hundred candles. The catafalque was guarded by penitents in their hooded costumes – black, white, blue or red, depending on the confraternity to which they belonged – each holding a torch. They chanted the Office for the Dead, walking ahead of a silent and vaguely uneasy crowd to the Requiem Mass.[25] The actual influence of a great missionary like Abbé Bridaine greatly transcended the towns he visited. When, in 1740, he was invited to Clermont-Ferrand, he had as collaborators the priests of the Hermitage who were responsible for preaching in the villages of the diocese.[26]

In the same way, Father François-Xavier Duplessis, SJ, whose fame was as great north of the Loire as Bridaine's south of it, was invited by the King of Poland, Stanislas Leszczynski, who had in 1737 become Duke of Lorraine, to ensure the success of a foundation he had just established: the royal missions. These were directed towards the prince's territories, with emphasis on the most isolated villages, which were to be visited, in turn, by small teams of Jesuits who would stay, on average, eight days in each place. They preached, they taught the catechism and they took confessions in the usual way. Distribution of works of piety was provided for. Stanislas added to this alms in money for the most necessitous or for the most urgent needs of a parish. A nursing brother of the order of Saint John of God travelled with the preachers and dispensed his care or his medicines to the sick. This foundation, carried out thoroughly until the Jesuits left in 1768 – and, even after that, by other religious – made possible a considerable intensification of missionary activity[27] (see Map 10). It was extended southward by the

---

[23] Le Quéré, François, *Un Missionnaire au XVIIIe siecle (J. J. Bridaine)*, Paris, Le Scorpion, 1959, pp. 68–9.

[24] *Ibid.*, pp. 43–5.

[25] *Ibid.*, pp. 57–8.

[26] Randanne, Abbé, *Etude historique sur l'ancienne mission diocésaine de Clermont et ses quatre maisons, L'Hermitage, Salers, Banelle, La Chasse*, Clermont-Ferrand, 1885, pp. 218–21.

[27] ADMM, G252; Delattre, *Les Etablissements de Jésuites*, vol. III, cols. 757–8.

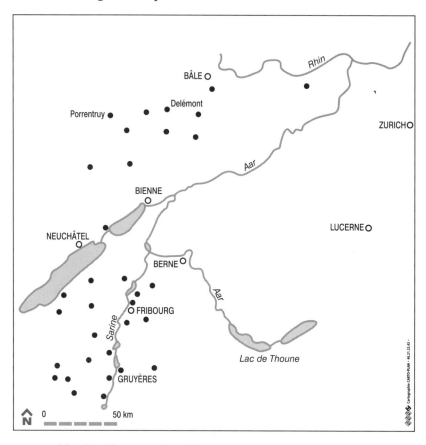

Map 7   Three years' work by a missionary. The missions of Father
Mailliardoz in Switzerland 1715–18.

priests of Beaupré, who performed in Franche-Comté more than 260
missions between 1700 and 1750, not counting repeats and retreats.[28]

On the other side of the Jura a comparable effort was made by Father
Charles Mailliardoz, SJ, who, after studying carefully the methods used
by his colleagues in the provinces of Champagne and Lyons, undertook
a systematic visitation of the parishes of the Swiss canton of Fribourg,[29]
to which he added a large part of the canton of Basel[30] (see Map 7). In

[28] Bergier, *Prêtres missionnaires de Beaupré*, pp. 108–9.
[29] BH, Munich, *Jesuiten*, 563, fos. 168–71, letter from Charles Mailliardoz to his
Provincial, presenting his plan for rural missions.
[30] ASJ, Zurich, MSS, *Compendium missionum ex et a Collegio Friburgensi institut. ab anno
1715*, n.p., n.f.

Alsace the Jesuits of the colleges and residences pursued more than ever their preaching and catechising in the villages, right up to the Sundgau, bordering on the Swiss cantons.[31]

From Central to Northern Europe

An initiative taken in Germany had very great consequences both because of the extent of the field in which it operated and because of the length of time in which it applied. The Elector of Bavaria decided in 1718 to send Jesuit missionaries into every district of his realm, in order 'to rescue the people from darkness and ignorance, instruct them in the pure doctrine and instil into them the proper virtues'.[32] This great enterprise of moral and religious education lasted all through the century and was not interrupted even by the disappearance of the Society of Jesus in 1773.[33]

The Bavarian missions were the culmination of an extensive movement which had begun in Italy.[34] In 1705, reports the biographer of Father Fulvio Fontana, when the latter was preaching 'a mission to the Airolo country, at the foot of Mount Saint Gotthard', which separates Italy from Switzerland, a group of Swiss, both men and women, preceded by a crucifix, came to meet him after a long journey through the mountains'.[35] As they did not know Italian they did not understand the sermons, but they wanted to be present and to receive, along with the others, the solemn blessing accorded by the Holy See which concluded the mission. Thereafter Father Fontana made a habit of extending his apostolic travels to the lands beyond the mountains. In 1705 he visited Schwyz, then Lucerne, Zug and Valais. In 1710 he went to Tyrol, stopped over in Innsbruck, was summoned to Vienna, and returned to Italy through the diocese of Trent.[36] A contemporary set of prints enables us to reconstitute the way these impressive ceremonies proceeded.[37]

---

[31] Delattre, *Les Etablissements de Jésuites*, vol. IV, cols. 967–81 (Oelenberg), vol. IV, cols. 1165–79 (Strasburg), vol. II, cols. 776–82 (Haguenau), vol. I, cols. 1503–9 (Colmar); Barth, 'Die Seelsorgetätigkeit', pp. 350–61 (Molsheim); Adam, Paul, *Histoire religieuse de Sélestat*, 2 vols., Sélestat, Alsatia, 1971, vol. II, pp. 108–10.

[32] BH, Munich, *Jesuiten*, 564, p. 1 (1718).

[33] Cf. below, chapter 10.

[34] Orlandi, 'L. A. Muratori', pp. 159–60 (Duchy of Modena).

[35] Fontana, *Padre Fulvio Fontana*, p. 356.

[36] *Ibid.*, pp. 356–92; Hattler, Franz, SJ, *Missionsbilder aus Tyrol. Geschichte der ständigen tirolischen Jesuitenmission von 1719–1784. Beitrag zur Geschichte der religiös-sittlichen Cultur des Landes und der socialen Wirksamkeit der Volksmissionen*, Innsbruck, 1899.

[37] *Imagini de Persone della Elzevia Rezia Valesia, e Tyrolo intervenute in abito di Penitenza nelle Missioni fatte dalle PP.della Comp.di Giesu Fulvio Fontana e Giov.Antonio Mariani. Offerte all Illismo Signora Maria Eleonora Contessa d'Herbestain*, s.l., 1711.

One of the first organised exercises to which the entire population was invited was the procession of penitents, which is described at length. Everyone had a place and a particular costume to wear, from the principal officials of the canton and the plump canons who found it hard to keep up with the rest to the ordinary townsfolk, both men and women. There were also groups of persons of both sexes who carried crosses, and penitents who scourged themselves. Just as in Italy, the mission was carried out in the open air, owing to the great numbers present. A 'theatre', with a roof over it, was set up. The Father took the stage and addressed the crowd, standing beside a crucifix, while his two companions translated his sermon and indicated by expressive gestures how the faithful should react (see Fig. 2). The closing ceremony, as reproduced in the picture and described by a priest of Upper Valais in his parish register, was even more impressive. The crowd, divided into fifteen sections, like the mysteries of the rosary, climbed, chanting, to the mountain pasture where the final benediction was given. After an open-air Mass, communion was given to almost ten thousand persons, arranged on either side of an avenue, with several priests simultaneously distributing the sacred species. Then Father Fontana gave everyone the pontifical blessing.[38]

In this way Paolo Segneri's method was transplanted, quite unchanged, out of Italy. After Switzerland and Austria, Germany, too, was affected. The Count Palatine, who had married a Medici, summoned two Jesuits, Fathers Loferer and Herdegen, who had studied the Italian method under Fontana. In April 1715 they arrived to carry out a Lenten mission, as requested by the prince, in his residence in Düsseldorf and Jülich.[39] The prince then sent them off into his realms. At Jülich, an important stronghold, people beheld, for the first time in Germany, the spectacular exercises which had been performed in Italy. There was a penitents' procession involving several thousand persons from round about and even from Düsseldorf. They walked barefoot, learning to scourge themselves vigorously while beating their breasts with dull, repeated sounds, and to groan loudly when a preacher expounded the theme laid down by Vincent Ferrer: 'Either repent or burn in Hell.' This 'army of penitents' assembled on the parade-ground of the fortress and suddenly threw themselves to the ground, each one spreading out his arms, cross-like, as a sign of penitence. It may be that these Germans added a bit, showing that they were greedier of mortifications than the

[38] According to Klaus Anderegg, *Durch der Heiligen Gnad und Hilf. Wallfahrt, Wallfahrtskapellen und Exvotos in den Oberwalliser Bezirken Goms und Ostlich-Raron*, Schriften der Schweizerischen Gesellschaft für Volkskunde, 64, Basel, 1979, pp. 168–9.
[39] Duhr, *Geschichte der Jesuiten*, vol. IV, 2, pp. 193–5.

Fig. 2   The sermon. (Missions of the Jesuit Fathers,
seventeenth-century engraving, Library of the Society of Jesus,
Chantilly, Cliché Flammarion.)

crowds who followed Father Fontana. When, during the second procession of penitents, Father Herdegen exhorted them, crying: 'I yearn for blood, for blood like Christ!' the howls of the flagellants and those loaded with chains or crosses grew so loud that they drowned the preacher's voice.[40] Once these experiments had proved successful on German soil, it was only a matter of repeating them. This was done in Bavaria and Swabia through the duke's efforts.[41] Founders, helped by the bishops and even by the Emperor, followed this example in Tyrol and in Upper and Lower Austria.[42]

The Italian method was also introduced in Bohemia in 1735 and in Silesia four years later.[43] Everywhere observable was the forming of teams of missionaries who worked the countryside systematically, from a centre such as Schweidnitz in Silesia. In Pomerania the college at Wałcz (Deutsch Krone) was especially active. In 1726–7 the five Fathers of the residence visited fifty neighbouring parishes.[44] In 1735 the number of their missions rose to one hundred.[45] The German Jesuits of the locality complained about their Polish colleagues, who had introduced scourging sessions in the churches. Thus the practices current in Italy were penetrating Eastern Europe, though not without adaptation, sometimes, to the religious sensibility of the local populations. A report sent to Rome by the Jesuit Provincial of Lithuania drew attention to the particular fervour of the inhabitants of his constituency, which extended as far as Warsaw, for the cult of the saints. He noted that the missions were occasions for mass-scale communions which were regularly repeated thereafter, on fixed days of the week, thanks to the recently introduced practice of novenas (1714).[46]

The Eastern countries underwent in the eighteenth century upheavals which were, in part, connected with religion. This was the case in Hungary, where the reconquest launched by the Habsburgs after 1683 often assumed the character of a crusade. The Jesuits, who were the chief agents of the Catholic restoration, acted simultaneously on several fronts, from Koloszvar (Clausenburg, Cluj) in Transylvania to Gorizia in Carniola, through Eger, Tyrnau, Sopron, Kőszeg and Komarno (see Map 8). They followed the advance of the imperial troops, re-establishing worship in towns and villages and replacing absent priests.

[40] BH, Munich, *Jesuiten*, 563, fols 1–10 (1715).
[41] See above, p. 69.
[42] Duhr, *Geschichte der Jesuiten*, vol. IV, 2, pp. 230–59; Hattler, *Missionsbilder aus Tirol.*
[43] ARSI, Boh, 194 (Bohemia and Silesia); Duhr, *Geschichte der Jesuiten*, vol. IV, 2, p. 250; Hoffmann, 'Die Jesuiten in Schweidnitz', pp. 105–6.
[44] *Historia Residentiae*, pp. 202–4.
[45] *Ibid.*, pp. 225–8.
[46] CPF, Rome, SOCG, 592 (1714), fos. 577–8vo.

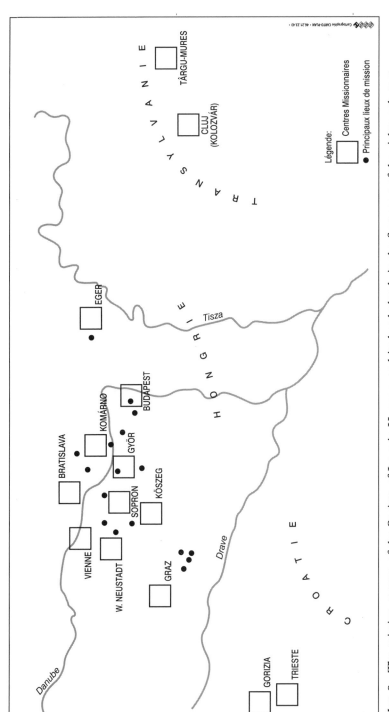

Map 8   The mission centres of the Society of Jesus in Hungary and its borderlands in the first years of the eighteenth century. (*Sources*: Arsi and Szilas, 'Die österreichische Jesuitenprovinz im Jahre 1773', *Archivum Historicum Societatis Jesu* (1978), 107–58.)

The mission then took the form of temporary help being brought to small, scattered Catholic communities. This was so in 1703, between the Danube and the Drava, when two missionaries alone visited 111 villages.[47]

The crusading spirit found other expressions, too. When missions were organised in 1717 between Komarno and Szentgotthard, near Styria, three processions took place. The first, in which adults and children were separated, served the aim of endowing with greater solemnity the proclamation of indulgences. The second was a night-time procession of penitents, in the Italian manner, with flagellants, torches and lamentations by the sinners, crying as they beat their breasts: 'Rather die thousands of times than sin again.' The third, however, was perfectly adapted to the circumstances, for 'they went, near Mogersdorf, to the plain where, 53 years earlier 14,000 Turks and barbarians had been repulsed by General Montecucculi, to the indescribable joy of all Christendom'. It was on the very spot where the imperial army had overcome the Ottomans in 1664 that the pontifical blessing was given.[48] This reminder of the past and of present hopes on so solemn an occasion was not intended solely to draw attention to the divine protection that Hungary had enjoyed. It also aimed to make everyone conscious of the eminent role played by the Most Catholic Emperor in this process of liberation. There was more in this than a sign of divine favour for the Habsburg dynasty and for the truth of the religion they defended. In a partly Protestant country where, once the Ottomans were gone, the Jesuits had only the Reformed churches to fight, the argument was a weighty one. In fact, the chronicler did not hide the fact that these towns and villages of the Raab valley had not been chosen at random, but that it was considered expedient to confirm the population in its new confession.[49] What was true of this region reunited 'to the orthodox [i.e., Catholic] faith a few years ago' was true also of most of Hungary and Transylvania. The Jesuits' mission in Hungary actually expressed a programme of counter-reformation drawn up many years before by the Bishop of Wiener-Neustadt, who had become Archbishop of Esztergom and Primate of Hungary, Cardinal Kollonitsch.[50]

One of the distinctive features of these missions of the first half of the eighteenth century was their extension to almost exclusively Protestant

[47] ARSI, Austria, 160, fos. 98vo-99 (1703).
[48] *Ibid.*, Austria, 229, fo. 104, leaves i to o (1717).
[49] *Ibid.*, fo.104, leaf i.
[50] *Ibid.*, fo. 13. Observations by the Bishop of Wiener-Neustadt, presiding over the Chamber of Hungary, on all that has been done to advance the Catholic religion, 1674. On Cardinal Kollonitsch, see *Die Bischöfe des Heiligen Römischen Reiches 1648–1803*, ed. Erwin Gatz, Berlin, Duncker u. Humblot, 1990, pp. 234–6.

areas from which they had hitherto been barred. The word 'mission' lacked here the meaning it had in countries where Catholics were the majority. It signified an ecclesiastical organisation that was fragile and supple, without bishops or property, even sometimes without churches, which depended directly on the *Propaganda* in Rome. That authority appointed the missionaries, and might confer wider powers on one of them, making him its representative (apostolic delegate).[51] This was the position of Catholic worship in England and the United Provinces.

The Jesuits who operated in the latter country recorded in their annual letter of 1695 that they no longer had to fear persecution or threats and that their freedom, though still restricted in some places, had, on the whole, never been so complete.[52] This was in fact so much the case that at certain times of the year their chapels became veritable mission centres like those that existed in wholly Catholic countries. In Holland (at Amsterdam) as in Gelderland (at Zutphen) and Friesland (at Leeuwarden), special catechism sessions were organised for Lent. Both believers and the merely curious came in great numbers – young and old, poor and rich among them. 'Devout girls', true helpmeets of the clergy, busied themselves with instructing the little ones and preparing the older children for their first communion.[53] Instruction on the Ten Commandments was given. In the evening a meditation on Christ's Passion was directed, before the salvation of the Holy Sacrament.[54] Confessions and communions usually resulted from this intense preparation. All the missionaries mentioned the crowds of participants and the thousands of hosts distributed. However, the missionary at Zutphen added some qualifications. 'Our community', he wrote, 'has increased by a third in the last two years, not through converts and neophytes but through bringing in the lukewarm and the ignorant, apart from the semi-Catholics both of this church and of the surrounding villages.'[55] The crowd was of mixed composition, as with every mission, including those in old Catholic countries. Some Protestants might even join their Catholic neighbours, out of mere curiosity or for other reasons. This happened with some Zeeland peasants who came to Zierikzee with their churn and their cream to meet a missionary who sprinkled plenty of holy water on their product. When they returned

[51] According to John Bossy, *The English Catholic Community 1570–1850*, London, Darton, Longman and Todd, 1975, pp. 203–16; Metzler, Johannes, *Die apostolischen Vikariate des Nordens. Ihre Entstehung, ihre Entwicklung und ihr Verwalter. Ein Beitrag zur Geschichte der nordischen Missionen*, Paderborn, 1919.
[52] ARB, Brussels, *Fonds jésuitique*, 1422 (Mission to Holland), *Litterae Annuae*, 1695, n.p. The remark was made with reference to Zutphen, in Gelderland.
[53] *Ibid.* On the 'devout girls', see the Utrecht and Nijmegen rubrics.
[54] *Ibid.*, Leeuwarden.   [55] *Ibid.*, Zutphen.

home 'they got a copious quantity of butter from it, to the amazement and joy of their Protestant husbands'. 'Blessed be God in all His works, praise and glory be to Him', concluded the good father.[56] At Oudetougue, on the little islands that form the border between Zeeland and Holland, there was an old man, crippled with pain and haunted by remorse after giving false witness, who was suddenly restored to health and went away in peace with himself after making his profession of faith and confession.[57] As in Brittany in the time of Dom Le Nobletz and Father Maunoir, the mission was accompanied by miracles. It was continued by means of devotions which were introduced in this exceptional period and which gradually took root in the community, helping to emphasise its specifically Catholic character. These were the cult of the Holy Sacrament (reinforced through the new solemnity given to Corpus Christi) and the devotion in honour of souls in Purgatory. The latter took shape among the faithful through a confraternity of the Good Death which was instituted in this area just as it may have been at the same time in Bavaria or in the Milanese.[58]

The situation in Ireland was similar. There the mostly Catholic population was subject to laws which forbade any public manifestations of their faith. The religious began, at any rate, to make their 'Mass houses' veritable mission centres. From 1720 the Holy Sacrament was exposed there on Sundays and feast-days. People gathered in them to say the hours and the prayers appropriate to confraternities, and they set forth in procession, to the strong disapproval of the archbishop, who was extremely exasperated by 'these friars wearing scapulars on their shoulders and at their belts and holding candles'.[59]

In north Germany and Scandinavia the missionaries were certainly obliged to show greater discretion. Nevertheless, they were increasingly present and active, even though success did not always reward their efforts. 'Heresy was never put down by preaching alone', a correspondent of the *Propaganda* at Schwerin remarked, quoting St Augustine.[60] In other places, though, the change effected was spectacular – for instance, at Heidelberg, which had been a citadel of Calvinism in Germany before the Thirty Years War. A century later the Jesuits organised, with participation by the Bishop of Worms, a procession of the Holy Sacrament in the midst of the town, on the occasion of the enlargement of their church (1713).[61]

[56] *Ibid.*, Zierikzee.   [57] *Ibid.*, Oudetougue.   [58] *Ibid.*, Oudewater.
[59] Corish, Patrick J., *The Catholic Community in the Seventeenth and Eighteenth Centuries*, Helicon History of Ireland, Dublin, Helicon, 1981, p. 85.
[60] CPF, Rome, SOCG, 587 (1713), fos. 370–1.
[61] CPF, Rome, SOCG, 587 (1713), fos. 513–4.

Just as notable was the transformation of the town of Marktbreit, in Franconia. In the middle of the seventeenth century its population was wholly Lutheran. At the end of the century a few Catholic families settled in the locality. The Capuchins came to give them the sacraments and say Mass on Sundays.[62] Everything went on modestly, almost clandestinely, since Mass was said in a private house. A foundation changed all that. This was done for the Jesuits of Würzburg who, in accepting it, undertook to send two of their company to live at Marktbreit. A chapel was built. The offices were celebrated there, regularly accompanied by instruction and preaching. On feast-days there were grand processions. In 1704 a confraternity of the Sacred Agony was formed and, in order to make its merits known, a play was performed in the open air. Then the religious preached their mission in the neighbouring villages. In 1714 an epidemic of plague caused the believers to go on pilgrimage to the sanctuary at Bettelbach. Two years later, when a chapel on a hill had been restored, the members of the Sacred Agony confraternity who wished to go there every Sunday erected the elements of a Way of the Cross. Within a few years all the structures of Baroque piety had been created and set up and were functioning. The landscape itself bore its marks and was altered. At the same time (1716) the annalist of the Würzburg college recorded that Catholics who, thirty-five years earlier, had made up only a tenth of the population of Marktbreit, now constituted more than two-thirds. The change brought about was consecrated by the building of a church and the appointment of a parish priest.

Seduced by novelty

To be sure, in Franconia as in the Palatinate the transformation observed could be put down to the presence of a new, Catholic prince. The famous rule, applied since the Peace of Augsburg (1555), of *cuius regio eius religio* was still in force in the Holy Roman Empire. It could even happen, as in the case of Hungary in the time of Cardinal Kollonitsch, that it was put into effect with new vigour where Protestant communities and their pastors were concerned.[63] Salzburg was the scene, in 1731–2, of measures so unprecedentedly violent that they astonished the population of the neighbourhood and of all Germany.

---

[62] SA, Mainz, *Jesuiten Abteilung*, 15,230, *Historia Missionis . . . Markbreid*, n.p., in which we find the account of this establishment; see also Châtellier, Louis, 'Mission et conversion dans l'espace rhénan et germanique à la fin du XVIIe siècle', in *Les Réveils missionnaires en France du Moyen Age à nos jours (XIIe–XXe siècle)*, Proceedings of colloquium in Lyons, May 1980, Paris, Beauchesne, 1984, pp. 119–27.

[63] ARSI, Austria, 229, fo. 13 (1674); *Die Bischöfe*, pp. 234–6.

The Prince-Archbishop Eleutherius von Firmian ordered the Jesuit missionaries to investigate the orthodoxy and correctness of the religious practices of the inhabitants of the Pongau, some of whom were suspected of Lutheranism. Twenty thousand peasants were compelled to leave their homeland.[64] Those who remained were placed under surveillance, while the Emperor and the Duke of Bavaria took rigorous steps to prevent the refugees from staying in their realms.[65] These manifestations of intolerance prolonged, well into the eighteenth century, those which had marked the Thirty Years War or the reign of Louis XIV and, since the Jesuits were involved, they exposed once more the ambiguity of missionary activity in Europe.

That ambiguity was apparent also in the use made by rulers of this missionary activity. Ecclesiastical historians customarily praise the Dukes of Bavaria or Lorraine for the pious foundations they established for the benefit of their subjects. But had they not a direct interest in doing that? When Maximilian II Emmanuel of Bavaria returned to his duchy after several years' absence, and after much devastation due to the War of the Spanish Succession (1701–14), a work of restoration was urgently needed. This had not only to be material but also to aim at re-establishing the authority and prestige of the Bavarian ruling house, badly shaken by the occupation of their realm by the powerful Austrian neighbour.[66] A mission might, in this very Catholic country, help to consolidate the ruler's credit while at the same time soothing tensions and contributing to the return of civil peace. At the time (1718) when the Duke founded his mission, refractory elements were still at large and terrorising the townspeople a few miles to the east of Munich. 'The most pious prince', wrote the compiler of the annual letters, 'found no remedy more efficacious than the mission.'[67] To the south, at Schöngau, there was an open split among the inhabitants and the peasants of the vicinity. Those who had collaborated with the Austrians during the war on the one hand, and on the other the loyal Bavarians who had suffered greatly under the occupation, could no longer live together. The Jesuits succeeded, apparently, in 'restoring peace and concord'.[68] There had been a revolt against the occupying army in

---

[64] OP, Munich, Abt. II, 11 (letter from Father Michel Zeck, SJ, to the Rector of Munich on the reasons for his summons to Salzburg, 10 August 1732). On Archbishop Eleutherius von Firmian, see *Die Bischöfe*, p. 112; BH, Munich, *Jesuiten*, 565, 566, 567. Here we perceive that the measure had been prepared since 1728 by the dispatch of missionaries among the incriminated populations.

[65] BH, Munich, *Jesuiten*, 566, n.p., years 1732, 1733, 1734.

[66] Hartmann, Peter Claus, *Bayerns Weg in die Gegenwart vom Stammesherzogtum zum Freistaat heute*, Regensburg, Fr. Puster, 1989, pp. 248–53.

[67] BH, Munich, *Jesuiten*, 564, p. 8, year 1719.

[68] *Ibid.*, *Jesuiten*, 565, n.p., year 1723.

1705–6, with the slogan: 'Rather die Bavarian than live and be corrupted by the Emperor's crimes.' It had been severely repressed and during Christmas night, 1705, many rebel peasants had been massacred at Sendling, near Munich. Was not the mission sent to that place a few years later a way of commemorating the event while at the same time helping to strengthen or create attachment to the ruling family?[69] Study of the maps, which shows the extent to which the border areas, both north and south, were specially favoured, leads us to that conclusion (see Map 9).

The Duke of Lorraine, the former King of Poland Stanislas Leszczynski, was in an even more uncomfortable situation when he took possession of his duchy in 1737.[70] Imposed from without and unknown to his subjects, he had to overcome their hostility, or at least indifference, and try to win their sympathy. The 'royal missions', accompanied as they were by almsgiving and distribution of medicines, were not without their use in achieving that result. The choice of regions for receiving special attention – the heart of the duchy, the western borderland with France, and the north-east adjoining German territories which were constantly under threat during the War of the Austrian Succession and the Seven Years War – gives support to this assumption (see Maps 10a and 10b). One even wonders if, in the age of enlightened despotism, the mission was not, in Catholic countries, one instrument among others that the rulers used to keep an eye on their subjects. With military bluntness, an administrator of Napoleon's time remarked that, 'independently of the moral benefit they [the missions] brought, they made it easier to collect taxes'.[71]

All the same, these measures could not, on their own, account for the dimensions of the missionary movement of the eighteenth century, which is so plain to see on the maps of Bavaria and Lorraine. Its extension to the smallest villages and its systematic character indicated that this was an action resolved upon for the Catholic world as a whole, even in Rome itself. Mere examination of the registers of the *Acta* of the congregation *De Propaganda Fide* shows, by their thickness and their numbers, how active this institution was in the first half of the eighteenth century.[72] The interest taken by the Popes, especially by Clement XI (1700–21) and Benedict XIV (1740–58), is revealed by the numerous

[69] *Ibid., Jesuiten*, 568, n.p., year 1748.
[70] Cabourdin, Guy, *Histoire de la Lorraine: les temps modernes*, vol. II, *Encyclopédie illustrée de la Lorraine*, Nancy, PUN, pp. 151–76.
[71] Quoted by Le Quéré, *Un Missionnaire*, pp. 244–50.
[72] Metzler, 'Die Kongregation'; Kowalsky, N. and Metzler, J., *Inventory of the Historical Archives of the Congregation for the Evangelisation of Peoples or de Propaganda Fide*, Rome, Pontificia Univ. Urbaniana 1988, 3rd edition.

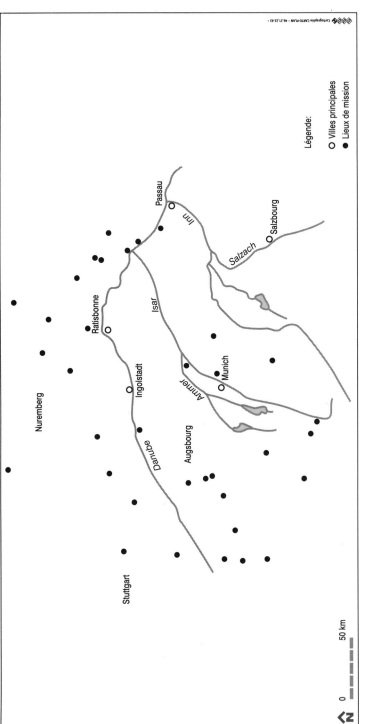

Légende:

○ Villes principales
● Lieux de mission

Passau

Inn

Salzbourg

Salzach

Ratisbonne

Isar

Ingolstadt

Munich

Ammer

Nuremberg

Danube

Augsbourg

Stuttgart

N

0   50 km

Map 9a   The Jesuit missions in Bavaria in the eighteenth century (1718–52): first period, 1718–22.

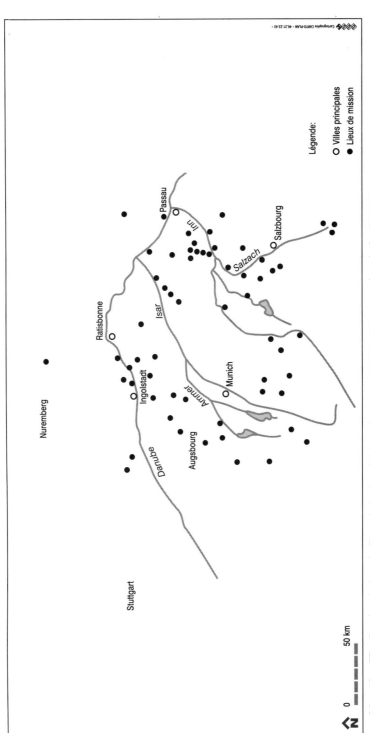

Map 9b   The Jesuit missions in Bavaria in the eighteenth century (1718–52): second period, 1723–32.

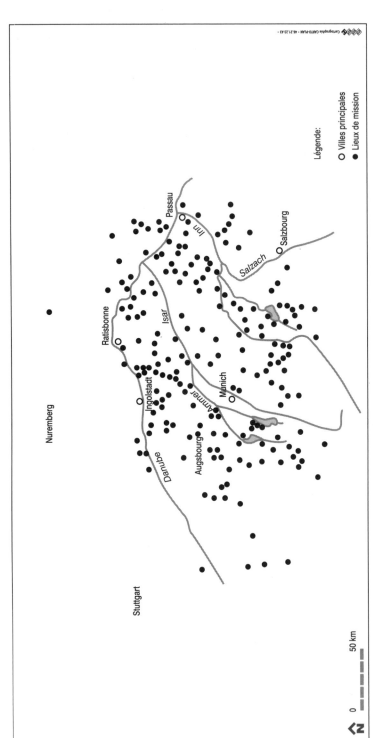

Map 9c The Jesuit missions in Bavaria in the eighteenth century (1718–52): third period, 1733–52.

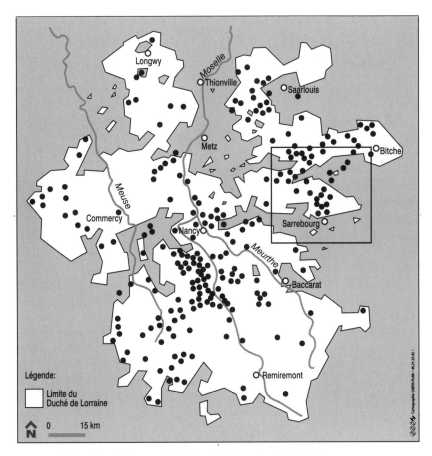

Map 10a   The royal missions in Lorraine, 1741–66.

decisions they took with a view to developing missions.[73] In their own way, the Jesuits expressed their conviction of the great importance of this apostolic work by choosing as their General, in 1678, Father Tirso Gonzalez, a Spaniard who was a former missionary.[74]

It was by then quite clear that, in 1750, at least where most of Europe was concerned, the decisions taken by the Council of Trent had borne fruit. Assiduity in founding diocesan seminaries and supervising the

[73] *Juris Pontificii de Propaganda Fide. Pars Prima complectens Bullas Brevia Acta S.S. . . . cura ac studio Raphaelis de Martinis*, 7 vols., Rome, 1888–97, vol. II (Clement XI), vol. III (Benedict XIV).

[74] Orlandi, 'S. Alfonso Maria de Liguori e l'ambiente missionario', p. 38; Evarisisto Rivero Vazquez, 'Galicia e los Jesuitas', in *Galicia Historica*, Fundación Barrie de la Maza, 1989, pp. 477–89, at pp. 487–9.

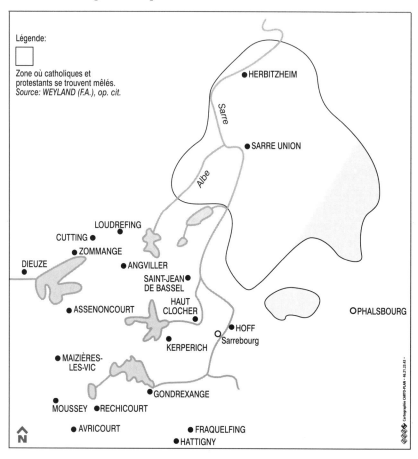

Map 10b   The village missions of Jean-Martin Moyë in Lorraine, 1783–91.

training of clergy was present everywhere. The same applied to the good behaviour of parish priests and their pastoral zeal.[75] The bishops, or their representatives, had at heart the fulfilment of their duties as these had been brought home to them by the Council. The necessary visitation of all the churches in a diocese every two years was being performed with increasing care. It had never been done so systematically, in France

[75] *Histoire de la France religieuse*, ed. Jacques Le Goff and René Rémond, vol. III, *Du Roi Très Chrétien à la laïcité républicaine (XVIIIe–XIXe siècle)*, ed. Philippe Joutard, Paris, Seuil, 1991, pp. 369–88 (Dominique Julia).

for example, as in the period 1670–1730.[76] It gave the visitor the opportunity to issue ordinances for the rebuilding of places of worship and their decoration, on how ceremonies should be conducted, on the distribution of the sacraments, education both religious and secular and the confraternities to be set up in order to foster the piety of the parishioners. Once the structures were in position it remained to carry out the essential task, changing people. This was what caused the missionaries to traverse entire regions methodically, from the big cities to the smallest villages, so as to try and reach everyone individually and lead him to conversion. There had been nothing like this gigantic enterprise since the early centuries of Christianity.

Was it really feasible? There was no shortage of sceptics or even of opponents. Among the latter was the priest of La Chèze, in the diocese of Saint-Brieuc, who urged his parishioners to stay at home and work for their living instead of going off to 'waste their time with the mission'. Yet that was a mission by Grignion de Montfort.[77] Father de Mailliardoz met with similar setbacks in the diocese of Lausanne.[78] As for Abbé Bridaine, he was the target of regular attacks by the Jansenists. 'These apostolics never vary in the slightest', one read in the *Nouvelles ecclésiastiques*: 'the same exercises, the same plan, the same processions, spectacles, contortions, and, if this may be said, the same howlings, which is what Bridaine is particularly good at'.[79] The criticism levelled by the writer of that article goes beyond the person of the famous missionary, to affect the mission itself. This was also what was aimed at when Father Labat, a Dominican and a great traveller, described with humour his colleagues at Civitavecchia, in the Papal States. They gave themselves furious blows with their scourges while managing, thanks to a clever knack they had, to avoid even grazing their skins. They preached penitence most feelingly. On returning to the refectory, however, they had themselves served with copious rations, well washed down with cool wine, so as to restore their strength and wet their whistles.[80]

Father Labat, who was a little bit of a *philosophe* and disposed to make fun of the ways of the Mediterranean countries, was not the only one to

[76] Froeschlé-Chopard, Marie-Hélène and M., *Atlas de la réforme pastorale en France de 1550 a 1790*, Paris, CNRS, 1986.
[77] [Grandet], *Grignion de Montfort*, p. 133.
[78] ASJ, Zurich, MSS, *Compendium*, missions to Gruyères (February 1717), Wünnewil (September 1717), and Rechthalten, with the parish priest of Tafers (October 1717), n.p.
[79] Le Quéré, *Un Missionnaire*, p. 68.
[80] Labat, Jean-Baptiste, *Voyages en Italie*, Paris, Gallimard, 1989, pp. 139–51. The scene is set in 1715.

find fault. Here is a Spaniard, a Jesuit to boot, who was the author of a novel which enjoyed success in the eighteenth century. Its title, *Fray Gerundio*, refers to the chief character, a preacher.[81] A strange preacher indeed, this simple-minded son of a rich peasant of the Tierra de Campos (between Valladolid and Sahagun), the steward of a confraternity who, because he has lived in the shadow of the clergy, wants to see his son mount with dignity the steps of the pulpit and address the people with authority. The son fulfils with ease the father's wish. 'If somebody understands nothing of the *ergos*', writes the author (Father de Isla), 'or gets bored with the dullness of scholastics, then provided he has a good voice, a good memory, a fine presence and plenty of boldness, I will make you a preacher, overnight: I will arm you from head to foot as a knight of the pulpit, with great bundles of sermons by others, good or bad, and half-a-dozen printed collections of sermons, bad or good: and so manage as best you can.'[82]

Father de Isla knew what he was talking about. His colleague Father Calatayud was even worse equipped, at the beginning of his career, than the hero of the novel. 'I carried few sermons with me,' he admits in his memoirs, 'so that when I entered the pulpit [for the first time] with the sermon written, in his own hand, by Father Jeronimo Lopez, I found myself lacking in resources and yet wielding a sort of authority over my audience.' Happily for him, a fire that broke out in the village caused his audience to leave in a hurry, much to his relief.[83] Father Calatayud, who had the apostolic spirit, himself joined in helping save the house which had caught fire. But Fray Gerundio, who thought only of his own glory and whose first sermon was uninterrupted by any accident, inflicted on his fellow-citizens a horrible patchwork in which Cybele, Saturn, Bacchus and Ceres marched in procession beside Tlaloc, Chivaltianno and Citcolt, who had come specially from Mexico to the Tierra de Campos.[84] Was it because of such excesses that some superiors of orders began to voice reserve regarding an activity that their predecessors had encouraged? 'The holy exercise of missions', the Superior-General of the Capuchins deplored in 1698, 'which earlier was useful for the conversion of souls, gradually became subject to abuse.'[85] A provincial of the Society of Jesus, responsible for a region where Father Paolo Segneri had done much work, did not hesitate to call for abandonment of 'solemn and clamorous' missions and a return to preaching without

[81] Gaudeau, Bernard, *Etude sur Fray Gerundio et sur son auteur le P. José Francisco de Isla (1703–1781)*, Paris, 1890.
[82] *Ibid.*, p. 322.
[83] BN, Madrid, MSS, 5838, *Algunas noticias*, fo. 3.
[84] Gaudeau, *Fray Gerundio*, pp. 272–3.
[85] AN, Luxemburg, *Abteilung* 15/39, 'Mémoires', vol. I, fo. 220vo.

pomp, simple teaching of the catechism, direction of confraternities, administration of the sacraments and those spiritual exercises which are 'the work proper to our ministry'.[86]

There was something more serious. Some people took pleasure in stressing the meagreness of the effect these missions had on the populations they were intended to transform. The father of Fray Gerundio, when, as a young man, he was looking for a wife, ended by winning the favour of his lovely neighbour when he appeared in a penitents' procession, dressed in a sack and wielding a scourge. 'Everyone knows', the author goes on, 'that this is one of the spectacles most to the liking of the girls of the Tierra de Campos, where, according to observations over a long period, most marriages are arranged on Good Friday or on the Day of the Cross in May, just as in the evenings when dancing takes place.'[87] The parallel he drew must have been particularly distressing to the missionaries who strove so hard to discourage dancing. That was only something in a novel. But in Modena a malicious observer noted that the carnival which followed the so-famous mission conducted by Father Segneri Junior in 1712 was just as brilliant, merry and frequented as in previous years.[88] Were the missionaries no more than a passing attraction for idlers? Concerning Abbé Bridaine's visit to Tours in 1752 the compiler of the *Nouvelles ecclésiastiques* noted: 'The common people gathered round just as they usually do when there is anything unusual to be seen and as they hasten to watch the entertainers who set up their stage in the public squares.'[89] A century later, in southern Italy, a missionary admitted that the crowd had come mainly 'out of curiosity to see the damned soul', the skull made up, or capped with insignia of rank, which the preacher waved about from the height of the pulpit.[90] Was the Baroque mission, like the frescos painted on church ceilings, so much make-believe?

This was, perhaps, what an increasing number of churchmen, more or less influenced by the spirit of the Enlightenment, were inclined to suggest. Evidently, though, they were not followed by the majority, since the mission phenomenon assumed, in this eighteenth century, a scale never before seen, and the crowds who participated were more and more dense, as though insensible to the criticisms sometimes uttered by their priests, or else unaware of them. All things considered, one wonders

---

[86] Orlandi, 'L. A. Muratori', p. 167. [87] Gaudeau, *Fray Gerundio*, p. 267.
[88] Orlandi, 'L. A. Muratori', p. 180. [89] Le Quéré, *Un Missionnaire*, pp. 68–9.
[90] Orlandi, Giuseppe, 'La missione popolare redentorista in Italia dal Settecento ai giorni nostri', *Spicilegium Historicum Congregationis SSmi Redemptoris*, 1985/1, pp. 51–141, at p. 117.

whether the immense missionary movement which developed across Europe during the century of the Enlightenment was not stimulated both by the apostolic activity of the religious *and* by the ardent desire of the crowds who welcomed them, took part and co-operated with them. No less than as a method of evangelisation undertaken by the church, the mission may have become, in the eighteenth century and in certain regions, the favourite form chosen by the people in which to experience their religion. In the mission one found, while the church as an institution was becoming more consolidated, a free space in which the individual, taken in isolation, was appealed to, had a decision to make and a task to accomplish. He was offered, in the form of new devotions, unfamiliar practices and teaching presented in an unprecedented way, paths previously unknown to him for obtaining salvation. The considerable success achieved was doubtless explicable, to some extent, by the seduction of novelty. But it was not a matter of fashion or of superficial taste for the exotic. The often abrupt change made in the way religion was presented resulted either in one's discovering what had hitherto been hidden or else in a sense of mounting enthusiasm linked with initiation into a new religion.

The case of the conversion of part of the Franconian town of Marktbreit, already mentioned, was perhaps an example of that behaviour. Whereas the missions organised in France after the Revocation of the Edict of Nantes with a view to bringing Protestants to Catholicism by trying to minimise the differences between the two confessions proved a complete failure, the mission to Marktbreit, which was marked throughout by the Tridentine spirit, without making any concessions, obtained maximum success. The Jesuits' activity took the form first of solemn processions – that of the Holy Blood during the octave of Corpus Christi, and those of the Rogation Days – and of veneration of the relics of Saint Francis Xavier. In the following weeks a confraternity of Christ's Agony was created, with, as its aim, help to souls in Purgatory, and a play was performed to introduce it to the people. Then came the organisation of pilgrimages in neighbouring places, re-establishment of a chapel in honour of the Fourteen Holy Helpers, and the making of a Way of the Cross . . . In short, no more flagrant break with the practices and content of the Lutheran doctrine could be imagined. If they had wanted to show how completely that doctrine was irreconcilable with Catholicism they could not have proceeded differently. Therein, maybe, lay the full attractiveness of the Jesuits' mission. They, at least, offered a religion that was entirely different, so that it aroused interest among people dissatisfied with Lutheranism, the nostalgics for the past, of whom there were not a few in a region of mixed religions. The pastors were all of a flutter and called on the ruler to suppress these 'novelties'.[91] The attractiveness of those novelties was certainly just as strong for the old Catholics who were used to a form of religious life that was rather stuffy, and perhaps dull and monotonous. For them, equally with those who were thinking of abjuring Protestantism, the religion that they discovered during the mission had all the attraction of something new.

The first half of the eighteenth century can therefore be called, without exaggeration, the golden age of the mission in Europe. Basically, the great enterprise of apostleship in country areas was advancing at the same rate as the other works of reform or deepening of Christianity which emerged from the Council of Trent. But it also had its own dynamic. At the very moment of this apogee the first signs of a profound change appeared. The mission started to lose the features it had inherited from the Dominicans and the Council. Created in order to impose orthodoxy and crush heresy, it was sometimes accused of spreading dubious doctrines. Established in order to strengthen the authority of the Roman Church, it was now suspected of encouraging the faithful to escape from control by their proper shepherds. Once strongly asked for by bishops and parish priests, it was now worrying some of them, who nevertheless had to bend before the desire expressed by their flocks. The former Tridentine mission was perhaps changing into a force for renewal and, sometimes, for contestation within the Roman Church.

In four centuries, from 1350 to 1750 approximately, an immense work of apostleship in the rural areas had been accomplished. Every region had its missionaries and in some periods several teams were at work simultaneously. This considerable achievement, on the details about which we are far from well informed for all the regions of Europe, was undoubtedly of decisive importance for the evolution not only of the religious feelings of the Christian populations but also for popular mentalities, everyday behaviour, in short for civilisation generally.[92] In any case it would be remaining content with approximations if we were to see the effects of these millions of instructions, sermons and directions of conscience, given over centuries by these itinerant preachers, merely as the diffusion of the Church's doctrine as defined at Trent. The situations of these crowds of penitents were various, their needs and

[91] SA, Mainz, *Jesuiten*, *Abteilung* 15/230, 'Historia Missionis Marktbreid', n.p., years 1703 and 1716.
[92] See the remark by the Spanish historian D. Ortiz on the role of the missions in eighteenth-century Spanish society quoted by Saugnieux, Joël, *Les Jansénistes et le renouveau de la prédication dans l'Espagne de la seconde moitié du XVIIIe siècle*, Lyons, PUL, 1976, p. 313.

their reactions differed from one region to another, just as missionaries' instructions were far from all composed in the same spirit. There was indeed change brought about through the missions, but we need to look into its nature.

Part 2

The world disillusioned

It was to be expected. The preachings of itinerant missionaries in rural areas that were farther and farther off the beaten track, more and more numerous and increasingly well adapted to their public, resulted in mass-scale confessions and communions and, according to the missionaries themselves, in countless 'conversions'. But how long did those 'conversions' last? When Grignion de Montfort was staying, in 1713, in the neighbourhood of Nantes, not far from Vallet, where he had conducted a mission a few years previously, he exclaimed: 'No, no, I am not going to go to La Valette [Vallet] – they have given up my chaplet.'[1] Many others had suffered deep sadness which sometimes bordered on discouragement when, on returning to places where they had worked, they discovered how little of the result remained.[2] It even happened that the memory of their mission had completely faded.[3] At most, the local priest was trying, as best he could, to maintain the devotions, prayers, confraternities and sacramental practices which had been established amid the fire, tears and enthusiasm of the concluding ceremony of a mission. But it was very difficult to save them from becoming, eventually, just the habits of a small clique of devout persons who were themselves caught up in the routine of parish life to the extent of identifying themselves with it.

Yet the effects of the European missions were undoubtedly substantial: but they were of a different order. Their consequence was a profound change, which came about little by little in everyone, in the very idea of religion. The 'Our Father', the fundamental prayer that all Christians learnt as children, gradually disclosed its meaning. Thanks to the missionaries, each of its formulations, or group of formulations, instructed the faithful regarding the 'evil' that was to be repudiated. One

[1] Picot de Clorivière, *Grignion de Montfort*, p. 185.
[2] BN, Madrid, MSS, 4503, *Ejercicios y Misiones desde año de 1753*, fos. 233 sq. (year 1759), missions by Father Calatayud in Andalusia.
[3] Birsens, *Manuels de catéchisme*, p. 171. Mention, in 1729, of persons in the Luxemburg countryside who are being 'taught for the first time the elements of Christian doctrine', although this region had been worked over by missionaries for a century.

after another the Christian had presented to him his three principal duties: to glorify God, to imitate Jesus Christ and to love his neighbour – with, in conclusion, the path leading to the necessary reconciliation. What also emerged, however, in counterpoint, was that mixture of good and evil which the missionaries found when they arrived anywhere at all.

Being free from illusions about human nature they knew that it was not enough to speak of good for good to be done. Better was it to take account of this initial situation and try, bit by bit, to raise each group of people, in line with their particular temperament, to the level of the three basic demands of the *Pater*. This was the Baroque spirit that was put into practice in most of the missions. This slow, twofold movement – taking root and uprooting – is what has to be studied more closely, since we can perceive in it an important cultural mutation which occurred in the rural areas in the modern period.

5 God

Whether they were in Mexico, Poland or Castile, the missionaries' primary concern was to make sure of the masses' beliefs. We may wonder whether, before the wide circulation of the question-and-answer catechism, the humble folk of Europe were more advanced, in that respect, than the heathen of the Far East or the Far West. Defining the three-in-one God of the Christians is a tough task which theologians themselves found hard to accomplish. However, it was the men of the Enlightenment who insisted on a definition, together with their successors who flatly declared that Christ had stopped at Eboli because the people who dwelt beyond that point had an idea of God that differed from theirs.[1] In traditional societies what mattered more than the concept was the way in which one imagined God, how one invoked Him, and the intimate knowledge that one had of Him. The missionaries started from those data, and from their highly tangible experience of evil and the works of mankind's enemy, in order to succeed in their teaching.

On the difficulty of saying 'Our Father'

The problem appeared at the very outset. How to get people to say 'God', to call him 'Our Father', when he remained hidden and his nature was a mystery? When Julien Maunoir landed on Ushant in 1641 he discovered, with alarm, that the population, almost to a man, were ignorant of 'the mysteries of the Trinity and of man saved by God'.[2]

[1] On this question see the survey by Gabriele De Rosa, 'Pertinenze ecclesiastiche e santita nella storia sociale e religiosa della Basilicata dal XVIII al XIX secolo', in *Società e Religione in Basilicata*, Atti del Convegno di Potenza, Matera (25–8 September 1975), 2 vols., s.l., D'Elia, 1977, vol. I, pp. 15–73, at p. 73.
[2] Croix and Roudaut, *Les Bretons*, pp. 227–8. See also Minois, Georges, 'Les missions dans les îles bretonnes dans la première moitié du XVIIe siècle', in *Foi chrétienne et milieux maritimes (XVe–XVIIIe siècle)*, Proceedings of Paris (Collège de France) colloquium, September 1987, assembled by Alain Cabantous and Françoise Hildesheimer, Paris, Publisud, 1989, pp. 19–37.

However, it is rather the shock felt by the missionary that surprises us. Must we deduce from this that in the middle of the seventeenth century all Catholics were able to answer correctly the first questions of the small catechism? That was undoubtedly not the case, since, in other regions at the same time, Father Maunoir's colleagues encountered the same need to give priority to their sermons on the Trinity and the Incarnation.[3]

The task was all the harder in that any analogy, comparison or even image might lead their listeners astray and cause them to fall into the gravest of heresies. In the fifteenth century a missionary had thought it clever to explain the dogma of the God who is simultaneously one and three by referring to the sun. He put it to his audience that although the sun was the centre of the firmament, the source of light and also the source of heat, it was nevertheless one.[4] The risk entailed by this approach was that the preacher never knew how it would be taken. There was danger that the sun, a mere object of comparison for the preacher, could become God himself in the minds of his listeners. When Vincent Ferrer found worship of the sun – also known as 'Saint Orient' – to be widespread in the Geneva region, with its chief feast-day the morrow of Corpus Christi, he declared relentless war on everything that might risk preserving or bringing back this cult. He desired that everyone, as well as himself, cease to employ exclamations which might seem like prayers, such as: 'Welcome, Sun, graciously favour us with enough bread, wine and fruit.'[5] A century and a half later, in the spring of 1561, the students of the Roman College and their teachers, having gone on mission to the villages around the Eternal City, found a similar situation. There, they wrote, the people knew 'no other God than the sun, whose authority extended over all the universe, and to worship it they recited, seven times a day, the Lord's Prayer and the Angelic Salutation'.[6]

In the opinion of the authors of this account, such idolatry was due to ignorance. But, since the inhabitants of these villages were perfectly capable of saying the *Pater noster* and the *Ave Maria*, they evidently did not live in one of those forgotten corners of Europe where Christianisation was still incomplete. They were not ignorant of their prayers or, doubtless, of the chief rites of the Christian religion, but they were mistaken regarding to whom they were to be addressed. Was their mistake not easily understandable? When the priest presented to them God in Majesty, on occasions of the greatest solemnity, and especially at

---

[3] In Pomerania, for example. See *Historia Residentiae*, pp. 22–3 (1631).
[4] Martin, *Le Métier de prédicateur*, p. 299.
[5] Gorce, *Saint Vincent Ferrier*, p. 181.
[6] Guidetti, *Le missioni popolari*, p. 32.

Corpus Christi, it was in the form of a huge gilded 'sun', shining brilliantly, which he or some ecclesiastic of still higher rank carried with the utmost respect and great devotion and lifted up when he reached the top step of the altar. At once the crowd bowed, going down on one knee. Before the monstrance (often called 'the sun' in the old documents), adoration was permissible, even required. The traces, observable here and there in the fifteenth and sixteenth centuries, of an alleged cult of the sun were thus, perhaps, derived from the feast of Corpus Christi which became widespread precisely in that period.[7] The missionaries' reports thus show that a symbol or image was perceived by the faithful so intensely that they sometimes ended by feeling a closeness to the divine being which could amount to quasi-identification. Hence the dilemma faced by all the preachers. They had to bring people to knowledge and love of God as a person while preventing this image from being taken not only for the Godhead but even for its representation. For the Godhead, stated the Council of Trent's catechism, cannot be made the object of any figure whatsoever. 'But the priests will teach that by these [these images] are expressed certain qualities or actions which are attributed to God. Thus we depict, like Daniel, the Ancient of Days sitting on a throne with open books before him, whereby are signified the eternity of God and the infinite wisdom which examines and judges the thoughts and actions of men.'[8]

In this way, following the Council of Trent, the rule was laid down by which images were allowed – and even recommended – on condition that they be explained, and their precise meaning shown, by the priest speaking from the pulpit. It was the same with them, basically, as with Scripture, to which the layman could not have access without guidance from the priest.[9] 'Our Father which art in heaven' might, therefore, appear in the shape of that magnificent old man reigning over the clouds who logically had his place at the top of the retable of the high altar. In a setting suggestive of the creation of the world – but which could also be its end – he pointed with a sweeping gesture to his beloved Son, who was at a lower level, with the Holy Spirit above his head.[10] This representation of the 'heavenly Trinity' which was so often used in the Baroque age to accompany the 'earthly

---

[7] *Saint Martin, Mémoire de Liège*, Liège, Du Perron, 1990. This contains studies of Corpus Christi and its development (role played by Julienne de Cornillon in the thirteenth century, pp. 31–53; the confraternity of the Holy Sacrament founded in Liège in 1573, pp. 165–76; the chapel of the Blessed Sacrament in Liège Cathedral, pp. 177–95).

[8] Boespflug, François, *Dieu dans l'art: Sollicitudini Nostrae de Bénoit XIV et l'affaire Crescence de Kaufbeuren*, Paris, Cerf, 1984, p. 195.

[9] *Ibid.*, p. 264.

[10] Menard, Michèle. *Une Histoire des mentalités religieuses aux XVIIe et XVIIIe siècles: mille retables de l'ancien diocèse du Mans*, Paris, Beauchesne, 1980, pp. 161–249.

Trinity' (the Holy Family), or the crucifixion, evoked those words in Scripture which contained the mystery of the Godhead one and threefold and that of the Incarnation: 'This is my beloved Son, in whom I am well pleased: hear ye him' (Matthew, XVII, 5).

If this reminder did not suffice, the missionaries and educators would explain to the believer how he was supposed to behave before such an image. The best interpretation and the most fruitful, thought Father François Coster at the end of the sixteenth century, was simply to make the sign of the cross. This could be done with three fingers, which was a way of recalling that, while Christ sustained and endured his Passion alone, yet 'the whole Trinity was involved'. Crossing oneself with two fingers served to recall 'the two natures, divine and human, in the one person of Jesus Christ'.[11] Father Lejeune, of the Oratory, reminded his hearers whenever he preached 'that the son of God was not always man and, being God from all eternity, he made himself man out of love for us and will be man forever, and that he is in the Holy Sacrament in flesh and blood, and that this is not like the Crucifix in the church which is only an image made of wood or stone, whereas Jesus Christ is in the Holy Sacrament in his own person'.[12] In this way, he thought, after a warning repeated every Sunday and throughout all missions, the risk of people slipping into idolatry would gradually be averted.[13]

On a matter so fundamental as this – what is God? – the post-Tridentine church could not let anyone and everyone imagine and stray as he chose. Certain images exclusively, as permitted by the supreme authority, the papacy, enabled the imagination to settle.[14] The missionaries provided the correct interpretation of these images through their doctrinal commentary on them. Imagination and Reason, those two powers of the mind, were mobilised for the greater glory of God. That was the strategy of the Baroque.

The name of God

The fact that a debate like this could take place on the subject of how the Eternal should be depicted in churches might seem to be a sign that

---

[11] Coster, François, Le Livre de la Compaignie, c'est à dire les cinq livres des institutions chrestiennes dressées pour l'usage de la Confrérie de la très heureuse Vierge Marie, mis en français du latin de François Coster, Antwerp, Plantin, 1588, pp. 308–9.

[12] Lejeune, Le Missionnaire de l'Oratoire, vol. I, 'Avis aux jeunes prédicateurs', n.p.

[13] This was the strict application of the Council of Trent's decree of 2 December 1563 on invocation, veneration and the relics of saints and on holy images. See in Héfelé and Leclercq, Histoire, pp. 592–600.

[14] Boespflug, Dieu dans l'art. See text of and commentary on Benedict XIV's Sollicitudini Nostrae, pp. 23–172.

his presence in this world was being perceived less precisely by the men of the seventeenth and eighteenth centuries. In Old Testament times the mere name of Yahweh was enough to bow all heads. Uttering it in the temple, in the solitude of one's house or of the wilderness was the first and greatest of prayers. Moses began his hymn with: 'Because I will publish the name of the Lord' (Deuteronomy, XXXII, 3), and the Psalmist declared, in the translation given in the Vulgate: 'Blessed is the man whose trust is in the name of the Lord' (Psalms, XXXIX, 5). [This reference is to the Douay Bible. In the King James version it is Psalm XL, 4: 'Blessed is that man that maketh the Lord his trust' (*translator's note*).] There lay the root of the oldest of prayers, traces of which were still observable at the beginning of the present age. Religious saints repeated the name of Jesus throughout their death-agony. A great Breton mystic, directed by Father Maunoir, Catherine Daniélou, could say, as a child, only '*Pater noster, ne oun quen*' and '*Ave Maria, ne oun quen*', which, translated from Breton, meant '*Pater noster* (or *Ave Maria*), I don't know anything else'. She kept on saying that in the churches of Quimper which she visited during the day.[15] Francis of Assisi and his followers employed this prayer in the form of continuous invocations of the Lord's name. To him and Bonaventure were due the devotion to the Holy Name of Jesus which enjoyed immense success in the Baroque period.[16] The litanies recited on that occasion, together with those addressed to the Virgin of Loretto or to all the saints, resumed this very old prayer in a somewhat more elaborate and developed form.

The biblical model also survived in another way. The name of God was always the emblem and banner of the Chosen People. Ignatius Loyola accordingly placed at the centre of his *Spiritual Exercises* the meditation on the two standards, after which the Christian decides to enlist and fight under Christ's name.[17]

To speak that name or to call upon it signified more than a commitment. It also meant appealing to a powerful supernatural force capable, in an instant, of putting to flight enemies of God, whether the Devil in person or his instruments.[18]

This accounts for the zeal shown by most of the missionaries of the

---

[15] AJF, Vanves, Fonds Maunoir, 2Aa, 'La vie de Catherine Daniélou par le P. Julien Maunoir de la Compagnie de Jesus, son directeur', p. 13.

[16] Thureau-Dangin, *Un Prédicateur populaire*, pp. 78 and 79.

[17] Ignace de Loyola, *Ecrits, Exercices spirituels*, paras. 136–48, pp. 122–9 (fourth day of the week).

[18] *Kurzer Innhalt des Johann Joseph Gassnerschen Systems durch die Kraft des heiligsten Namens Jesus gegen den Teufel und alle höllische Anfechtungen in Leibs- und Seelen Krankheiten zu streiten*, Sulzbach, 1775.

Baroque period in attacking blasphemy.[19] Worse than an insult to God – which is true of every sin – the crime here denounced was perversion of something that ought to serve as praise of God, as prayer sent up to him: an appeal to God by name. Calling upon the Eternal in order to insult and mock him meant acting as if every bond between creature and Creator was thenceforth broken, without hope of redemption and through man's fault alone. The blasphemer who already behaves like one of the damned is acting in truly diabolical fashion. It is therefore not surprising that the fight against swearers was considered by the clergy as a continuation of the repressive activity of the judges against witches and sorcerers.[20] In the eyes of theologians it was as though Satan, having failed in his plan to bewitch the world, was resuming in a more insidious way his work of perverting human nature, by getting inside every individual and causing him to speak like a demon.

It was between 1630 and 1640 that there frequently appeared in the annual *Letters* of the Jesuits of the German-speaking countries manifestations of a systematic campaign directed against the 'sins of the tongue'. Founding confraternities of Saint Isidore, specially aimed at those sins, or of the Holy Name of Jesus (Dillingen, Kaufbeuren), stage-plays with the seriousness of the sin of blasphemy as their theme (Freiburg-im-Breisgau), instructions focused on this theme (Munich), candles lit before images of Christ in the streets (Trent) – all these methods were used to follow up the effect of sermons.[21] Nevertheless, after a century of effort, the missionaries had to accept that the task was a great deal more difficult than had at first been foreseen. In 1725 a religious of the mission in Bavaria estimated that 'a large number of blasphemies form part of everyday language, to such an extent that we have to persuade people to speak differently (*et linguae usus restitutus iterum*)'.[22]

The task was substantial, and all the more so because, in the course of a century, through the penetration of the Catholic Reformation into people's minds, what was required had greatly increased. For people to greet each other with 'Good day' became, if not blasphemous, then at least the sign of a lack of Christian feeling even in the smallest of

---

[19] The preachers of the seventeenth and eighteenth centuries were only doing what their medieval predecessors had done. See Casagrande, Carla, and Vecchio, Silvana, *Les Péchés de la langue*, Paris, Cerf, 1991.

[20] This is clearly seen in an article by Wolfgang Behringer, 'Scheiternde Hexenprozesse. Volksglaube und Hexenverfolgung im 1600 in München', in Richard von Dulmen, *Kultur der einfachen Leute: Bayerisches Volksleben vom 16. bis zum 19. Jahrhundert*, Munich, Beck, 1983, pp. 42–78.

[21] BH, Munich, *Jesuiten*, 104, fo. 256 (Trent); *Jesuiten*, 105, fo. 7vo (Dilligen), fo. 138vo (Freiburg-im-Breisgau); *Jesuiten*, 106 (Munich, the congregation of the Immaculate Conception against the habit of swearing, 1644), *Jesuiten*, 110, fo. 112 (Kaufbeuren).

[22] *Ibid.*, *Jesuiten*, 565, pp. 27–8 (1725).

matters. What one was supposed to say was '*Grüss Gott*' ('Salute God') –
and this is still what people say in Bavaria – so as to make clear that
whatever happened during the day must be put down to the glory and
honour of God. Harder still was it to prevent those cries of anger against
Heaven due to despair after the death of a dear one. In Andalusia a
woman particularly scandalised Father Pedro Calatayud by telling him
that Paradise mattered little to her unless she were to find there her
daughter who had just died, and that she would rather go to Hell if that
was where the girl was.[23] Women, though, according to this zealous
missionary, were more often guilty of 'curses' than of blasphemies in the
strict sense. The distinction, however, was often difficult to draw. At
Corunna, in Galicia, a mother of thirteen children, worn out by their
cries and her toil, had gone so far as to say: 'Won't death carry you off?'
('*No os llevara la muerte?*') Three months later, nine of her children had
been buried.[24] Undoubtedly, the Devil had answered her appeal. He
had also come, the preacher believed, when a little girl of six who had
said to her mother one day: 'You'll see that I shall be burnt' was found
by her parents, on their return from Mass, burning with fever, with two
marks on her cheeks. These could only be scratches from the claws of
the Evil One.[25] In this case the 'curse' which she had allegedly uttered
had been turned against herself. Nothing, though, equalled the crime of
the 'blissful person' – a pious woman who assiduously frequented the
conventicles organised by her parish priest – to whom her husband had
administered some blows with a stick to punish her for neglectful
housekeeping. In open court, before the Inquisition of Valladolid, she
dared to say: 'May God alone repay my husband for the punishment he
inflicted on me.'[26] Here the curse was worse than blasphemy because it
took God for Satan, who alone finds pleasure in deeds of hatred.

By means of these examples Father Calatayud – who must have been a
bit of a woman-hater – sought to show the young religious who were
being trained by reading his notebooks that women were just as guilty as
men of the crime he was prosecuting so ardently. It was not to be
expected that he would show any mildness towards the swearwords that
resounded in workshops and stables.[27] They were proceeded against
with maximum vigilance and were the subject of a ceremony of
expiation, partly devised by Calatayud himself, which was intended to

[23] BN, Madrid, MSS, 5838, fo. 97vo (mission to Velez Rubio, 1732).
[24] *Ibid.*, fo. 32vo (1730).
[25] *Ibid.*, fo. 15vo (mission to Valderas, near Benavente, 1727).
[26] *Ibid.*, fo. 10vo (mission to Mota del Marquès, west of Valladolid, 1723).
[27] *Ibid.*, fo. 20vo: case of a soldier who swore and was made to kiss the ground by boys
who followed the missionary's exercises (mission to Sepulved, north-east of Segovia,
1729).

influence participants to the end of their lives. This was how he described one such ceremony, which took place at the very conclusion of his career, in 1758, at Utrera in Andalusia. On Wednesday, 19 April, there was to be a sumptuous procession of penitents, bringing together all the confraternities. The previous day, in order to 'sanctify the streets', an 'office' against blasphemy was held. In the principal church, which, as was proper, looked out on the Plaza Mayor, the men and women of the town were assembled. The proceedings began with the ritual sermon that the missionary usually delivered on such occasions. Then, crucifix in hand, and speaking from the pulpit, he called on the men to leave by the door on the north side of the church. This crowd was then split. Led by the Fathers and the diocesan clergy, each of the two separated groups had to traverse the little town and its chief thoroughfares by a different route. As they left the church a missionary cried: 'Hail Jesus!' and everyone repeated 'Hail Jesus!' then the Father cried: 'Down with curses!', which was followed by another 'Hail Jesus!' And this dialogue was repeated, with reference to swearwords and blasphemies, mingled with cries of 'Hail Jesus!' At certain points, decided on beforehand, rather like the 'stations' of a Corpus Christi procession or of a Way of the Cross, the leader brought the column to a halt and shouted loudly the command: '*Bocas a tierra*' ('Mouths to the ground'). All threw themselves down to kiss the soil, as in the old pilgrim rite. They stayed in that attitude of extreme penitence while the Father addressed them, holding high the crucifix in his right hand. The act of contrition having been recited, the whole group continued on its way, punctuated by shouts of 'Hail Jesus! Down with blasphemy!', and, after further halts, re-entered the principal church. There they met again Father Calatayud, who, being old and ill, had not been able to lead the procession. From the pulpit he now ordered the women in his audience to perform the same exercise as the men. While, thanks to the men's loud cries, the spirit of penitence filled the church, the old missionary, clutching his crucifix, hurled forth '*saetas de fuego*' (arrows of fire), scriptural verses appropriate to the occasion which, he wrote without false modesty, 'rent hearts that were already overwhelmed'. The act of contrition which followed was said amid plenty of tears, groans and deep sighs.[28]

Despite features derived from the great model constituted by Paolo Segneri's processions of penitents, this ceremony contained several original elements. First, the role played by the community, though it was inherent in every mission, assumed here an importance all the greater in that the community was, so to speak, entrusted with the task of carrying

[28] BN, Madrid, MSS, 4503, fos.162–163vo.

out a rite of purification for the entire town. Those cries glorifying Jesus which rang through the streets, that kissing of the ground, were so many means of washing away the blasphemous filth with which the walls and the soil and been covered by men's fault. It was a way of restoring it to the condition it should never have lost, that of a city of God. Father Calatayud had constructed this ceremony by using practices long established in Spain, such as the pilgrim's kissing the Promised Land when at last he reaches it, and the spontaneous praise (*saeta*) that springs from a gypsy's heart as the floats of the Holy Week procession pass by. In this ritual there was a strange mixture. On the one hand, a memory of the Old Testament was certainly present, in the concern to avert divine vengeance. On the other, however, under a seeming fidelity to tradition, was not a new relationship to God, less direct, effected by the Church's mediation and under its control, being established?

From waiting for God to God present

The crowds mentioned in their reports by all the missionaries doubtless did not come impelled solely by fear of divine punishment or by the attraction of picturesque ceremonies. Through repeating, morning and evening, 'Thy Kingdom come', many might wonder whether these devout religious, dressed as pilgrims, were not, like the Angel of the Apocalypse, emissaries of the Almighty. Vincent Ferrer seemed like that when he announced at Murcia that the world would end in forty-five days precisely.[29] In the seventeenth century the Portuguese Jesuit Antonio Vieira warned his contemporaries of the imminent arrival of the Fifth Monarchy, which would be ruled by Christ in person. Meanwhile, it was his compatriots' duty to bring the Gospel to all the nations of the earth.[30] When the prophetic spirit manifested itself in events more modest than that, it proved to the faithful the supernatural origin of the missionaries' undertaking. That happened when, during the preaching at La Chèze (between Saint-Brieuc and Vannes) by Grignion de Montfort, people recalled how Vincent Ferrer, 'the great apostle of Brittany', had said that the work would be continued by a man whom the Almighty would cause to be born in a 'distant time'.[31] Similarly, Dom Le Nobletz announced that Julien Maunoir would one day take over from him, though he did not yet know the man.[32]

[29] Gorce, *Saint Vincent Ferrier*, p. 144. Cf. above, chapter 1.
[30] Cantel, Raymond, *Prophétisme et Messianisme dans l'œuvre d'Antonio Vieira*, Paris, Ed. Hispano-Americanas, 1960, p. 72, pp. 141–5 and 212.
[31] Picot de Clorivière, *Grignion de Montfort*, pp. 154–5.
[32] Boschet, *Le Parfait Missionnaire*, 1697, pp. 4–5.

Just as wonderful seemed the gift of probing hearts and pointing out unhesitatingly the great sinners who were present amid a crowd of unknowns. At Corunna Pedro Calatayud preached in the street, as was his wont when he arrived in a town, on a theme that spontaneously came to his mind. 'There is a woman here who has not lived with her husband for the last five years', he suddenly declared, without knowing that the guilty one was near him. A few days later, having been told that there was also a man who had deserted his wife two years previously, he went up to a group of men and cried: 'Where is this accursed fellow!', grabbing at random the shoulder of one of them, who turned out to be the offender.[33]

People told each other about the wonders that had occurred when some missionary visited them. The preachings of Paolo Segneri in central and northern Italy were accompanied by extraordinary events.[34] Julien Maunoir, at Ushant, cured sick children.[35] One of these miracles reveals the full power of the evangelical model. 'While we were walking along', Father Maunoir recorded, 'on our way to celebrate Mass, we were told that this girl had asked for us to visit her. At her house we taught her about the mysteries of the Most Holy Trinity and of mankind saved by God, and caused her to make an act of faith in Jesus Christ. Then, after washing her eyes with water in which Saint Joan's bead had been dipped, we called to her, saying: *"Sellit ouzomp!"*, that is, "Look at us!" and she immediately recovered her sight.'[36] The allusion to the miracle of Christ healing the blind man is obvious here.

Somewhat different was the miracle performed by the Jesuits at the beginning of their mission in Bavaria. This event took place at Oberessendorf, in the diocese of Augsburg, in 1719. The population were showing only slight interest in the mission. The drought which had prevailed for several weeks seriously endangered the harvest and the survival of the flocks and herds. Public prayers and supplications ordered by the bishop had produced no effect.

In face of the general affliction the missionary, afraid that they might turn to the futile superstition to which some of the inhabitants were given, and which was a huge sin, proposed that they turn to God. He ordered the villagers to say five *Paters* and five *Aves* before the holy sacrament exposed on the mission's platform, this to be followed by a solemn undertaking made by the whole community to renounce the use of superstitions. Hardly had the prayers been concluded [wrote the annalist], than clouds appeared on the horizon. They gradually condensed and covered the entire sky, and soon abundant rain followed. [The weather continued like that for several days.] When, on the fourth day, the rain seemed

[33] BN, Madrid, MSS, 5838, fo. 32–32vo (1730).
[34] Guidetti, *Le missioni popolari*, p. 105.
[35] Croix and Roudault, *Les Bretons*, p. 228.   [36] *Ibid.*

likely to hinder the procession, a missionary caused prayers to be said again, for the clouds to stay closed during the procession . . . The rain held back while the ceremony proceeded, and most of the participants were already back in their villages when, as if permission had been given for this to happen, rain fell so plentifully, for a whole day, that it brought back life to the meadows and ploughed fields. Thereafter the preachers were seen as possessing the power to open and shut the heavens as they wished, and whatever they said was taken as oracles (*veluti oracula*).[37]

The memory of Christ permeates this story, too. But, even more than in the previous one, we see here the attribution of supernatural powers to the Jesuits, who are not just the 'holy fathers' (*tadou santel*) of Brittany but real demigods capable of acting upon the elements and diverting the wrath of God. What was called Saint Ignatius' or Saint Francis Xavier's water, obtained by immersing relics of the two saints in holy water, and which people came in great numbers to collect in bottles and demijohns, added to this reputation as healers which they enjoyed. Not without some emphasis, the chronicler who reported the results obtained by the Society in Bavaria in 1720 described a number of miracles attributed to Francis Xavier and concluded: 'There were many others for whom the Saviour's words were fulfilled: the blind see, the deaf hear, the lame walk, the sick are healed. The poor were instructed in the Gospel.'[38] This was, basically, the image of themselves that the missionaries wanted to give: envoys of God the supernatural origin of whose office was proved, as in the time of Christ, by miracles.

There was thus a close connection, in the minds of the faithful and in those of many missionaries, between the work of moral uplift that they were carrying out in the country districts and manifestations of the sacred. This equivalence was nowhere plainer than in the places of pilgrimage to which crowds hastened in hope of receiving divine favours.[39]

At Piekary, in Poland, a town in the far west of Cracow diocese, there was an old wooden church with, on a side-altar, a beautiful picture of the Virgin and Child. In the seventeenth century this picture was considered miraculous and was the object of a cult and a minor pilgrimage. All remained at a very modest level in the middle of the century, attracting only peasants from the neighbouring district, while for others it was merely a halt on the route of the great pilgrimage to Czestochowa, the catchment area of which extended far beyond the region. In 1669 the Austrian Jesuits set up an establishment not far from

[37] BH, Munich, *Jesuiten*, 564, pp. 23–4 (1719).
[38] *Ibid.*, p. 61 (1720).
[39] Dupront, Alphonse, *Du Sacré. Croisades et pèlerinages. Images et langages*, Paris, Gallimard, 1987.

Opole (Oppeln), in Silesia, and immediately benefited from the Emperor's protection. Very soon they were invited to Tarnowskie Gory (Tarnowitz), where they busied themselves, from 1675, with the German minority living in a region where Protestants formed the majority (see Map 2). The Catholics of Opole, who possessed a copy of the famous Virgin of Czestochowa, led the Jesuits to take an interest in this picture. The Catholics of Tarnowitz informed the Fathers about 'the German one at Piekary'.[40] What led the Silesian missionaries to devote all their efforts to promoting the cult of that picture? Political considerations were certainly not absent, since, in the difficult negotiations which the Jesuits had to pursue with the Bishop of Cracow, the Emperor was their loyal supporter, thanks to whom they secured the unification of the parish of Piekary with their college at Opole. Thus, through the Virgin of Piekary, German influence in Poland was advanced far eastward. Apparently, Polish pilgrims at the end of the seventeenth century were heard to say of their King (Jan Sobieski): 'What do our priests do for our King? The Jesuits do much for their Emperor.'[41] Had the Jesuits been sent on special mission to the advanced posts of the Empire, under orders, like the Teutonic Knights of olden times, to carry the imperial eagle farther eastward? But the Black Virgin of Czestochowa, emerging like an icon from a gilded background, should she not also, unlike 'the German one at Piekary', give the Jesuits cause for some anxiety? Was she truly Catholic? Besides, the Poles who jostled each other on the communion bench and were incapable of marching in order in processions, unlike the Silesians, inspired no confidence among the missionaries.[42] What seemed to them preferable was an authentically Germanic sanctuary, more conformable to the Catholic Reformation as they understood it. However, that must have counted little compared with what seemed to the missionaries the essential thing. One of them gave in his report what was doubtless the chief explanation for all this zeal. The miraculous picture was in the church at Piekary like 'a visit from the Lord and an opportunity for souls, in this time when plague threatens, to prepare themselves for the black death'.[43] And indeed, not long after the first miracles and the subsequent arrival of floods of pilgrims, plague broke out afresh in the Empire. The Emperor, who was in Prague at this time, asked for the picture and it was brought to him (February 1680). After being the object of private devotion by the sovereign and his family it was transferred to the church of the Holy

---

[40] Hoffmann, Hermann, 'Die Jesuiten in Oppeln. Die Tätigkeit der Jesuiten in den Fürstentumern Oppeln und Ratibor', *Zur schlesischen Kirchengeschichte*, 8, Breslau, 1934, p. 95.

[41] *Ibid.*, p. 247.   [42] *Ibid.*   [43] *Ibid.*, p. 237.

Saviour where, exposed on an altar under the cupola, it was venerated by a countless number of people. The Archbishop said High Mass before it. Sermons, instructions, confessions and communions followed each other without interruption. To conclude, the Archbishop decreed a solemn procession through the three towns that made up Prague (the Hradčin, the old town and the new town).[44] The picture, conveyed in a coach hung with cloth, drawn by six horses and lit by as many torches, was first taken to the church of St Ignatius, where it was presented for veneration by the citizens. Then it went to the Ursulines and, finally, to St Vitus' cathedral, where it was met by the Archbishop and his chapter, who accompanied it to the high altar, where high mass was sung. Next day the holy picture began its triumphant return journey to Piekary.

After such success the renown of the Virgin of Piekary was an accomplished fact. Crowds now came from afar to venerate her. The King of Poland, Jan Sobieski, marching to fight the Turks who were besieging Vienna, halted at Piekary to ask for her protection. In that same year, 1683, however, we find mentioned for the first time in the Jesuits' chronicle a confraternity of Christian Doctrine and also of the Forty Hours' Prayer. Two years later the children of the catechism class performed a 'Passion play'. In the statistics which they carefully compiled the Fathers were much more interested in the number of communions than in the miracles reported.[45] For these pilgrims who arrived in their thousands were the audiences for their sermons and instructions, the penitents who crowded before their confessionals and the first members of their confraternities. In this way 'a place visited by the Lord' became a major mission centre.

The origin of the Piekary residence showed how closely the presence of something holy was linked with a mission. Declaring God's word was not enough. It was further necessary that the man who came to meet the people should seem to bear a supernatural mandate to perform this task. Or else the place where this Good News was proclaimed must enjoy a special status demonstrated to all by a miracle or wonder. Such a situation was common in the seventeenth and eighteenth centuries. It even happened that certain missionaries systematically chose chapels which were targets of active (or declining) pilgrimages as the places to preach from. The Jesuits of the province of the Upper Rhineland, established in Alsace, at Haguenau, Molsheim and Sélestat, made it their business, as soon as they arrived, to restore or develop sanctuaries of the Virgin which had suffered from the Reformation or had fallen into decay owing to the wars. Examples were Marienthal, near Haguenau,

[44] *Ibid.*, p. 238.   [45] *Ibid.*, p. 256.

Altbronn, near Molsheim, Wiversheim, between Saverne and Strasburg, and Neukirch, near Sélestat.[46] The religious who were given charge of these chapels, and who bore, in the Society's lists, the unequivocal name of *missionnarii*, committed themselves to the ordinary tasks of this function. Was this not also a way of supervising old-established pilgrimages, the devotions practised in them and the customs which had become routine among the pilgrims, so as, where necessary, to make some corrections?

However, another situation was already taking shape. This was when the death in a certain place of one of a mission's 'holy fathers' who had preached there had the effect of consecrating that place and giving it, because of the presence of a venerated corpse, the character of a centre of pilgrimage. Examples were the village of Lalouvesc in Vivarais, after the death of Jean-François Regis in 1640, and Pomeur, in Lower Brittany, when M. de Trémaria passed away there in 1673.[47] In 1655 there died at Saint-Cirq-Lapopie, in the diocese of Cahors, Father Michel Le Fèvre, companion of the famous Oratorian missionary Jean Lejeune. His reputation of great piety sufficed for him to be regarded as a potential saint. A peasant who sat up with him took a button from his habit. A canon of Brive-la-Gaillarde who was ill rushed to occupy the dead man's bed as soon as he had been placed on his bier, convinced this would bring him relief. As the body was borne by, the inhabitants rent their clothes. Miracles began straightaway. One, two, three persons declared that they had benefited from these. The peasants naturally wanted to keep the body and would not let the Fathers of the Oratory take it away, despite 'the so-persuasive eloquence of Father Lejeune' and the 'singular esteem in which he was held . . . so convinced were they that they possessed the body of a saint'.[48] The same thing happened at the death of Louis-Marie Grignion de Montfort in 1716 at Saint-Laurent-sur-Sèvre (between Angers and Fontenay-le-Comte), where his body remained.[49] When the popular Capuchin preacher Diego José of Cadiz died in 1801, at Ronda, between Seville and Cadiz, the crowd rushed to the Governor's house, where the religious had died, and demanded that his body be placed in a ground-floor room giving on to

---

[46] Châtellier, *Tradition chrétienne*, pp. 193–205.
[47] Dompnier, Bernard, 'Les Jésuites et la dévotion populaire. Autour de l'origine du culte de saint Jean-François Régis (1641–1676)', in *Les Jésuites parmi les hommes aux XVIe et XVIIe siècles*, Proceedings of Clermont-Ferrand colloquium (April 1985), Clermont-Ferrand, Publications de l'Université de Clermond-Ferrand, II, fasc. XXV, 1987, pp. 195–308; AJF, Vanves, Fonds Maunoir, 2Ae/2, 'Vie de M. l'abbé de Trémaria composée par le Révérend P. Julien Maunoir' (copy), pp. 73–94.
[48] Batterel, *Mémoires domestiques*, vol. III, pp. 74–5.
[49] [Grandet], *Grignion de Montfort*, pp. 244–5.

the street. The population gathered to contemplate the holy man on his bed and held out, to the priests who were beside him, jewels, linen, chaplets and loaves, to be brought into contact with the corpse and then returned to their owners.[50] The missions, which took their place in the geography of holy things in this world, contributed also to enrich it, so perfectly did they fit into a world which they aimed to change, not to overturn.

The missionaries who arrived in the rural areas did not find a people without God. Indeed, they were perhaps frightened by the ease with which he was appealed to, taken to task and even seen in the persons of these preachers who came to teach them the Word. The *tadou santel* of Ushant, and still more those who, in Bavaria, opened and shut the heavens like gods, seemed to possess a supernatural power beyond the understanding of human beings. These powers were enhanced still more when the churches in which they proclaimed the Word were also holy locations where natural graces abounded around a venerated image. The existence of pilgrimages, the arrival of 'holy' preachers, the acts of penitence performed in common, to wash away sins before God, were not, taken separately, anything new for the masses. But their bringing together emphasised the exceptional nature of the event. What the missionaries sought to suggest by means of teaching heightened by these practices was a new idea of God. For a familiarity with Him which could go so far as vulgar swearwords they tried to substitute the sense of divine transcendence. The undertaking was a delicate one because, at the same time, they wished to demonstrate God's omnipresence in the whole universe and in every person's life.

[50] Damase de Loisey, Father, *Le Bienheureux Diego-Joseph de Cadix*, Paris, Poussielgue, 1902, p. 260.

6   The cross

Though Europe was Christian, Christ was still remote, impressive, even terrifying, taking the form of that enormous crucifix that dominates the transepts of churches and whose face, sad and sombre, is barely distinguishable in the shadow of the arches. Was it not very difficult to talk to him, confide in him, repeat what he had said to his father in the Garden of Olives: 'Thy will be done on earth as it is in heaven'? Did people even think of doing that? To be sure, there had been *The Imitation of Jesus Christ* and the *Spiritual Exercises* of Ignatius Loyola, but these books, though known to and used by the devout in the towns, had, even in adapted or abridged form, little circulation in country districts. The most novel and essential thing that the missionaries brought was the cross – in the most literal sense of the word. From the end of the seventeenth century the ceremony of planting the cross assumed increasing importance in the procedure of a mission. Once done, it was a permanent reminder of what had been said and promised in those days of fervour. Set up in the centre of the village or on the top of the hill overlooking it, present constantly to everyone's gaze, the cross recalled the famous hymn popularised by Grignion de Montfort:

> *Vive Jésus, vive sa croix!*
> *N'est-il pas bien juste qu'on l'aime*
> *Puisqu'il nous montre sur ce bois*
> *Qu'il nous aimait plus que soy-meme?*
> *Chrétiens, chantons à haute voix:*
> *Vive Jésus, vive sa croix![1]*

(Hail Jesus, hail his cross! Is it not right indeed that we should love him, since he shows us, on this piece of wood, that he loved us more than himself? Christians, let us sing at the tops of our voices: Hail Jesus, hail his cross!)

---

[1] *Les Œuvres du [Bienheureux] de Montfort. Ses cantiques*, critical study and notes by R. P. F. Fradet, S. M. M., Paris and Angers, Beauchesne-Grassin, 1929, p. 655. The editor states that this hymn was taken and adapted by Grignion de Montfort from a collection widely known at the time of his first missions.

Just as the cross changed the familiar landscape, so was it intended to change men's lives.

A taking of possession

During Holy Week in 1651 at Wałcz (Deutsch Krone) in Pomerania the Jesuits organised a procession of penitents to the top of the hill near Mönchsberg. There they planted a cross 'as a sign of possession', wrote the chronicler.[2] Workmen soon set to and there appeared the foundations of a school and a chapel. The cross, like the one which, a few years later, was set up at Papá, in Hungary, to proclaim the victory won at Szentgotthard, was a rich political and religious symbol in the eastern marches of the Holy Roman Empire.[3] It was a sign of the triumph of the True Church over heretics and infidels. In a sense, it gave material form to the frontier of Christendom. We find such crosses, in great numbers, on the borders between Catholic and Protestant territories, and also in those places where it was believed that, in former times, witches had assembled.

The crosses which some religious, from the 1670s onward, habitually caused to be erected at the end of their missions had a more spiritual significance. Their value was none the less for a whole village or a whole region, as a consecration to Christ, who thus became, from his cross, the sole and true master of that place. An example was the famous calvary installed at Pontchâteau by Louis Grignion de Montfort in 1709–10.

M. Grignion had long been trying to spread around him a lively devotion to the cross. His first biographer tells us that, during his pilgrimage to Rome, he obtained permission from the Pope to bless little crosses made of paper and cloth, which he handed out at the end of each mission to persons who had attended thirty-three sermons.[4] At La Chèze, in the diocese of Saint-Brieuc, in 1708, he was unwilling, despite the bad weather and his poor state of health, to refrain from the final exercise which concluded his missions. He 'ordered the people to carry it [the cross] barefoot and, so as the better to get them to do that, he suited the action to the word by taking off his own shoes, whereupon more than two hundred men came to him barefoot, seeking the honour of carrying the cross'.[5] In this account, however, the ceremony appeared to be primarily penitential. Things went differently at Pontchâteau where the monumental constructions had so lasting an effect on men's minds. It seems that he was obsessed with desire to set up a great calvary close to the places where he had preached. Was this to be a memorial,

---

[2] *Historia Residentiae*, p. 92.   [3] ARSI, Rome, Austria, 229, fo. 268.
[4] [Grandet], *Grignion de Montfort*, p. 101.   [5] *Ibid.*, p. 137.

more imposing than usual, to his mission? Was he thinking of creating a place of assembly for believers that was outside the familiar parish setting, so as to renew their faith by means of a new kind of pilgrimage? Or, quite simply, did he just want to share with others his devotion to the crucified Jesus?

In any case, the initiative was his. When he was working in the diocese of Saint-Brieuc, under the direction of M. Leuduger, canon of the cathedral, he met a clever craftsman – perhaps he was even a sculptor – from whom he ordered an image of Christ. This was no ordinary figure, for it was nearly two and a half metres tall.[6] And as the price was not ordinary, either, Canon Leuduger told him that he must meet the full cost himself. Montfort undertook a collection for the purpose and dreamt of an imposing construction. However, other apostolic work claimed his attention. The Jesuits of Nantes asked him to help them. Then he was summoned to the villages and small towns of Campbon, Besné, Crossac and Pontchâteau, all of which were situated beside the Brière, north of the Loire estuary. Around those marshes the firm ground stood out so clearly that anything built on it could be seen from afar. He noticed a stretch of heath near Pontchâteau which struck him as particularly suitable. Then, during his mission to that place, in July 1709, he revealed his plan to build a calvary there. He called on his listeners to dig a ditch so as to keep animals from coming too close. 'But when he saw what a great number of people had gathered, he conceived a grander design, to make not a ditch but trenches around this calvary. He took a rope and made a circuit of 400 feet, then a second circuit of 500 feet, so that the mountain made from the earth dug from the trenches was 133 feet across: the trenches, 15 feet wide, were 500 feet round on the inner side and 600 on the outer side where he made a bank at the two ends of which he had shrubs planted, so as to decorate this walkway'. The enterprise had thus expanded – from a simple cross erected on a heath it became a calvary mounted on an immense pedestal made from the earth and stones drawn from the ditches. This was the 'mountain'. Meanwhile, Montfort had gone to the nearby village of Missillac, from where he could also watch how the works were progressing. His first setback came when the owner of the wood in which someone had found a fine chestnut tree that would serve for the base of the cross failed to respond to the requests put to him. Eventually M. Grignion had to take steps 'to wrest a slight consent from him'. As they were afraid that the man might go back on this, the workers hastened to the wood, cut down the tree and, with 'twelve yoke of oxen',

[6] *Ibid.*, p. 152.

dragged it to the site for the calvary. That place became a regular building-site, with the crowd at work there continually growing. On some days there were more than 500 persons present, with a hundred oxen to pull the carts. Despite the surprising amount of heavy work that these men and women performed, they were happy with only a piece of black bread to sustain them. Everything proceeded in perfect order, to the sound of the hymns which the crowd sang with fervour. As a reward, once their working day was over, they were permitted to 'pay their respects to the crucifix which was placed in a little grotto covered with earth brought thither, and in which it was impossible to see without a candle. Besides the crucifix there were figures to be seen of the Holy Virgin, St John and St Mary Magdalene, and also of the Two Thieves – a spectacle which, being visible only with the aid of a lamp which was kept alight, stirred the people to solemn feelings and brought tears to their eyes.'[7] While this was going on, M. Grignion and his companions were continuing with their missions around the Grande Brière marshes. Herbignac, Camoël and Asserac were visited in turn (see Map 11). He then moved to Bouguenais, near Nantes, where a rehearsal was carried out for what was intended at Pontchâteau. The 10,000 persons who participated in the closing procession were divided into fourteen squadrons, each of which was preceded by its standard 'of white satin, an ell and a half long and an ell wide'. 'They were led into a great plain on the banks of the Loire where there was a very rich temporary altar on which to place the holy sacrament.'

When the missionary returned to Pontchâteau, in August 1710, the 'mountain' was complete. The time had come to set up the calvary itself. At the top of the hill was a wall surmounted by a rosary all the beads of which were as big as bowls.

Within this ring three crosses were planted. The middle one, made from the fine tree of which I spoke, was painted red, and at its foot was a little chapel on which were fifteen good wooden steps that served to climb up all round this cross. On the right thereof was a green cross, and on the left a black one. To the red cross was attached the eight-foot-tall Christ, with, above, the Holy Spirit. On the green cross was put the Good Thief, who had been brought there in a triumphal float on which rode a large number of angels, ending a fine procession adorned with standards, come from half a league away. On the black cross was put the Bad Thief, who was rending his heart. At the foot of the cross were placed the Holy Virgin with St John and St Mary Magdalene. At the gate in the ring-wall there was a pipe filled with water which discharged through the mouth of a serpent, representing the Brazen Serpent of the Old Testament. At the approach to the gate there was to be an *Ecce Homo.*[8]

---

[7] *Ibid.*, p. 157.   [8] *Ibid.*, pp. 158–9.

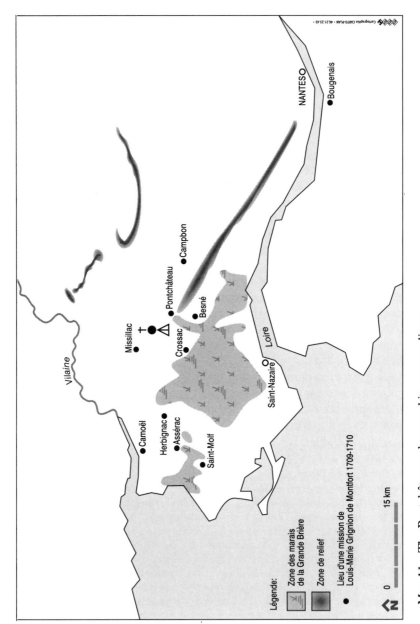

Map 11   The Pontchâteau calvary and its surroundings.

Légende:

Zone des marais
de la Grande Brière

Zone de relief

● Lieu d'une mission de
Louis-Marie Grignion de Montfort 1709-1710

0   15 km

The rest of the building work was still in the planning stage. The intention was for the hill to be surrounded by a wall protecting a road 'like a snail's shell' by which people could climb up to the calvary. There would also be three chapels 'in which 14 mysteries of the Rosary would be depicted, adjoining the original grotto, which would have shown the 15th'. The wall around the hill was to be hidden by firs and cypresses planted in groups of ten, 'so that, when in this avenue between the wall and the trenches, one might say one's entire rosary on these trees while walking round the calvary'. The entrance would be situated facing the cross, with a garden on either side: the earthly paradise and the Garden of Olives.

M. Grignion had chosen the feast of the Exaltation of the Holy Cross, 14 September 1710, for his solemn benediction. The preachers had already been appointed and pilgrims were arriving from all quarters. The calvary was visible from afar, and news of this imposing construction work, involving hundreds of men and women, had spread even beyond the region. In connection with it people recalled prophecies and wonders. An old peasant remembered having seen, about forty years earlier, crosses surrounded by standards descending from the sky, in broad daylight, upon this heath where the missionary had built his calvary. The event had been accompanied by so great a noise that the cattle which were grazing there had fled into the neighbouring villages. After that, the country rang with the sound of an infinite number of voices, forming a veritable heavenly concert. People were already talking of miracles. Was it not said that many cures had been effected by means of earth taken from the pious building-site?

But now, on the eve of the celebration, when the heath was already covered with pilgrims and arrangements were being made to accommodate them, a priest arrived to announce that the bishop forbade the benediction. In the following days severe measures were taken, one after another. First, Montfort was invited to get on with his missions. Then the bishop forbade him to return to the calvary, which was to be destroyed by court order. According to the author of this account, the crowds who had continued to arrive, and to hope, were now gripped by sobs of grief. Soon, those who so enthusiastically had erected the monument in honour of the cross were ordered to take it down. They were seen to lower the figure of Christ with every sign of love and piety. A witness said that he 'did not believe that the descent from the cross carried out in Jerusalem was as sad as this one. Everybody knelt while others performed the task of Nicodemus and Joseph of Arimathea.' Once this pious task was completed, the people took their time over work which was hateful to them. 'It seems', wrote the author of this report, 'that the men had arms of iron when erecting [the calvary] and arms of wool when destroying it.'[9]

This event shows how, at the beginning of the eighteenth century, the planting of crosses in certain places and circumstances released an emotional charge which was as strong in the case of the humble folk as in that of the men of power. The former were present from the outset of the enterprise. To what extent, moreover, were they its instigators? It was they who contributed to pay for the image of Christ ordered by M. Grignion. When he hit upon the heath of Pontchâteau as the place where his project could be put into practice, they came in such great numbers at his appeal that he was induced to conceive something much more substantial. It was they who accomplished his project, subjecting themselves to labour-discipline and taking initiatives (the tree selected in the neighbouring wood). They quickly endowed the enterprise with a wondrous aura through tales of prophecies or miracles that were passed around. When they had to pull it all down, they kept their hope alight as long as possible and put aside religiously the carved figures of Christ and the other personages, placing them 'in a chapel which is now honoured by the inhabitants'.[10] As for the crosses themselves, these were preserved in even more secret fashion by the peasants. On the other hand, this popular enthusiasm which responded to, and sometimes went beyond, Montfort's appeals, had been aroused by him alone. Recognised as a man of God, Montfort's words and deeds acquired sacred value. The establishment of a calvary in this empty stretch of land looking out over a vast countryside was felt by the Breton population as something much more than a gesture of devotion. It was perhaps the act of foundation of a real place of worship, new and close to them.

This was perhaps the reason for the emotion provoked by the event among the men of power and ecclesiastics. Montfort was accused of unintentionally causing to be built a regular 'fortress', with 'trenches' and 'tunnels', which could provide an enemy with a solid strongpoint if he were to land (this was during the War of the Spanish Succession, 1702–13). The argument might seem to have weight. Yet, once the crosses had been taken away, the 'mountain' was left practically untouched. It was as though only the crosses were objected to by the authorities. Shortly afterwards, at Sallertaine in the diocese of Luçon, Montfort had a similar experience. He managed to have built, outside the town, 'in a high place where formerly there had been a cemetery', a great calvary with a chapel, statues of saints, and a rosary. Its destruction was ordered just as had happened at Pontchâteau.[11]

[9] *Ibid.*, pp. 160–6.   [10] *Ibid.*, p. 166.
[11] Picot de Clorivière, *Grignion de Montfort*, pp. 258–60 and 270.

All this seemed to imply that Montfort was suspected of seeking, through the constructs he was building, to establish a new cult in that place, competing with what existed in the parish churches. The charge was the more convincing in that the missionary did not hesitate to make changes in the churches put at his disposal. The dead buried in the nave were exhumed and moved to cemeteries and the arms of the local lord were erased, on the principle that 'churches should contain only the bodies of Jesus Christ and the saints'.[12] This way of emphasising in the most conspicuous way the reign of Christ over the world could seem a sign of the divine origin of the mission and also as heralding the return of the Son at the end of the world. Can one be surprised that a missionary-prophet like this was followed, in the words of a hostile observer, 'by everyone', meaning the poor people?[13]

Yet Montfort was not an exception. Between 1680 and 1750 there were crosses everywhere. A real frenzy had seized the countryfolk, who set them up in great numbers, in east and west alike.[14] Research which is still at its beginning, and is difficult owing to the destruction which goes on all the time, shows how extensive this movement was. Crosses appeared in the fields and on the heaths, on the tops of hills and in the depths of valleys. In certain mountain parishes we can still find thirty or more, as though isolation increased the need felt for these emblems of Christianity.[15]

Each region had its preferred type of cross. In Alsace the 'Bildstock', with its little niche containing a statuette of the Pietà, accompanied by some flowers, was widespread. On the other side of the Vosges, in Lorraine, high crosses with smooth uprights were more numerous. Often a name or two revealed who the founders were. A date and prayers to be said in order to obtain an indulgence indicate the circumstances in which the cross had been erected. Sometimes the worn state of the arms or the upright of the monument shows that they had not only served to arouse pious feelings among the peasants who worked nearby but had also been used for sharpening their tools. Perhaps the stone of which a cross was made was thought to have exceptional

---

[12] [Grandet], *Grignion de Montfort*, pp. 143–7.

[13] *Ibid.*, p. 164.

[14] Studies include: 'Croix rurales anciennes des environs de Saverne et du Kochersberg', *Pays d'Alsace. Société d'histoire et d'archéologie de Saverne et des environs*, 2–3, 1974, special number; Martin, Hervé, 'La fonction polyvalente des croix à la fin du Moyen Age'; Castel, Yves-Pascal, 'La floraison des croix et des calvaires dans le Léon sous l'influence de Mgr Roland de Neufville (1562–1613)', *Annales de Bretagne et des pays de l'Ouest*, 90, 1983/2, special number, 'L'espace et le sacré', pp. 295–310 and 311–19.

[15] Véron, Michel, *La Vie religieuse dans l'ancien doyenné de Remiremont sous l'Ancien Régime (XVIe–XVIIIe siècle)*, mémoire de maîtrise, typescript, University of Nancy II, 1989, 2 vols, 200 pp. and 133 pp.

qualities, just as the wood of the mission crosses planted by Father Honoré de Cannes at the end of the seventeenth century was supposed to induce miracles.[16] These crosses were also frequently objects of veneration which was expressed, as the Salzburg Jesuits noticed, in superabundant decoration with flowers, rosaries and votive offerings hung from their arms.[17] Being supremely sacred objects, they ended by having attributed to them a mysterious power which worried some bishops.[18] The Bishop of Arras took serious precautions. He explained to the people of his diocese that 'the Adoration of the Cross' (an expression consecrated by long use), which strictly signified 'honour and worship in the highest degree', meant, in fact, no more than 'bowing and showing respect'. For, 'the Catholic Church adores God alone . . . but it respects the Cross to which the Man-God was fastened for the world's salvation'.[19]

Considerations of this sort did perhaps lead some missionaries to show extreme prudence. Charles Mailliardoz, who carried out missions in his native country, the Swiss canton of Fribourg, in 1715 made this ceremony central from the start. At Rue it took place at Whitsun. After a grand procession, everyone gathered near the newly erected crucifix. The Father gave an exhortation on the theme of the Passion, and then, after blessing the crowd, he and his companions, 'drawn to the cross', kissed it before reciting, arms outstretched, the five *Paters* and five *Aves* required to obtain an indulgence.[20] The same ritual was followed in the other places they visited. In 1716 at Albeuve, south of Gruyères, their success was all the greater because the ceremony was held on 25 April, Saint Mark's day, when, as on the Rogation Days, a procession traditionally toured the parish boundary, to ask for a good harvest. Would not the cross bring an additional blessing to the occasion?[21] And yet, a few weeks later, after a sermon on superstitions the missionaries wondered if it would be opportune to make known the extension of the indulgence which had been obtained in the previous year.[22] At the end

---

[16] At Gougenheim (Bas-Rhin) the roundedness of the upright of a cross is due to the sharpening of tools upon it at harvest-time. For sketches and beliefs connected with this, see 'Croix rurales anciennes des environs de Saverne', p. 43. Regarding the mission cross planted by Father Honoré de Cannes in Toulouse in 1678, see above, chapter 3.

[17] BH, Munich, *Jesuiten*, 566, n.p., n.f., year 1731.

[18] *Ibid.*, *Jesuiten*, 567, n.p., year 1735. 'We have set up crosses in the dioceses of Regensburg and Salzburg, but not in that of Passau, as the Bishop was unwilling and did not grant indulgences.'

[19] *Avis et pratiques pour profiter de la mission et en conserver le fruit à l'usage des missions du père du Plessis de la Compagnie de Jésus*, Paris, 1742–4, p. 197.

[20] ASJ, Zurich, MSS, *Compendium Missionum*, mission 1 in the diocese of Lausanne (Rue), 11th day, 9 June 1715.

[21] *Ibid.*, mission 5 in the diocese of Lausanne (Albeuve), 7th day, 25 April 1716.

[22] *Ibid.*, mission 8 in the diocese of Lausanne (Saint-Martin), 9th day, 15 June 1716.

of his mission in Switzerland, in 1718, the 'planting' had become a perfectly organised ceremony in which everyone had his proper place, walking behind children dressed as little angels along a predetermined route and singing hymns that had been carefully planned – a procession during which moments of enthusiasm and improvisations such as had occurred at Rue in 1715 were no longer possible.[23]

But there was no tendency to 'routinise' this ceremony. In March 1738 Father François-Xavier Duplessis gave Lenten sermons in Arras. The cross which was to be solemnly planted was being offered for the devotion of the faithful in the Jesuits' church when a miracle happened. Isabelle Legrand, a disabled fruit-seller, felt, after she had kissed the crucifix, that her whole being was in upheaval. Perturbed, she was able to get up unaided and without using her crutches, and went to repeat her devotion. Spontaneously copying the behaviour of pilgrims in bygone days she walked several times round the cross, kissed Christ's feet once more and was then perfectly cured. We can imagine the crowds next day, when the procession set out. Everyone wanted to see the beneficiary of a miracle, who walked where she could easily be seen. There followed a *Te Deum*, a thanksgiving service and the proclamation of indulgences. The mission cross had become miraculous.[24] In the course of the next few months 252 processions came to Arras. According to Father Duplessis a single year saw the arrival of more than 1,200,000 persons.[25] Every town and village wanted to greet the preacher who performed such wonders and to receive from his hands a cross that would be equally beneficent (see Map 12). Stanislas Leszczynski, the Duke of Lorraine, wanted to have both of these missionaries to inaugurate his 'royal missions' (15 August 1738). He caused a cross surmounted by a dome and protected at its base by a casing of gilt iron to be set up in the great approach-drive of his château of La Malgrange. In this way he endowed the Lorrainers, at his accession, with a new centre of pilgrimage.[26]

A religion of the cross

In the 1730s Father Duplessis was not the only zealous promoter of this devotion. Abbé Bridaine was promoting it in the South of France. The imposing ceremony with which the 1734 mission to Arles concluded

---

[23] *Ibid.*, mission 6 in the diocese of Basel (Saignelégier), 12th day, 30 March 1718.
[24] *Avis et pratiques*, order by Mgr the Bishop of Arras, published as appendix, pp. ix–xxxvi.
[25] *Ibid.*, p. 194.
[26] *Ibid.*, order by Mgr the Bishop-Count of Toul and description of the cross at Nancy, pp. LVI–LXVI.

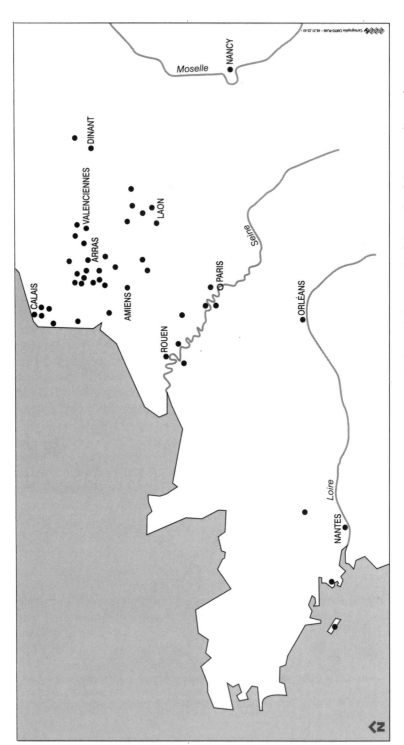

Map 12   The missions of Father François-Xavier Duplessis, SJ, and the spread of the cult of the cross in northern France, 1738–44.

had struck people's imagination.[27] From 1731 the Jesuit missionaries in Bavaria and Upper Austria devoted to crosses a special section in their annual *Letters*. They did not merely describe the ceremony of setting-up the crosses and the miraculous cures that resulted from contact with them, but also showed the place these crosses held in the day-to-day piety of the faithful. The latter had learnt, during the mission to Laufen, near Salzburg, to come in procession every evening to the calvary in order to sing a hymn drawn from the collection the Father had left with them, and on that spot to examine their consciences. 'So as to make this practice perpetual', wrote the author of this account, 'and even to increase it, the Provost of Laufen, Baron Rheling, and his wife, wanted to decorate this cross, at their own expense, with paintings bearing their names, and they called on the peasants to join in the pious work by contributing their labour.'[28] In the valley of the Inn, near Munich, these evening prayers by the community were perfectly organised. At Wasserburg the bell warned the inhabitants, as night fell, that the time had come to start out. At the foot of the cross a dignitary of the collegiate church awaited them. He conducted the singing and invited everyone to call to mind his sins of that day, so as to ask forgiveness for them. Not far away, at Mühldorf, the villagers' daily meditations were facilitated by contemplating a fine group of statues in which the chief items were the suffering Christ and his 'dolorous' mother at his feet. An innovation attracted all eyes: between the arms of the victim had been placed a big heart, painted red, surrounded by golden rays.[29]

This was like an illustration to a passage in a little book which had circulated widely in Bavaria a few years earlier. 'Venerate the image of the Sacred Heart both at church and in your home', it said. 'May the mere contemplation of it fill you with gratitude and overwhelming love, and may it engender in you the desire to immerse yourself wholly in the living heart of Jesus, so that you may live by his Spirit.' The writer added: 'If it often happens that you are inflamed with guilty love when you see your beloved, how greatly is it to be wished that the same should happen with sacred love, through the image of the most adorable heart of Jesus!'[30] In this vibrant exhortation the missionary was only translating and making accessible to the Christian masses the extraordinary revelations with which had been favoured, fifty years before, Sister Marguerite-Marie Alacoque, a nun of the Order of the Visitation,

---

[27] Le Quéré, *Un Missionnaire*, pp. 57–8.
[28] BH, Munich, *Jesuiten*, 566, n.p., n.f., year 1731.
[29] *Ibid.*, year 1733.
[30] Pinamonti, Johannes Petrus, *Kurtzer Begriff der nothwendigsten Stücken der christcatholischen Lehr . . . zum Gebrauch der heiligen Mission zusammengetragen*, Stadt am Hof, 1725, p. 289.

at Paray-le-Monial, and which had been made widely known in Europe through the book by Father Croiset, SJ.[31] Published a year after the nun's death (1690), it had at once been translated into several languages. The formation of confraternities had followed.[32]

As for the missionaries, they were undoubtedly the most ardent and most effective propagators of the new devotion. Giovanni Maria Martinelli, the future founder of the missionary college of Rhó, in the Archdiocese of Milan, translated Father Croiset's book in 1698. He passed on the spirit of this work to the numerous priests whom he trained in his institute, and they carried out no less than 1,500 missions in the towns and, especially, the rural areas, during the first fifty years thereafter.[33] In Germany Father Philipp Jeningen, who was one of the most famous missionaries at the end of the seventeenth century, concerned himself in his last years (he died in 1704) with making the Sacred Heart known and loved. Attached to the Principality of Ellwangen, where Catholics and Lutherans lived side by side, he employed, for promoting the new devotion, the expressions and the spirit of the nun of Paray-le-Monial. 'What is offered to me is mine', he wrote. 'The Heart of Jesus has been offered to me, so the Heart of Jesus is mine, and through it I love Jesus and will love him in the highest and most perfect fashion, with the Heart as though mine and belonging to me' ('*mit seinem Herzen wie mit dem meinen das mir gehört*').[34] This was close to the words of Marguerite-Marie in her autobiography. 'Afterwards, he asked me for my heart, which I begged him to take, which he did, putting it in his own adorable heart, and made me see it in there like a little atom being consumed in this fiery furnace, from which he drew it forth looking like a flame in the shape of a heart, and put it back in the place wherefrom he had taken it.'[35]

It is not pointless to ponder on the speed with which this devotion spread in the world of missions, before any decision had been taken by the *magisterium* and while the Church was markedly divided on the question.[36] Was it thought that here was a way to bring the most uncouth spirits more easily to confession or communion? Or did the missionaries sense a desire among believers, which perhaps they

---

[31] *Vie et Œuvres de Sainte Marguerite-Marie Alacoque*, presented by Raymond Darricau, 2 vols., Paris and Fribourg, Saint-Paul, 1990, vol. I, p. 22.

[32] The first confraternities of the Sacred Heart were reported, notably in eastern France, in the last decade of the seventeenth century.

[33] Barbieri, *Martinelli*, pp. 48, 67, 86.

[34] Hausen, Father Wilhelm, *Leben und Tugenden des apostolischen Dieners Gottes Philipp Jeningen aus der Gesellschaft Iesu*, Regensburg, 1873, p. 133.

[35] *Vie et Œuvres*, p. 83 (autobiography of Marguerite-Marie Alacoque).

[36] Taveneaux, René, *Le Jansénisme en Lorraine 1640–1789*, Paris, Vrin, 1960, pp. 683–6; *Dict.spir.*, vol. II, cols. 1023–46.

themselves shared to some extent, for a more tender religion, such as found expression in the Lutheran lands in the form of Pietism?[37] We know that in 1701 the Jesuits of Opole (Oppeln) in Silesia spoke of love for the Heart of Jesus in one of the three performances of sacred plays which it was their custom to put on during Carnival, on the occasion of the Forty Hours' Devotion.[38] Two years later the Sacred Heart entered Austria in an extraordinary manner, with great crowds and wonders, like a manifestation of the supernatural in this world, heralding salvation for bodies and souls.

As early as 1702 the Jesuits of Graz had probably begun to invite the faithful to practise the cult of the Sacred Heart. In the following year, the necessary indulgences having been obtained from Rome, Count Lengheim asked that a mission take place in his castle of Kapfenstein, on the border of Hungary, not far from Szentgotthard, at the time laid down for celebrating this new feast, namely, after the octave of Corpus Christi. On the eve of the day in question all the parish priests read from the pulpit, by order of the bishop, the exercises of piety to be performed and the prayers to be said. When the day came the whole province of Styria was on the march, from dawn, to the sound of bells. The crowd, in long columns, each village following its banner, climbed the road to Kapfenstein as though on some distinguished pilgrimage. Noblemen on horseback acted as rank-closers on either side of this endless procession. But when the leading parishes caught sight of the church tower they could not hold back. Everyone competed to be the first to reach this new seat of grace. The line broke. The horses whinnied. The horsemen tried to keep people and animals in check. It was no use. The scrimmage was such that a member of the Count's suite who was dangerously placed on the edge of a path at a point which overhung the river (Levada) far below, could not control his mount and fell with it into the water. A single cry then went up from the crowd: 'Oh most holy Heart of Jesus, have pity on him!' The miracle took place: the man, protected by his horse, was safe and sound on a rock by the river's bank. He, too, had appealed to the Heart of Jesus as he fell. After such a start as this the mission proved still more fervent. Three days were not enough for sixteen priests to confess all the penitents.[39] The new devotion, having thus fully demonstrated its efficacy, was thenceforth included among the practices of the Catholic masses.

---

[37] Spener, Philipp Jakob, *Pia desideria, ou désir sincère d'une amélioration de la vraie Eglise évangélique*, trans. Annemarie Lienhard, afterword by Marc Lienhard: 'Spener et le piétisme', Paris, Arfuyen, 1990; Jean-Baptiste Neveux, *Vie spirituelle et vie sociale entre Rhin et Baltique, au XVIIe siècle*, Paris, Klincksieck, 1967, pp. 179–202.

[38] Hoffmann, 'Die Jesuiten in Oppeln', p. 93.

[39] ARSI, Rome, Austria, 160, fos. 15–16 (1703).

The devotion to the Five Wounds of Christ was, in a way, as Sister Marguerite-Marie declared, a continuation of the devotion to the Sacred Heart.[40] The Breton missionary Jean Leuduger had offered the public, before 1700, *Réflexions sur les cinq playes et les cicatrices du sacré chef de Jésus* ('Reflections on the five wounds and the scars on the sacred head of Jesus').[41] These illustrated 'reflections' were intended to nourish the piety of their readers every day of the week. One began on Sunday with the wound in the heart, then came the wounds in the four limbs and, to conclude, on Saturday, attention was given once more to the first wound.

> *Dans votre Cœur, que j'ay moi-même ouvert,*
> *Souffrez, Jesus, que je sois à couvert*
> *De tous désirs dereglez de mon cœur,*
> *Que le Démon y forme à mon malheur.*[42]

(In your Heart, which I have myself opened, allow me, Jesus, to take shelter from all the unruly desires of my own heart which the Devil forms there, to my misfortune.)

The prefatory couplet for each day of the week was always conceived in the same way and lent itself to a development or 'consideration' in three points. First, the Christian was invited to contemplate the horrid wound. 'Behold the size and depth of this sacred wound, from which pours out what Blood he has left.' Then, turning inward, he must acknowledge his guilt. 'I admit, my Saviour, that it was the unruly desires of my heart, the evil thoughts of my mind and my wicked feelings that thrust that Lance into your sacred Heart.' There followed the resolution: 'I dedicate all my feelings to you, consecrating my heart to your holy Love.' The penitent ended his meditation for the day by saying a *Pater* and an *Ave* 'for the conversion of those who fill their minds with evil thoughts and unruly desires'. This was not merely an original method of learning to pray but a real initiation into meditation for everyone, starting with the simple countrymen and countrywomen. For, wrote Jean Leuduger, 'we must undeceive those who think that the countryfolk are incapable of mental prayer'.[43] In order to do that he urged them to 'cleave' to Jesus in the way that Bérulle had led select souls to do, at the beginning of the seventeenth century. The gaping wounds were so many ways of access to closeness with Christ.

'If, my Jesus, you will let me abide there', one said on Tuesday, meditating on the wound in the left hand. And on Thursday, with regard

[40] *Vie et Œuvres*, p. 85 (autobiography of Marguerite-Marie Alacoque).
[41] Appendix to [Leuduger], *Bouquet des retraites*, copy held in the ACJM, Paris.
[42] *Ibid.*, p. 5.
[43] [Leuduger], *Bouquet de la mission*, Rennes, 1747, p. 212.

to the left foot: 'Into your wound must I withdraw.' On Friday the scars caused by the crown of thorns led to this exclamation: 'Within your holes will I make my abode.' And the conclusion of a whole week of meditations came on Saturday, when the penitent was again called upon to contemplate the wound in the Sacred Heart:

> *Rentrons, mon âme, au fond de ce coté,*
> *Pour y trouver un lieu de seureté:*
> *C'est ma demeure et mon appartement*
> *Où je seray jusqu'au dernier moment.*[44]

(My soul, let us return to the depths of this side, so as to find a place of refuge there: this is my home and my abode where I shall stay until my last moment.)

Thus, in naïve verses, the lofty spirituality of the French School was brought, after correction and adaptation, within the reach of the most humble and ignorant of Christians, that is to say, the majority of them.

True, differences could be observed between one order and another. The Eudists, for instance, introduced their retreatants to this higher form of religious life through numerous hymns which punctuated the day's agenda. To this they added the recitation of litanies, repeated day after day, which eventually imprinted on the mind as many images or subjects for reflection as there had been invocations. The image, finally, had its role to play. 'After dinner', after explanation and singing of hymns, an hour was spent on 'explaining the pictures and statues'. We may suppose that this served as medium for mental prayer the next morning, which was focused, says the chronicler, 'on the mysteries of the Passion'.[45]

Another way of uniting oneself with Jesus and entering into his Spirit was to walk with him to the place of his torment, to step in his footprints and accompany him in his sufferings. The practice of the Way of the Cross was long established,[46] but in the eighteenth century it became very widespread, so that, in the German-speaking countries especially, it became the devotion *par excellence* of the Catholic Christian. A Capuchin missionary, Martin von Cochem, was its active propagator.[47] 'Here begins the ascent to Calvary', he wrote, 'in which the ten sorrowful secrets of Christ's Passion will be considered. Each pious Christian, following the example of our dear and pious ancestors, climbs this

---

[44] [Leuduger], *Bouquet des retraites*, pp. 5–17.
[45] ACJM, Paris, 'Annales de la Congrégation de Jésus et Marie', vol. XXVIII, fos. 149–50 (1703).
[46] *Dict. spir.*, vol. II, cols. 2576–606.
[47] On Martin von Cochem, Leutfried Signer, *Martin von Cochem. Eine grosse Gestalt des rheinischen Barock. Seine literarhistorische Stellung und Bedeutung*, Wiesbaden, Franz Steiner (Institut für europäische Geschichte, Mainz, Vorträge, no. XXXV), 1963.

mountain covered with bitter myrrh, and visits it in a pilgrimage either of body or mind. You can do this on Sunday afternoons or on feast-days, at home or at church, or, still better, by visiting the seven stations.'[48] These stations, usually set up along a steep path, punctuated a walk which, by itself, was a painful test. At Bad Tölz, in Bavaria, the whole set, still well preserved, shows us what this austere and testing exercise was that the good Catholics of that place and its environs practised, from the Mount of Olives at the foot of the slope to the sumptuous chapel which crowned the hill. Between these end-points small chapels in which the successive scenes of the Passion were depicted enabled the devout to collect their thoughts for a few moments before continuing their walk. One of these, especially imposing, was dedicated to the *Ecce homo*. A huge statue, partly hidden by a big gate made of wrought iron, opening and closing like a tabernacle, becomes gradually visible in all its grandeur to the person who, on his knees, climbs the majestic flight of steps leading up to it. This royal stairway is guarded by angels with opened wings, each holding a big candle. Nearby was the open-air cross under which there still exists the Holy Sepulchre, a dark and gloomy grotto where, at the turn of a little stairway, the visitor comes upon the corpse of Christ, under a ray of light.

The force of the images gave freedom of flight to the imagination, that other power of the mind which had to be liberated. The missionary worked on this, too, by means of themes he suggested for prayers. When confronting the spectacle of Jesus on the cross, Martin von Cochem wanted those who accompanied him to have before their eyes the dislocated body of the Saviour. 'With fury the butchers bored the holes as far apart as possible, so as to stretch to the utmost the feet and hands of Christ. They bound his limbs with ropes and tugged so hard this way and that as to cause them almost to be pulled from the trunk.' Then came the driving of nails into the limbs and the dragging by the executioners of the cross which bore Christ, gasping, 'fourteen paces farther'. It was then lifted and held in the air above a hole into which it was dropped. All the stages of the torment were carefully described and became themes for meditations.[49]

These meditations thus had as their basis a recapitulation, as exact as possible, of the Passion. When this could not be done *in situ*, the believer was advised to make do with an image, on condition that he use it with the greatest respect and most perfect love. 'When you hold an image of

[48] Martin von Cochem, Cap., *Der grossen Myrrhengarten*, Cologne, 1754 (the first edition was dated 1687), p. 149.
[49] *Ibid.*, pp. 149–57.

the crucifixion in your hands', wrote the German Capuchin, 'raise it so that you can kiss each of the five wounds, one after another.'[50] This way of praying before the cross might seem cruder than that advocated by Jean Leuduger and by those whose inspiration was Sister Marguerite-Marie. The two methods were certainly not contradictory. For, while the faithful who followed the missionaries were susceptible to the attraction of the new devotions, they nevertheless remained attached to older practices of piety in which the body had its place in a prayer that was inconceivable without hardship, and the culmination of which, at the end of the road, was a meeting with Christ. So true was it that, for many, true prayer was like the pilgrimage from which the Way of the Cross was derived.

Experiences

Assiduity followed by perseverance did not necessarily imply docility to the teaching received or perfect unity in themes of devotion or pious practices. The Man-God, torn and suffering on the cross, who was offered to Christians more and more insistently in order to touch their hearts led each individual to formulate his prayer in a way peculiar to him. The cult of the cross invited believers to address a personal prayer to God, or rather to Christ. What that meant is often, to be sure, most difficult to discover, apart from the narrow circle of mystics or devout persons who attracted notice in their lifetimes and whose words have been recorded. These exceptional persons had an influence on the spiritual life of their time. They practised, with precision, the exercises of piety that were expected of all believers, so that the evidence they provide must not be neglected since it shows us, mingled with matters unusual, the everyday experiences of both the saints and the rest.

Nicolas de Saludem, counsellor in the Parlement of Brittany and lord of Trémaria, was certainly not an ordinary man.[51] Though he had lived a long time 'in forgetfulness of God', his mother had thought on his behalf. This pious lady had summoned Father Maunoir in 1643 and 1644 to preach on her estates at Cap Sizun and Plogoff before she withdrew to live at Quimper. Her son became converted all of a sudden, one day in 1655, when, being about 'to commit a great sin', he heard a mysterious voice that seemed to come from the crucifix. He abandoned everything, entrusted his children to his sister and, on Father Maunoir's advice, went to Paris to join the little group directed by Father Bagot,

---

[50] *Ibid.*, p. 215.
[51] AJF, Vanves, Fonds Maunoir, 2Ae/2, 'Vie de M. l'abbé de Trémaria composée par le Révérend P. Julien Maunoir' (nineteenth-century copy).

SJ.[52] It was there in the course of one of his first mental prayers, when he was at a loss how to go on, that he set himself

to contemplate a picture of the crucifix with particular feeling. In a sudden movement he felt himself being divinely and powerfully inspired to enter into the wound in the side of Christ crucified. He found in that sacred side a school where he learnt in a short time more than books had taught him . . . He chose in that sacred wound one home for his memory, another for his understanding and a third for his will. He said, not long before his death, to his first director [Father Maunoir], who had decided him to leave his family and his country, that his soul had always remained since then in that sacred refuge, with all his powers and without any effort or trouble.[53]

This form of simultaneous choice and surrender in the gaping wounds of the Saviour was perhaps not something that just anyone would manage.

Marie des Vallées, the Norman mystic who played so important a role alongside Jean Eudes and who was, before Marguerite-Marie, one of the pioneers of the cult of the Sacred Heart, had a much simpler prayer to honour the five wounds of Christ. Having received an *écu* for a pilgrimage she had made, on someone else's behalf, to Notre-Dame de la Délivrande, near Caen, in 1643, she said:

This *écu* represents Jesus Christ, with his five wounds. The wound in the right hand is for M. Potier [her confessor], who stands for the humanity of the Son of God, who is the right hand of the Deity. The wound in the left hand is for little sister N . . . , who stands for the Church. The one in the right foot stands for our sister . . . , who is older, and represents the Synagogue. The one in the left foot is for . . . , who has a crippled foot and represents the Gentiles, who had only the foot of Nature. The wound in the heart is for myself and represents the Passion, which is the heart of Christ and will do away with all sins. These five people will one day be united just as five francs make an *écu*. And there will no longer be more than one faith, one law, one sheepfold and shepherd.[54]

This extraordinary sermon which brought together, in a few very simple words, the whole story of Salvation with the most perfect charity towards others living in this world was understood by all. If necessary, the scriptural references could be dropped by the less educated, who confined themselves to saying a *Pater* and an *Ave* while contemplating each wound for the sake of some other person, while keeping, like Marie des Vallées, the wound in the heart for themselves and their sins.

---

[52] *Ibid.*, pp. 9–10; on Father Bagot, Châtellier, *L'Europe des dévots*, pp. 87, 110 and 201 (Eng. trans., *The Europe of the Devout*, pp. 71, 94, 183)).

[53] AJF, Vanves, Fonds Maunoir, 2Ae/2, 'Vie de M. l'abbé de Trémaria', p. 11.

[54] Dermenghem, Emile, *La Vie admirable et les révélations de Marie des Vallées*, Paris, Plon, 1926, p. 231; on Jean Eudes and the devotion to the Heart of Jesus, Milcent, *Un Artisan du renouveau chrétien au XVIIe siècle*, pp. 449–58.

Sister Crescentia, born at Kaufbeuren, near Augsburg, in 1682, was a Franciscan Tertiary and the daughter of a poor tailor of that place. At 30, in 1712, she had a strange experience. Not only did she have so precise a vision of the crucifixion that she was able to guide a painter in the representation of it that he wished to make, but she also felt in herself the sufferings of the Passion. 'Do you want to follow me?' the voice apparently asked her. 'If you want to follow me, you must go with me in my Passion.' She carried the cross, fell under it, had her right hand nailed to it, then her left, and so on. All this happened 'secretly', without anything to show on her body. Yet this inward 'stigmatist' distinctly heard a voice telling her: 'Now you will always carry my sufferings with you, for there is no love without pain.'[55] Like Marie des Vallées she did not isolate herself in sorrowful contemplation of Christ. At night her cell was filled with the howling and clamour of the souls in Purgatory who came to ask for her prayers.[56] Was this the effect upon the mind and sensibility of this daughter of St Francis of the instruction imparted by the Capuchin Martin von Cochem?[57] It was certainly the case that this instruction, illustrated by the visions of this simple girl, acquired almost supernatural power. Jesus was there, just as the Sister had seen him and had asked the painter to reproduce him. It was enough to get Crescentia to touch or bless an image or a rosary in order to be united with Jesus as she was constantly. The unitive way, the highest degree of spiritual life, became communicable to an entire people, even if only in the most naïve form.[58] The worthy women of Mühlenbach, in Baden, refused to sit at their spinning-wheels on Thursday: they were unwilling, they told the church official who questioned them, to spin the flax that would be used next day to tie Christ to the pillar for his flagellation.[59] What the missionaries taught, through the image and through the edifying example of such as Marie des Vallées or Sister Crescentia of Kaufbeuren, had ended by becoming an object of meditation, but meditation so natural, simple and spontaneous that it permeated the actions and thoughts of everyday life, becoming merged with it.

Moreover, this development was not confined to the Catholics. In a

[55] Miller, Arthur Maximilian, *Crescentia von Kaufbeuren: Das Leben einer schwäbischen Mystikerin*, Stein am Rhein, Christiana, 3rd edition, 1968, pp. 206–7.
[56] Weitlauff, Manfred, 'Die selige Maria Crescentia Höss von Kaufbeuren (1682–1744)', in *Bavaria Sancta*, ed. Georg Schwaiger, vol. II, Regensburg, 1971, pp. 242–82.
[57] *Ibid.*, p. 263: suggestion by Manfred Weitlauff regarding the acute sense that Sister Crescentia had of the bond between her and souls in purgatory, and which we also find in Martin von Cochem's work entitled *Goldenen Himmel-Schlüssel.*
[58] *Ibid.*, p. 272; Boespflug, *Dieu dans l'art*, p. 82.
[59] Châtellier, *Tradition chrétienne*, pp. 449–50.

Europe of intermingled religions it was indeed difficult to know whence had come this emotional devotion centred on Christ's sufferings. In the times of Marie des Vallées and then of Martin von Cochem, the first Pietists, Philipp Jakob Spener and August Hermann Franck, were engaged in arousing a similar form of piety in Lutheran Germany.[60] Count Nicolaus Ludwig of Zinzendorf, the founder of the community of Moravian Brethren at Herrnhut, received the first shock that determined his apostolic vocation when he was contemplating an *Ecce homo* in the Prince-Elector's gallery in Düsseldorf in 1719. This Christ in bonds and with a crown of thorns, painted by Domenico Fetti, was the very model of the pictures offered in the churches for meditation by the faithful, being surmounted by an inscription in big letters: 'This is what I suffered for you: you, though, what have you done for me?' (*Ego pro te haec passus sum: Tu vero, quid fecisti pro me?*) 'My blood so throbbed', Zinzendorf recorded later, 'as I cannot describe, and I prayed to my Saviour that he take me with him by force to participate in his Passion, should my senses by themselves be unwilling to go in' (*mich in die Gemeinschaft seines Leidens mit Gewalt zu reissen wenn mein Sinn nicht hinein wollte*).[61] The founder of the Moravian Brethren thus expressed with admirable brevity and force the spontaneous prayer of an eighteenth-century Protestant before the sorrowing Christ. The desire for union, for communion (*Gemeinschaft*) was as strong as with the Catholic mystics or spiritual writers, with this difference, that it was for God to place the individual close to Himself, and not for the individual to seek refuge in the holy gaping wounds.

Was it fear of the allure of this emotional Protestant piety that led the Jesuit missionaries of Moravia and Silesia, who were preaching close to the Herrnhut centre, to emphasise still more strongly the heart's devotion to the cross? The great mission of 1739 in that region had as one of its purposes the struggle against Pietism. But this served to show what a place that devotion now held in the everyday religion of the Catholic masses. In Breslau the mission was opened with the publication of a work entitled 'Ardent love for the mission's cross'.[62] Then, in all the towns and larger villages great demonstrations were held, to show this love and increase the number and fervour of those who shared it. At Jauer (Jawor), half-way between Breslau and Görlitz, in a region of contact where adherents of the different Christian confessions had long

[60] Spener, *Pia desideria*; Neveux, *Vie spirituelle*, pp. 179–202.
[61] Beyreuther, Erich, *Nikolaus Ludwig von Zinzendorf in Selbstzeugnissen und Bilddokumenten*, Hamburg, Rowohlt, 1965, p. 46, with reproduction of the picture by Domenico Fetti.
[62] Hoffmann, Hermann, 'Die Marianische Männer-Kongregation Maria Reinigung in Breslau 1638–1938', *Zur schlesischen Kirchengeschichte*, 35, Breslau, 1938, p. 58.

been intermingled, together with sects, not to mention the *illuminati* of Jakob Böhme, the missionaries preached, as everywhere else, against Pietism. At the end of his sermon the preacher 'took the crucifix, knelt, put his arms round it, pressed it to his chest, kissed it and spoke to it as though it were Jesus Christ himself. He ended by telling everybody: "Kiss your Jesus, who has suffered so harshly for your sins".'[63] If he had wished to show that, in their tender love for the crucified Christ, Catholics had no cause to be jealous of the Pietists, he could not have acted differently. Was not what was being presented as a return to the sources due, just as much, to the stimulating effect of the neighbouring Protestant communities?

In Ireland, however, an absolutely contrary reaction was observed among the Catholic clergy. The bishops and the Archbishop of Armagh tried to prohibit, not always successfully, the processions of religious and even the Ways of the Cross that they set up.[64] They did not want their flocks to be confused with those who were following with enthusiasm, in Ireland as throughout the United Kingdom, the first Methodist preachers. Perhaps they were also afraid of the attraction that what those preachers were saying might exert on the masses of poor people who made up the great majority of their own community.[65] For it was among these preachers, expelled by the Anglican Church and often obliged to speak in the open air, that were to be found a tone and a teaching comparable to those of the missionaries who were sometimes welcomed in great state by the priests and bishops on the Continent. One of the first companions of John Wesley, George Whitefield, preached to the poor, uprooted people who came to look for work in the mines or factories near Bristol or Newcastle. When once he was describing the tottering gait of a man without God who, like a blind man, was trying to find his way near a precipice, cries arose from the panting crowd: 'He's going to fall . . . There, he's lost.'[66] Emotion changed to edification when Whitefield described the Garden of Olives in the evening of Holy Thursday. 'I see my Saviour', he cried, 'my Saviour in agony.' And all his hearers were carried away like those who heard Martin von Cochem or who took part in a Way of the Cross. In

---

[63] Hoffmann, Hermann. 'Die Jesuiten in Hirschberg', *Zur schlesischen Kirchengeschichte*, 7, Breslau, 1934, p. 106.

[64] Corish, *The Catholic Community*, pp. 85–9. In 1759 the Bishop of Wexford wanted to demolish the stations of a Way of the Cross which had been erected by religious thirteen years previously.

[65] *Ibid.*, pp. 73–81.

[66] Rataboul, Louis J., *John Wesley, un anglican sans frontières 1703–1791*, Nancy, PUN, 1991, p. 95; La Gorce, Agnès de, *Wesley maître d'un peuple (1703–1791)*, Paris, Albin Michel, 1940, pp. 163–4.

John Wesley, who owed some of his training to Zinzendorf's Moravian Brethren, there was that same exacerbated sensibility before the sufferings of Jesus.

> For whom didst thou the cross endure?
> Who nailed thy body to the tree?
> Did not thy death my life procure?
> O let thy pity answer me![67]

sang the congregation while waiting for the voice of the founder of Methodism to confirm what those verses said. Here was again that violent desire for union with the Man-God with a heart of flesh, expressed with faith by suffering mankind. A whole tradition showed itself here, going back to the *Imitation of Jesus Christ*. A tone and a spirit were manifested which were not very different from those expressed on the other side of the Channel, in the sermons or treatises of direction of the missionaries who called on the sinner to cleave to the wounded Heart of Jesus as the only way to salvation.[68]

The transcendence of God-the-Father was tempered by the closeness of God-the-Son, whose humanity was constantly stressed. Christocentrism was at the source of the spirit of reformation in the sixteenth century – first Protestant, then Catholic. But it remained in the domain of lofty spirituality, or of theological thought, both with Luther and in the work of Bérulle. What was remarkable in the period of the missionary enterprise at the beginning of the eighteenth century was the central position occupied by Christ's Passion in the teaching that they carried on. Was this the expression, on the apostolic plane, of the movement of spirituality which, in the same period, came to birth around Marguerite-Marie Alacoque or Martin von Cochem? Was it a matter of responding, while giving them the desired direction, to traditional devotions of the Christian populations? Or did the missionaries think that by drawing inspiration from the one and taking account of the others, they could make themselves better understood by all? In any case, by preaching Christ suffering on the earth, it was a religion closely bound up with the world, with men's miseries and hopes, that they were proclaiming.

---

[67] La Gorce, *Wesley*, p. 146; on Wesley and the Moravian Brethren, *ibid.*, pp. 89–110.
[68] Rataboul, *John Wesley*, p. 75–84.

7   Bread

The abrupt demand of the Lord's Prayer: 'Give us this day our daily bread' brings to mind the sad reality of the world of humble folk. It was a world in which poverty always threatened and life itself was precarious, as is emphasised by the repetition of the same idea – 'this day' and 'daily'. There was no certainty of tomorrow in that world of the lowly, nor should such certainty be looked for by the Christian, since it was written 'Take no thought for your life, what ye shall eat, or what ye shall drink; nor yet for your body, what ye shall put on . . . Behold the fowls of the air: for they sow not, neither do they reap, nor gather into barns; yet your heavenly Father feedeth them. Are ye not much better than they?' (*Matthew*, VI, 25–6). That was indeed why there were so many edifying stories about pious persons like Job in the Old Testament, who abandoned themselves wholly to God's will. If necessary, the missionaries did not shrink from appearing in the form of instruments of divine Providence.

Nevertheless, it was not possible for them to be unaware that since it was the consequence and penalty of original sin, hunger could not fail to be, in many cases, an evil counsellor. Better was it, all things considered, to ascribe a sanctifying value to work, even at the risk of seeming inspired by Calvinist models. That was what gradually came to the fore. All the same, bread, as symbol of life, did not vanish from the preachers' language. But it changed into spiritual food, becoming the bread of souls.

Hunger

We find the whole misery of a land without bread in the story of a miracle by Gerard Maiella, the saint of the hungry land, which is reported by Gabriele De Rosa.[1] In the depths of southern Italy, in a convent not far from Potenza, lived a poor little lay brother serving as a doorkeeper. His

---

[1] De Rosa, *'Pertinenze ecclesiastiche'*, pp. 51–69.

body was nothing but one bleeding wound owing to a series of mortifications, each more cruel than the last. His face – thin, pale, sad – was the face of Christ. People who met him thought they were seeing a ghost. When Gerard was still a child he had received a piece of white bread from little Jesus, carried in his Mother's arms. White bread in deepest Basilicata! That had to be a miracle! Later, in the convent where among his other duties was the distribution of food to the poor, a gentleman who was completely destitute came to him after this distribution was over. Everything had been given and the community's oven was out. Nevertheless, Brother Gerard brought from the kitchen a steaming pancake which he held close to his breast as though it had, again, been given him miraculously. No more was needed for this man, holy but shortlived (1726–55), to be recognised, in that desolate region, as the last resort in face of life's worst miseries.

This story could, of course, be taken as an illustration of the special worth of the poor and of their power. Paolo Segneri wrote: 'Far, then, from our poverty separating us from God, it is a reason why we should approach him and put our requests to him. He will never reject an appeal from such a quarter when he sees it accompanied by humble trust.' On whom should he cast his eyes if not upon the poor?'[2] But the story also shows us the tragic condition of many to whom the rural missionaries addressed their preaching. Vincent de Paul was one of the first to become aware of how widespread this poverty was. As a result, he never left a place without setting up a charitable confraternity whose task would be both to relieve the poor and to keep alive the spirit of the mission.[3] The latter, moreover, in its strict meaning, gave way, during the period of great distress in the middle of the seventeenth century, to purely charitable activities which were, so to speak, missions in deeds. This was particularly the case in Lorraine, which had been devastated by the Thirty Years' War.[4] Fifty years later the priests of Vincent de Paul's society, the Lazarists, acted in the same way in the diocese of Montauban. During the terrible year 1693 they were obliged to replace many exercises with distributions of 'bread and soup to the poorest people'.[5] In the previous years, in Franche-Comté, the Beaupré missionaries encountered parents who asked if they might kill their children so as to save them from further suffering and themselves from having to watch the children's slow agony. Alms were inadequate for

[2] Segneri, *Méditations*, vol. I, pp. 29–30.
[3] Coste, *Le Grand Saint*, vol. I, pp. 311–21. Vincent de Paul had told his priests: 'Establish confraternities wherever you go on mission', vol. I, p. 312.
[4] *Ibid.*, vol. II, pp. 581–617.
[5] APM, Paris, unclassified MS entitled 'Missions performed by the missionaries of the seminary [of Montauban] 1654–1714', p. 39 (mission to Brials, May 1693).

dealing with this evil, and so, being unable either to preach or to relieve, the missionaries were compelled to suspend their activity for over a year and a half.[6]

Except in these extreme periods the preachers took care to provide distributions of bread and clothing to the poor who came to hear them. When he arrived in the Ile d'Yeu, Grignion de Montfort said, after speaking highly of works of charity, that 'it was his practice, in the missions he conducted, to see that the poor of the neighbourhood were fed during that time, so that they might also profit by the instruction given'. It was resolved that, every day, a cooking-pot should be provided for the poor, with food supplied at the general expense. The ladies themselves prepared the meals. The poor people turned up at the appointed hour. 'They were read to, and, after the meal, the missionary instructed them, feelingly, on how to hallow their condition, or on one of the most essential duties of religion.'[7] During one of their first expeditions in Franche-Comté the Beaupré missionaries themselves baked the bread which was distributed each day, between the exercises, an event which recalled the Gospel model of the Sermon on the Mount. The missionaries also bought linen to make 'sheets' for distributing to families who had no means of screening children from parents or brothers from sisters.[8]

In the time of Honoré de Cannes the Capuchins used to set up wherever they preached a charity office staffed by priests and pious laymen.[9] Sometimes they collaborated in benevolent works with the magistrates, and tried, through a reconciliation office, to secure the restitution of ill-gotten goods.[10] These recoveries were sometimes so numerous and took up so much attention that the success or otherwise of a mission came to be judged by them.[11] Jean Leuduger, in Brittany, thought it more expedient to attach to his team a former lawyer who had become a priest, Abbé Dorauleau, who 'rendered great service by the care he took in settling suits and other disputes'.[12] Usury was regarded as one of the major evils weighing upon the poor country people, so Father Charles Mailliardoz, in central Switzerland, always devoted a day, in the places he passed through, to the crime of lending

[6] Bergier, *Histoire de Beaupré*, p. 79.
[7] Picot de Clorivière, *Grignion de Montfort*, p. 251: see also Henry, Jean-François, 'La mission du père de Montfort à l'île d'Yeu 1712', in *Foi chrétienne*, pp. 38–49.
[8] Bergier, *Histoire de Beaupré*, p. 36.
[9] Mauzaize, *Le Rôle des capucins*, vol. II, p. 1015.
[10] *Ibid.*, pp. 1015–16.
[11] BN, Paris, MSS, Nouvelles acquisitions françaises 4135, 'Recueil de ce qui s'est passé de plus notable en ce couvent du Marais, depuis son establissement en l'année 1622', fo. 63.
[12] ACJM, 'Annales de la Congrégation', vol. XXVII, p. 1239 (1692).

at interest, with, as the usual conclusion, repayment being made by all who had behaved badly to their debtors.[13] As for the Oratorians, they continued in M. Vincent's line of conduct. In his *Direction pour les Missions* (1646), Father Bourgoing advocated 'the establishment of a charitable society to aid all the helpless, shamefaced, sick and disabled poor'. He wanted to be associated with this work 'ladies of the highest rank, so as to stimulate all the rest. There should be a lady director with a lady assistant and some others assigned to each district, so as to visit and help the sick poor whenever necessary, even to ensure that they received the Holy Sacraments in good time.'[14] The last clause is important, for it shows how, in the rural areas as in the towns, this charitable activity pursued moral and religious ends.[15] The distributions of alms were accompanied by inspection of bedrooms (to see that boys and girls were separated) and preparation of the sick for death, as well as care for young widows burdened with children, or orphan girls who were alone in the world, so as to save them from falling into prostitution.

In the months that followed the Revocation of the Edict of Nantes a terrible famine descended upon the Cévennes. This 'extreme destitution' happened, according to the Intendant of the Languedoc *généralité*, M. de Baville, 'because the wheat and the chestnuts failed there'. He added: 'Many peasants are at present surviving on acorns and grass.'[16] This offered an opportunity to cause the inhabitants to welcome missionaries and listen to their instruction. 'When they heard about the alms available from the mission at Alais', the writer of this letter continued, 'eight hundred persons came down from the mountains and are now living on His Majesty's generosity. This great need has made me think that it would be very useful, after Easter, to establish, in the heart of the Cévennes, four or five missions through which I would distribute bread. In this way the poor would receive at one and the same time help for their temporal needs and instruction.'[17] Without displaying the cold cynicism of the King's representative in the province, the missionaries did hope that religion would gain from the charitable activity they carried on in the Cévennes. Father de Chevigny, of the Oratory,

---

[13] ASJ, Zurich, MSS, 'Compendium missionum', mission no. 1 in the diocese of Lausanne (Rue), sermon of the 8th day.

[14] [Bourgoing], *Direction pour les missions*, pp. 161–2.

[15] Châtellier, *L'Europe des dévots*, pp. 144–51 (Eng.trans., pp. 129–35).

[16] Boilisle, A. M. de, *Correspondance des contrôleurs généraux des Finances avec les intendants des provinces*, 3 vols., Paris, Imprimerie nationale, 1874–77, vol. I, pp. 65–6, letter of 29 March 1686.

[17] *Ibid.*

distributed alms from his funds to a large number of needy families, clothed many poor people . . . paid small pensions to the convents for over forty girls, . . . and fed, at his own expense, over 200 poor people three times a week in a sort of house of charity managed by a layman from his entourage and appointed by him. He took pleasure in sometimes going to eat with them and serve them. Besides these charities, he distributed devotional books costing nearly a hundred pistoles.[18]

The Jesuits manned charity offices in the larger centres of the Cévennes, using 'money furnished to them by the King for this purpose'.[19] None of these religious expected gratitude from the people they helped. They thought that, to start with, they would attach the people to themselves through material interest. Then, the wonders that they were able to perform in this time of wretchedness would, they believed, give credence to their words and cause them to be recognised, like Gerard Maiella, as men of God.

The ransom of sin

But would the beautiful Gospel image of the poor man receiving from the priest's hands bread that came from heaven stand up to the test of reality? As they pressed on farther and farther into regions little-known to them, the missionaries were going to encounter hard, suspicious men who, far from greeting them with outpourings of joy, would be quick to hasten away from them, when they did not express the hatred they felt by spitting in their faces. This was because hunger is a consequence of original sin, the theologians may have thought, and the hungry people wandering about those wastelands already showed the marks of the damned, whose spectres they seemed to be. More simply, years of atrocious misery had made these men and women insensible to many things – Hell, to start with, which could not be more horrible than what they had experienced for so many years, all through their lives. Perhaps these newcomers who had arrived in their village were priests, but what of that? What mattered was that they were strangers and would be a burden on the community in one way or another.[20]

Las Hurdes did indeed appear, from the notebooks of Father Calatayud, to be a part of Spain under damnation. When he arrived at Miranda de Castañar after an exhausting journey over the rocks the missionary was lodged, by order of the magistrates, in the house of a

---

[18] AOF, Paris, MSS, 4°, 5, 'Troisième partie', fo. 264.
[19] Boilisle, *Correspondance*, vol. I, pp. 100–1, letter from the Intendant Baville, 24 July 1687.
[20] Several cases of flight by peasants at the missionaries' approach. This was still happening in Bavaria in 1720 – BH, Munich, *Jesuiten*, 564, year 1720, p. 12.

man who seemed suitable in every way since he was the brother of a
Franciscan. But hardly had the religious entered under his roof than
their host began treating them roughly, in words at first and soon with
blows of his stick. When mealtime came the host, after being asked,
brought the Jesuits their ration. As it seemed to them very small, they
protested. This provoked fresh fury from the peasant, directed against
these insatiable men who were not satisfied, like everybody else, with
'the contents of an ordinary pot'.[21] In a much less deprived region,
Lower Normandy, the Eudists had a similar experience. 'We were so
little wanted before this mission [to Cérences in 1712]', wrote the
order's chronicler, 'that we were accommodated very badly and had to
fetch even mattresses from Coutances. These were laid on the bare floor
in a hay-loft, where we lay down with our noses against the thatch that
covered it and with nothing but straw to block the door and the little
hole that served as window.'[22] In southern Italy, too, acts of open
hostility by the poor were not infrequent.[23] Thus, missionaries who
wished to devote themselves to instructing 'men who were rough and
boorish and most ignorant', according to Rule XXIV of the *Apostoliche
Missioni* of Naples, encountered indeed the very persons they were
looking for.[24] No doubt those men did not always behave as the
missionaries imagined they would, before meeting them in the flesh.

Another cause of conflict was work. Of course, man could not do
without it. Besides, nobody liked idle people. But given that one had to
work, it was best not to make too much of the fact and to show that
indifference to one's work that the missionaries liked so much in the
case of the farmer who left his farm for a day, or half a day, to come and
hear a sermon, or of the day-labourer who gave up several days' wages
for that purpose.[25] Men like these were the real poor whom one
cherished, poor people encountered by chance, for whom alms had been
reserved so as to reimburse them for their losses. In contrast, those
wretched creatures who were always poor and yet were always at work in
their fields seemed somehow victims of a curse which distanced them
from the compassion of the faithful. 'Their poverty bound them to their
work', noted the Lazarists, concerning the inhabitants of a village near
Montauban.[26] That mere mention in the form of a reproach seemed to

---

[21] BN, Madrid, MSS, 5838, fo. 6–6vo (June 1719).
[22] ACJM, 'Annales de la Congrégation', vol. XXVIII, p. 334.
[23] Rienzo, 'Il processo de Cristianizazione', p. 468.   [24] *Ibid.*, p. 464.
[25] *Ibid.*, p. 462. 'At Chieti in 1747 many were obliged, in order to make their confessions,
    to leave work and suffer hunger.' Comparable situations occurred in Spain during the
    passage of Father Calatayud, and in France in the towns visited by Abbé Bridaine.
[26] APM, Paris, *Missions données*, p. 15 (mission to La Ville-Dieu-du-Temple, January
    1678).

seal forever, even into eternity, the fate of this community which had not seen fit to profit from the benefits of the mission. Worse still, obsession with bread which was so hard to get might lead not only to sin but even to impiety, to repudiation of Christianity, to paganism. When passing through the Sierra de Bacares on his way into the province of Murcia, Father Calatayud met a peasant who was finding it difficult to negotiate his mules and his plough through the trees. It was a Sunday, and even the one in the octave of the nativity of the Virgin (8 September). 'My son, where are you going to plough on a feast-day?' asked the Jesuit. The other replied, woefully: 'Father, you ought rather to ask me "Where are you going to start ploughing?"', because I have not been able to get those mules moving all day.'[27] The animals' strike on the Lord's Day had already punished the sinner sufficiently, so the Father had nothing to add. It was not the same when he found himself faced with hardened sinners who were sure of the permissibility of what they were up to.

At Utrera, south of Seville, in the plain of the Guadalquivir, everything came to a stop during the olive harvest. On the feast-day of Our Lady of Consolation (8 September), the people gathered near a chapel which was situated at some distance from the little town. Peasants flocked to this place from all parts of the region.[28] In the middle of the eighteenth century all one could see was men on horseback with their wives or their betrothed seated behind them, carts covered with white veils and lavishly decorated with flowers, leaves, garlands and long cords ending in gilded acorns, which bore whole families crowded together, full of excitement as they looked forward to the festival. On the eve of the occasion the roads were so dense with traffic that the draught-animals were head to head and the people they drew were packed so closely together that accidents frequently occurred, while even more frequent were exchanges of jokes, friendly words, gestures of affection – in short, 'licentious actions', wrote the ecclesiastical chroniclers – such as normally result from this sort of promiscuity. That was only the beginning. In the evening was held 'the horsemen's *feria*', watched by all the women, whether well-born or mere peasants, dressed in their holiday garb. Games, singing and dancing went on well into the night. In the small hours men, women and children huddled together, pell-mell, to snatch a few hours of sleep in an improvised camp, while some sought repose in the unhitched carts and others sought calm even farther off. 'A vile opportunity for improper words and indecent acts', complained Father Calatayud's correspondent, especially as there was no shortage of

[27] BN, Madrid, MSS, 5838, *Algunas noticias*, fo. 112 (mission to Lorca, September 1733).
[28] BN, Madrid, MSS, 4503, *Ejercicios y Misiones*, fos. 179–85 vo (1758).

prostitutes present. As though by magic the swearwords and frivolous expressions which the missionaries thought they had done away with for good were once more in everyone's mouth. When someone took offence at this the reply came: 'The Virgin doesn't mind that.' It was another way of saying that the priests' law did not apply any more.

For, at Utrera, everything was dominated by three partners – the horses, the people, and Our Lady of Consolation. In the morning Our Lady emerged in majesty from the parish church. She was carried by the dignitaries of the oldest of the confraternities, that of Campillos, a large village more than 60 kilometres distant. There were no parish crosses and no clergy in copes occupying the place of honour. A little beyond the Real gate, where the chapel was, another confraternity, that of Osuna, took over. Others followed, each carrying the Madonna for about an hour, along a well-determined route across the Huerta, like a proper procession. At that word, however, Father Calatayud's informant broke into protest. Because, he wrote, you need to see it in order to appreciate

the unheard-of impropriety with which these stupid confraternity-members treat the venerated and miraculous statue of the Virgin of Consolation. One moment they are turning it round and round several times; next, they are walking behind it crouched down like crabs; now they are lowering it to the ground, then they are lifting it up as high as their arms will reach; they rush ahead, then start walking backwards; they make circles, then, leaving the road, rush off with the statue through the olive-groves.

Behind the confraternities the crowd that followed copied, as best they could, the movements of those at the front. Pedestrians, riders, families in their carts, the military detachment which had been sent to do the honours, the religious who, for this occasion, had tucked their gowns up into their belts, everyone with a handkerchief on his head and a stalk of esparto grass in his hand, all came and went, ran, jostled each other and mingled amidst clouds of dust so thick that even those in the front ranks were unable to see the statue. When, at last, they drew near the town, the Utrera confraternity took charge of the statue and escorted it back to the church that was its resting-place, though not without stopping from time to time before the house of someone who wanted the statue to cure a sick person. It even happened, in 1748, that the Virgin required her bearers to make a detour to the prison, where, according to the confraternity-members, her faithful interpreters, she demanded that a prisoner be set free. The *corregidor* obeyed. How could one oppose the will of the Queen of Heaven?[29]

[29] *Ibid.*, fo. 184.

Father Calatayud, who carefully described this peasant festival, was sufficiently 'enlightened' to realise that it was an ancient agrarian rite. He was not in the least against (any more than were most of the missionaries of the Baroque period) those processions in the form of supplications that took place on St Mark's day, or at other times, to obtain good harvests. But he wanted them to proceed in conformity with the Church's rules, under direction by the clergy and in the presence of the municipal authorities. What exasperated him at Utrera was the absence of the latter, who were consequently accessories to disorder that resulted in this absurd and crazy ceremony, a veritable profanation of the holy statue of the Virgin. And that was the doing of '*unos hombres toscos, quales son todos los Hermanos de las Hermandades*' ('those few boors who are all members of the confraternities').[30] With them it was as if, all of a sudden, several centuries of apostolic activity had been wiped out. The 'image' of the Holy Virgin came alive and gave proof of this by its many movements. The dust that it thus stirred up passed on to the people, the animals, the trees and their fruits supernatural health and strength. The *feria* of Utrera showed that an entire form of popular behaviour in relation to religion which it was thought had vanished thanks to the missions remained very much alive beneath the tranquil appearances of a practice that was regular and in accordance with the Council of Trent. This ambivalence became clearly apparent when the troublemakers were questioned. 'But, after all', it was put to them, 'when in 1737, 1750 and 1753 this venerable statue was borne by members of the magistracy, did not the miracle take place just as well without any need for the confraternities or for wild rushing about the countryside?' Yes, they replied, 'but that was not the right day, the festival of the Virgin [of Consolation]'.[31]

Truly, these poor countryfolk concealed frightening abysses beneath the smooth waters of submission. And we can perceive, showing through the notebooks of the ageing missionary, after more than forty years of preaching in these regions, a profound discouragement which might be expressed thus: 'Are they even Christians?' The anxious striving for daily bread seemed to lead men into aberrations that might separate them forever from God.

When the bread of the angels becomes the bread of men

The programme for the mission that Father Calatayud was preparing to devote to Utrera was thus ready-made: it would be expiatory and aimed against these tiresome local customs which must be uprooted.[32]

[30] *Ibid.*, fo. 181vo.   [31] *Ibid.*, fos. 183–183vo.   [32] *Ibid.*, fos. 156–68.

But was this, in the opinion of a growing number of priests and faithful, the right solution? Already in the time of Grignion de Montfort some parish priests advised their flocks to resist the seductions of the mission and stay at home. 'You would do well', they said, to go to work 'to make a living for yourselves and your children'.[33] At Tours Abbé Bridaine was accused of distracting the workers from their work.[34] On their part, the bishops decreed a reduction in the number of feast-days when one was not supposed to work, so as not to reduce the incomes of the poorest inhabitants of their dioceses.[35] Were not peasant festivals and Baroque missions detrimental to work in the fields by taking the cultivator away from his plough?

Some missionaries began to take cognisance of this problem. Although the Lazarists of Montauban were quick to denounce absenteeism, at the very end of the seventeenth century they showed greater understanding. At Labastide-Saint-Pierre future preachers were advised to choose the Advent period, 'so as to have the day-labourers'.[36] At Montvalen they taught the 'doctrine' after the morning's preaching instead of at the beginning of the afternoon, 'so as to allow the shepherds and workmen to go to work for the rest of the day'.[37] At Saint-Porquier the leader of the team thought it useful to mention that this mission could take place only during Lent, 'because the people are very busy in winter and summer with spinning and growing tobacco, and in autumn with the wine-harvest and the harvesting of tobacco-leaves'.[38]

People's occupations gradually appeared in the texts as account followed account. They were no longer that anonymous crowd summoned at fixed hours to the foot of the pulpit, but farmers, day-labourers, spinning-women, shepherds and shepherdesses, craftsmen or sailors, whom one had to learn to know, with their specific needs and the constraints imposed by their different trades. It seems that in the northern countries and the German-speaking region this happened sooner and more naturally than elsewhere. One of the first missions carried out by the Society of Jesus in the diocese of Oldenburg, in north Germany, had among its principal themes the sanctification of labour (1689).[39] In Alsace the Jesuits made it a practice, from the end of the seventeenth century, not to make people break off from their work in the fields in order to take part in the mission. This mission happened on

[33] [Grandet], *Grignion de Montfort*, p. 133.
[34] According to the Jansenist journal *Les Nouvelles ecclésiastiques*, quoted by Le Quéré, *J. J. Bridaine*, pp. 68–9 (1752).
[35] E.g., in Alsace, Châtellier, *Tradition chrétienne*, pp. 395–7.
[36] APM, Paris, MS, 'Missions données', p. 32 (1689).
[37] *Ibid.*, p. 38 (1692).   [38] *Ibid.*, p. 47 (1698).
[39] Duhr, *Geschichte der Jesuiten*, vol. III, pp. 668–9.

seven or eight consecutive Sundays and involved, each time, a journey by one or two Fathers from Molsheim or Strasburg who could get to their destination and back in one day without having to find a place to stay overnight. Economy, a saving of everyone's time, and effectiveness thanks to a cycle which developed over a long period – these were the advantages of this method.[40] It applied likewise in Belgium and in the north of France, where there was a sufficiently dense network of colleges and residences. From among the personnel in these houses, a Father (sometimes two or three, as at Alost or Cassel) set out each Sunday to preach and teach the catechism in a neighbouring village.[41] It was thus, apparently, in urbanised areas that the missionaries first learnt to respect the constraints of labour and to allow it the value of a form of asceticism. All the apostolic expeditions among craftsmen in the towns had generated thinking which began to bring results in a much wider field of missionary activity.[42] These were also regions in which Catholic and Protestant communities were intermingled, or at least lived close to each other. To what extent was the Calvinistic ethic gradually imposed upon the Catholic preachers?

In any case, by the middle of the eighteenth century the point had been taken, in the Mediterranean countries as well. Alfonso de Liguori urgently requested the preachers he sent into the villages of the Kingdom of Naples to keep for the evening, 'when the workers came in from the fields', the most important and most fruitful exercises of their mission.[43] He stressed this again at the end of his *Instruction*, making his idea more explicit. He wrote:

Some parish priests, 'want the sermon to end before nightfall, saying that, if it were to end any later, scandals might result. But they are quite wrong. The audience for the mission is made up mainly of craftsmen who live from one day to the next and are therefore obliged to go to work every day. If the sermon is delivered in the daytime the only persons present will be the priests, a few burgesses and some devout, or over-devout, women who are in a position to leave their work, but most of the women and, above all, most of the men who are in greatest need will not be present. [And he concluded:] The chief fruit of the mission is conversion of the men: if the men persist in vice the women will do as they do.[44]

---

[40] Barth, *Die Seelsorgetätigkeit*, pp. 352–5.
[41] ARB, Brussels, Fonds jésuitique, L.1471, Prov. Flandro-Belgique, *Catalogi Functionum*, 1749–54.
[42] Châtellier, *L'Europe des dévots*, pp. 76–83, 136–44, 250–6 (Eng. trans. pp. 58–66, 120–9, 236–43).
[43] Liguori, Alfonso de, *Instruction pratique pour les exercices de Mission*, Avignon, 1827, p. 132.
[44] Ibid, p. 181.

Thus, the very purpose of the mission which was to have precedence over everything else compelled the Church to take account of the work-rhythm of persons with families. Heaven was not in sole command – Earth also had something to say in the matter.

It was doubtless not accidental that at this time the Holy Family, that earthly Trinity, came to assume the place of honour in many village churches and chapels.[45] Joseph the carpenter, hitherto somewhat neglected by painters and sculptors, was now the object of great veneration by the faithful, who saw in him not merely the model head of a family but also the patron saint of the 'good death', since he breathed his last in Christ's arms.[46] Jesus, Mary and Joseph also constituted a family of poor working people who, like all the humble folk who frequented the rural churches, had known bad times, perhaps even famine-years. When the priest, after opening the tabernacle, offered the bread and wine while uttering the sacramental words over the prepared table, then, despite all the Baroque ostentation, something like a convivial atmosphere spread through the church, making communion, formerly something out of the ordinary, the simple, natural, familial act of a child coming to take food along with his brothers and sisters.

It had been all very well for the Church, since the Council of Trent, to encourage frequent communion: it laid down very strict conditions on all who wanted to approach the sacrament. 'Purity of soul', meaning freedom from all mortal sin, was, of course, the first of these. To it were added purity of intention, sustained attention, inward and outward respect, and devotion, defined as 'a spiritual hunger, an appetite for the divine Eucharist'.[47] Further to that fine list, the Bishop of Strasburg, Cardinal Armand-Gaston de Rohan, concluded in 1748: 'To communicate one has to be a saint, and even more so for daily communion: to increase one's sanctity, to perfect, ensure and consolidate it, one has to communicate and communicate frequently.'[48] It is not hard to conceive the perplexity of most people confronted by this severe warning coupled with a pressing invitation.

Especially was this so as the preachers had taken care to accompany their explanations regarding the conditions required for receiving communion with frightening stories that could paralyse for a long time

---

[45] Menard, *Une histoire des mentalités religieuses*; Châtellier, *Tradition chrétienne*, pp. 135–7.
[46] Barth, Médard, *Die Verehrung des heiligen Joseph im Elsass*, Haguenau, 1970; Vovelle, Michel, *Vision de la mort et de l'au-delà en Provence du XVe au XXe siècle*, Paris, Colin, 1970.
[47] *Instruction pastorale de son Altesse éminentissime Monseigneur le Cardinal de Rohan évêque et prince de Strasbourg, sur la pénitence et l'eucharistie*, Strasburg, 1748, pp. 72–82.
[48] Archives départementales du Bas-Rhin, G.1946, letter of 13 February 1748 to Vicar-General Riccius.

the initiative of even the most enterprising. This is what Alfonso de Liguori, though he was far from being a rigorist, offered for meditation by his listeners.[49] 'Take good care to give not that which is holy unto the dogs', he began, quoting Matthew, VII, 6 – which was quite a programme in itself. Then he went on:

Tremble, then, you vengeful ones, be afraid lest by seeking to approach the holy Table this morning with hatred in your hearts, you will suffer the fate of the woman who wanted to do her Easter duty without having first become reconciled with her enemy. Since her hatred was well-known the priest had refused her communion. In order not to submit to this insult, she protested that she forgave her enemy. When, however, as she left the church after Mass, her enemy came up to thank her for that forgiveness, the wretched woman replied: 'What forgiveness? You'll see me die on a scaffold before I forgive you.' Hardly had she uttered those words than she fell down dead. Her face went black as a piece of coal and, her mouth falling open, the sacred host was seen to emerge from it and to remain hanging in the air until a priest came to receive it on a paten. The body of this wretched woman was refused Christian burial.[50]

There was also the alarming story of the holy man Pelagius who was a hermit in the first part of his life and a monk in the second, and was always engaged in fasting and the severest penances. On his deathbed he received the Sacrament, breathed his last and was buried 'in the odour of sanctity'. Yet, several nights in succession, his body left the tomb as if dissatisfied with the place where he had been buried. The abbot then spoke to him thus:

'Pelagius, you were obedient when you were alive, continue to obey now that you are dead. Tell me, as from God, is it the Lord's will that you be buried in some place apart?' 'Alas', cried the dead man, 'I am damned for having concealed a sin when I confessed: see, Father, the state of my body.' And at once his body looked like a piece of red-hot iron throwing out sparks. At this sight the religious fled. However, Pelagius recalled the abbot to him and asked that he take from his mouth the sacred host which was still there. When that had been done, Pelagius asked him to remove his body from the church and throw it on the rubbish-dump – which he did at once.

What, then was this horrible concealed sin which had caused the holy man to suffer damnation? When living in the desert he had had the misfortune to go along with an unworthy thought, just one. He had not dared, thereafter, to confess this to a priest. The most severe asceticism

[49] On the pastoral work of Alfonso de Liguori, Jean Delumeau, 'Morale et pastorale de Saint Alphonse. Bienveillance et juste milieu', in *Alphonse de Liguori, pasteur et docteur*, collected works, preface by Jean Delumeau, Paris, Beauchesne, 1987, pp. 138–59; Delumeau, *L'Aveu et le pardon: les difficultés de la confession XIIIe–XVIIIe siècle*, Paris, Fayard, 1990.
[50] Liguori, *Instruction pratique*, pp. 61–2.

Fig. 3   The good works performed during the mission: charity, mass, procession. (Missions of the Jesuit Fathers, seventeenth-century engraving, Library of the Society of Jesus, Chantilly, Cliché Flammarion.)

and most rigorous penance had been of no avail to this unhappy emulator of St Anthony. One moment of acquiescence in temptation had been enough to determine his eternity in Hell.[51]

These stories intended to instruct, these *exempla*, as they were called in the Middle Ages, were not without effect. Proof is furnished, once again, by Father Calatayud's notebooks. It was his custom, at his first sermon, to offer the host (*el panuelo*) to the assembly and warn them in these words: 'Soon, your conscience will tell you if you have dealt well or ill with this.'[52] In Old Castile, near Medina del Campo, hardly had he finished that first instruction when a man approached him to ask that he hear his confession. Next morning the man arrived and began by saying: 'I have brought the consecrated host.' He opened his hand and showed a thin flake of white bread, folded over. Then he explained. During Holy Week (this event took place in September) a priest had refused him absolution because he was living with a concubine. In order not to be conspicuous in the parish church he communicated all the same on Easter Day, but kept the host in his mouth without swallowing it. On his return home he put it above his bed (a curious place for someone who was living with a mistress, but perhaps he feared that he might die suddenly while in his state of sin) and when he had to go to work in the fields, or to travel to town, he carried it with him in his coat. After hearing this the priest asked the man to prepare himself for a general confession. Then he took the host, placed it between the communion-cloths and put it in a place of safety in the sacristy, where he noticed, a few days later, that it had recovered its original form.[53] This story shows how the consecrated host might be perceived by the faithful during the first half of the eighteenth century. The fear inspired by the preachers was certainly effective, since the penitent did not want to transgress the ban on his taking communion, but, at the same time, he wanted to carry off the sacred object for domestic purposes so precise that one wonders whether the refusal of absolution was not merely a pretext to justify, after the act, a misappropriation of something that had been consecrated.

This case was not exceptional. In 1715 the Jesuits of Schweidnitz, in Silesia, had faced a similar situation.[54] Nor was this an occasion of scandal. Proof of that was given by the 'miracle' at the end, the reconstitution of the host. It might seem like a putting into practice in a

---

[51] *Ibid.*, pp. 92–3.
[52] BN, Madrid, MSS, 5838, *Algunas noticias*, fo. 120 (mission to Cartagena, 1734).
[53] *Ibid.*, fo. 13 (mission to Nava del Rey, 1726).
[54] Hoffmann, 'Die Jesuiten in Schweidnitz', pp. 166–224. A man had attached with string a piece of the consecrated host in his throat.

most concrete way of the Church's injunction: 'Communicate frequently, but, above all, do not communicate when in a state of sin.' Unless, that is, the conduct of the peasant of Old Castile was inspired by a profound sense of the sacred, at once sought and feared, and by its very nature ambivalent.

Quite different was the case of Father Jean Pichon. This religious of the Society of Jesus, a missionary of some reputation in the second quarter of the eighteenth century, especially in Eastern France, taught a doctrine that gave rise to a fine scandal.[55] Communion, he said, should not be an exceptional event, nor even a pious act that one performed at regular intervals as though taking a medicine for one's soul, or preparing for a spiritual feast. No, he wrote, if Christ wanted 'to give us his adorable flesh under the appearances of bread, the daily food of our bodies, was this not to indicate to us that it ought to be the daily food of our souls?'[56] Otherwise, he added, he would have chosen the form of some 'exquisite and rare meat'. But 'it is rarely that we eat exquisite meats, whereas there is nothing more ordinary than eating bread. Nothing, therefore, should be more ordinary for a Christian than to eat the heavenly bread of the eucharist.'[57] All that remained for him to do was to pile on quotations from the Gospel to persuade his readers (and his listeners during missions) that daily communion was indeed fulfilment of Christ's will. The words of the Last Supper: 'Take, eat: this is my body' showed that 'he wants us to take this truly divine food every day or at least very often'.[58] The phrase 'My flesh is meat indeed' gave rise to this commentary: 'Now, food is taken every day, not once a year or once a month, nor even once a week: bread is eaten every day. It is the same with the Eucharist which Jesus promises to provide in order that it may be, every day, the food of our souls.'[59] Consequently, it was inevitable that the conditions regarded as indispensable by the doctors of the Church for a person to approach the holy table were somewhat upset. 'The only necessary and indispensable disposition', he declared, 'for worthily receiving Jesus Christ is to be free from any mortal sin.'[60] And what about the venial sins that one is constantly committing? He disapproved of them, of course, but he hastened to add that 'this ought not to stand in the way of communion, said the Council of Trent, following all the Church's Fathers and Doctors'.[61]

---

[55] Appolis, Emile, Le 'Tiers Parti' catholique au XVIIIe siècle, Paris, Picard, 1960, pp. 310–16.

[56] Pichon, Jean, L'Esprit de Jésus-Christ et de l'Eglise sur la fréquente Communion, Paris, 1745, p. 29. The BSJ at Chantilly has a copy of the first edition, censored, with corrections by the author.

[57] Ibid., p. 22.   [58] Ibid., p. 21.   [59] Ibid., p. 24.   [60] Ibid., p. 265.

[61] Ibid., p. 304.

The polemical intention of a work which appeared just a century after Antoine Arnauld's *Fréquente Communion* and which had been written and tried out in a region much affected by Jansenism, namely, Lorraine, was what primarily engaged the censors' attention.[62] In the ruling which the bishops published in this connection they showed that if the Jansenists had sinned through 'excessive rigour', that was no excuse for falling into 'excessive laxity'.[63]

But that was perhaps only the outward aspect of the matter. Inviting Christians to break bread with Jesus every day meant actually altering religion. Everything associated with an exceptional and sometimes disquieting encounter with something sacred gave place to conviviality with the Man-God, a poor man among poor men, who had come to feed them and strengthen them in their faith. In this way the idea crept in among some clergy that Paradise might well begin on earth if men would agree to live with Christ among them.

The multiplication of missions to the countryside caused the Church in the eighteenth century to get to know better the immense world of the poor. Thereby it perceived how little its ideal conception of poverty accorded with reality. The casting away of material goods is doubtless an evangelical virtue when it is the voluntary action of someone who wishes to come closer to God. When, though, it is the normal condition of someone who lacks everything and who is destined to spend his whole life in deprivation, there is great danger that the opposite effect may result. Hardness of heart, desperation to make the earth produce, interested behaviour regarding religion, exploiting it for the advantages to be got from it here below, all were the usual consequences of poverty. And yet not the least of the paradoxes of this story is the missionaries' attitude, at once so critical of the peasants' customs and yet inclined to take full account of what had been revealed to them – not only out of concern for effectiveness but also, perhaps, because some of them wondered, after two centuries of Tridentine theology, whether the idea of a God close to men and living among them did not deserve serious examination.

[62] Appolis, *Le 'Tiers Parti'*, pp. 310–16.
[63] *Instruction pastorale de son Altesse*, p. 12.

8   From pardon to salvation

'Forgive us our trespasses as we forgive those who have trespassed against us.' Here is the sign of God's grace, the distinguishing mark of the elect who act as Christ acted towards his executioners when he forgave them. Because, however, this meant behaving in a way contrary to that characteristic of most people, thousands of missionaries had to be sent forth to teach men the express will of the Lord. Many of these envoys were perfectly aware of the problem they faced. This gigantic work of reconciliation was their chief task. It was uplifting only for those who viewed matters from on high. For those who convinced themselves, more and more with every passing day, that 'man is a wolf to man' – 'And the brother shall deliver up the brother to death, and the father the child . . . ' (Matthew, X, 21) – what prevailed were lassitude, discouragement and terror before the monstrous crimes that they discovered. When, at the cost of considerable and constantly renewed efforts, they obtained a few reconciliations – regarding which they had to make sure that they were not matters of mere conformity, or were due to those who were less to blame in a quarrel – they did indeed feel that they had led their charges to the very gates of paradise. Perhaps God gave their reward, already in this world, to men who became reconciled with each other.

On the brink of hell

It was doubtless these divisions, these unatonable hatreds that made the strongest impression on the missionaries when they undertook their journeys across Europe. Almost the sole aim of the first Jesuit expeditions in the Kingdom of Naples was to re-establish a semblance of peace. They congratulated themselves when, after several weeks of preaching in the town squares and processions of penitents, 'the church became a place of security to which no one came armed any more'.[1]

---

[1] Guidetti, *Le missioni popolari*, p. 68 (first years of the seventeenth century).

Penitents bearing heavy crosses marched along the streets. At the missionaries' command they flung themselves down to lick the pavements of the streets or of the church which had been 'defiled by so much blood.' An observation made by a royal member of the missionaries' audience was reported with pride: 'What human justice could not achieve had been put right by divine justice.'[2] But for how long? Fifty years later, the Republic of Genoa appealed to Paolo Segneri the Elder to settle a quarrel which had broken out in the town, yet within two years the hatred kindled had resulted in the death of forty persons.[3]

Less conspicuous, and perhaps all the more dangerous, were the long-lasting hatreds in the villages which came to light in confessional handbooks or during a witchcraft trial. There were many casters of spells who, while relatives or old acquaintances were being married, tied laces together under cover of half-darkness in the church, so as to make the young couple childless, or who nailed a dead bird to the door of a cattleshed so as to cause the animals within to die.[4] The fact that a woman suspected of having made a pact with the Devil was capable of accusing, in her turn, many hundreds of others revealed what the relations between and even within families could be in Bavaria in the first half of the seventeenth century.[5] Were the witchcraft trials the North European form of the Mediterranean vendetta? Certainly, in a number of regions, the Jesuits never went around without demijohns of Saint Ignatius' or St Xavier's water, both of which were supposed to be beneficial against the deeds of malevolent creatures, alike living and dead (ghosts).[6] In Holland the miraculous water did much, according to the annual Letters sent to Rome, to enhance the prestige of the Society of Jesus. At Oudewater a widow's cattle were attacked by a mysterious illness: one after another, four cows died inexplicably. The farmer's people were sure that a spell cast by a witch must be the cause. It remained to find the witch, and they set about doing that. For what reason is not clear, a Jesuit arrived on the scene. He diagnosed a lack of faith among the members of the farmer's household. He persuaded them to approach the sacraments more often, he sprinkled the animals with holy water in the name of St Ignatius, and he stuck a picture of St Francis Xavier on the cattleshed door so as to dissuade the evil one from entering – also, perhaps, to reassure the anxious population. Then

[2] *Ibid.*, p. 69.   [3] *Ibid.*, p. 105.

[4] Thiers, Jean-Baptiste, *Traité des superstitions selon l'Ecriture sainte, les décrets du concile de Trente et les sentiments des saints pères et les théologiens*, Paris, 4 vols., 1697–1704.

[5] Behringer, Wolfgang, *Hexenverfolgung in Bayern: Volksmagie und Staatsraison in der Frühen Neuzeit*, Munich, R. Oldenburg, 1987, pp. 199–205.

[6] *Zehen Freytätige Verehrung dess Heiligen Patriarchen Ignatii von Loyola*, Selestat, 1736; Adam, Paul, *Histoire religieuse de Sélestat*, 2 vols., Sélestat, 1971, vol. I, p. 114.

he encouraged the widow and her people to begin a *novena*. As soon as that was decided (*verum dum novena instituitur*), the miracle happened. 'The animals that were still alive recovered their health.'[7] The spell had been taken off the cattleshed. This was doubly a victory: not only had the cows been cured, but a magical practice had been replaced (for good, it was hoped) by another that was fully Catholic.

Disunity among men, even when some of them remained crouched in the shadows, was not the only form encountered by the missionaries. Things grew still more serious and worrying when the spirits of the dead appeared on earth and started to attack the living. Was it in order to escape their intense gaze that the peasants of Upper Bavaria adopted the custom of removing the eyes from corpses and replacing them with wooden balls, a practice that the Bishop of Chiemsee had to forbid in the middle of the eighteenth century?[8] Was it fear of ghosts that gave rise to the habit, widespread in the hinterland of Naples and in Basilicata, of cursing the dead?[9] The story of a ghost who appeared at Geertruiden-berg, near Breda, in Holland, at the very end of the seventeenth century, completely justified people's fear of them. A man whose life had not been an edifying one had died without anyone being certain that his repentance was sincere. Soon, strange things started happening in his house: dull sounds of knocking on interior walls, and doors opening by themselves to admit a horrid spectre. All this was so terrifying that soldiers who were billeted in the house decamped in the middle of the night, having had enough. The man's widow, a pious woman who respected established customs, suspecting what the origin of the noises was, did not fail to have Masses said on the anniversary of her husband's death. But, apparently, that did not suffice. The dead man started to torment his son, who was boarding several kilometres distant from the house. He appeared both at night and during the day, when the boy was in class among his schoolfellows. The boy's masters, alarmed by the effect this was having on him, called in a person 'who knew how to talk to the dead.' When duly questioned, the spectre replied that he wanted six candles placed on the high altar at Geertruidenberg and that the holy sacrifice be offered on his behalf. Thus informed, the boy hastened to carry out his father's wishes. But he was not yet at the end of his distress. Next day the Mass took place as required, with the dead man's son

---

[7] ARB, Brussels, Fonds jésuitique, 1422, n.p., n.f., 1687.

[8] BH, Munich, *Jesuiten*, 568, n.p., n.f. (1750).

[9] *Histoire de saint Alphonse de Liguori fondateur de la Congrégation du T. S. Redempteur 1696–1787*, Paris, Poussielgue, 1879, pp. 162–3. According to the author, when Alfonso de Liguori examined the intentions of the blasphemers, he found 'much less hatred of the dead than anger against their living relatives'. However, his view is far from being shared by all.

serving. Throughout the proceedings those present observed that something strange was happening. The youngster, kneeling beside the priest, was prey to great agitation. Pale, and sweating heavily, he seemed to be in conversation with an invisible being who accompanied him in all his movements. In the course of this last dialogue, on the steps of the altar, between father and son, the former revealed that he had been condemned to spend a thousand years in Purgatory. Fortunately, the High Mass had obtained remission of his sufferings. He was vigorously expressing to the choir-boy his joy at this development when the lad, exhausted by so much mental conflict and emotion, collapsed unconscious. A few moments later he recovered, raised his head and shouted three times: 'There he is, going up!' (*Ecce ascendit*). This story was intended to remind the faithful of the necessity and efficacity of saying prayers for the dead and, especially, of having Masses said for them. At the same time, it showed how one was surrounded by a cohort of spirits from beyond the grave who were all the more encroaching, tenacious and dangerous the closer they had been to one when alive.[10]

The enmity that set people against one another was, perhaps, nowhere stronger and cruder than within the family itself. It was as if, since the Fall, a horrible inversion had taken place, making what should be the home of love the cell of crime and hatred. One of Father Calatayud's first missions was to Alberca, in the province of Salamanca, not far from the famous shrine of the Virgin at Nuestra Señora de la Peña de Francia. As usual, the Father had organised processions of penitents, which were all the more needed in that a drought was desolating the region. One morning, the procession left the village and made for a point from which the Virgin's shrine could be seen. The 'Nazarenes', children dressed as little angels, walked in front, followed by the grown-ups. At a cross-roads marked by a calvary a man had, not long before, laid down his dying wife. This had come about as follows. In a neighbouring village a married woman, profiting by her husband's frequent absences (he was probably a merchant) had taken his manservant as her lover. Eventually the deceived husband realised what was going on. Pretending to set off on a journey, so as to lull his adulterous wife's caution, he hid himself near the house. The effect of his stratagem was not long delayed. Having been told that his master had gone away, the servant hastened to take his place. He received several bullets from his master's carbine, which left him stone dead. Then the husband rushed into the house. He seized his faithless wife, tied her four limbs to the bed, and taking a few bullets, heated them over a candlestick and then poured the molten lead into the

---

[10] ARB, Brussels, Fonds jésuitique, 1422, n.p., n.f., 1695.

wretched woman's vagina. 'Whoever sins must pay for it, and where and by what he or she has sinned', was the justification which he kept repeating. After thus making himself the justiciary of crimes committed against Heaven, he could no longer remain there. When the punishment was completed he dressed his victim, who was already dying, and dragged her to the calvary where, later, the little 'Nazarenes' were to pass, in orderly ranks, dressed in their robes of innocence. It was a dark night, and he had plenty of time to place her in the posture of one praying before the cross. There she was found, dead, the next morning. The husband, feeling his duty done, went to collect his bag and his stick and set off whithersoever his business took him.[11]

We should not be too quick to condemn the savagery of the people of those harsh lands. The murderer was a believer, since he claimed to be only punishing sin, and placed his ravaged victim before the crucifix. Would he have thought of those words and that scenario unless he had learnt the catechism and without a probable visit by missionaries to his village? Moreover, the phrase this criminal uttered as he performed his act of vengeance was the sentence which the religious made the penitents say when they scourged themselves as they went through the streets at night: '*Quien tal hace, que tal pague*' (Whoever acts like that must pay for it).[12] Who was capable of perverting to that extent the words of the men of God? Satan himself, perhaps, come disguised as an ordinary villager to do his will and then vanish into the night after distilling the fire of Hell into the body of the adulteress. Thus this small news-item became a cautionary tale and a pressing invitation to penitence.

Pardon and reconciliation

It meant, then, a considerable change when the missionaries made reconciliation between all the faithful the main theme of their exercises. This happened more or less everywhere round about 1720.

The good priests had long thought that one of their chief duties was to put an end to any quarrels that might arise among their flocks. The exemplary Counter-Reformation parish priest Pierre Fourier performed with the greatest vigilance the functions of justice of the peace in his parish of Mattaincourt in Lorraine, at the very beginning of the seventeenth century.[13] In Ireland one of the first effects of the Catholic Reformation, of great consequence for the future, was the wish

---

[11] BN, Madrid, MSS, 5838, *Algunas noticias*, fo. 3–3vo (mission to Alberca, 1718).
[12] *Ibid.*, fo. 85vo (mission to Logroño, 1732).
[13] Taveneaux, René, 'La pensée et l'œuvre sociales de St Pierre Fourier', in *Lyon et l'Europe: hommes et sociétés (mélanges P. Gascon)*, Lyons, 1980, vol. II, pp. 267–78.

expressed by the bishops to be, first and foremost, peacemakers, by taking it upon themselves to deal with disputes which until then had been settled within families or by conflicts between rival groups.[14] Some missionaries on the Continent adopted these concerns, which conformed to the Tridentine ideal. Vincent de Paul and Jean Eudes both carried out reconciliations, some of which took spectacular forms.[15] However, they were responding to specific need and did not yet think of introducing a new exercise into the plan of their missions.

Everything changed at the beginning of the eighteenth century when Grignion de Montfort consecrated a hymn which was certainly intended as the continuation of a sermon on 'forgiveness of trespasses.' In his characteristically simple style he instilled into the people on whom he was working some principles which transformed the very spirit of the mission. He had them sing:

> Sans cet amour, sans ce pardon
> Dieu n'accepte aucun sacrifice.
> On serait martyr du démon
> Au milieu du plus grand supplice,
> Ni l'aumône de tout son bien
> Sans ce pardon ne sert à rien.

(Without this love, without this forgiveness, God will accept no sacrifice. In the midst of the greatest torment one would be the Devil's martyr, nor, without this forgiveness, would giving away all one's possessions in alms be of any use.)

> Un homme dans l'inimitié
> Demande à Dieu dans sa prière
> Qu'il le regarde sans pitié
> Et qu'il rallume sa colère:
> Il ne dit jamais son Pater
> Qu'il ne se condamne à l'enfer.

(When a man who is in a state of enmity prays to God he asks to be looked upon without pity and for his anger to be rekindled: he never says the Lord's Prayer without dooming himself to Hell.)

> L'inimitié tourne en poison
> Toutes les sources de la vie,
> Les sacrements et l'oraison
> Tout est un sacrilège impie
> Et le vindicatif de cœur
> Se perd malgré tout confesseur.

---

[14] Corish, The Catholic Community, pp. 35–6.
[15] Berthelot du Chesnay, Grignion de Montfort, pp. 170–2. Coste, Le Grand Saint, vol. III, p. 53: at Ludes, in Champagne, 'they go and kneel down in people's houses, to ask forgiveness from those they have offended'.

(Enmity poisons all the springs of life, the sacraments and prayer all become so much impious sacrilege, and the vengeful heart is lost, not to be saved by any Father-Confessor.)

Further on in the hymn, which, with its fifty-seven verses and its air of 'Hail Jesus, hail his Cross', was a veritable sermon, he laid down the conduct to be followed:

> *Sans tarder, allez promptement*
> *Voir cette personne contraire*
> *Et lui demandez humblement*
> *Pardon, mais un pardon sincere,*
> *Et n'en craignez pas un rebut*
> *Puisque Dieu seul est votre but.*

(Without delay, go promptly and see this opponent of yours and humbly ask his pardon – but a sincere one. Do not be afraid of rebuff, since God alone is your objective.)

The choice to be made, moreover, was dictated without possibility of appeal, since, a few verses previously, the preacher-poet had declared:

> *Vindicatif, va te venger*
> *Et dans l'enfer va te plonger.*[16]

(Go, vengeful man, take your revenge, and so plunge yourself into Hell.)

Henceforth the forgiving of offences occupied a central place among the exercises of the mission. This was not an act added on as something complementary but a work that was indispensable to every Christian. By referring to the Lord's Prayer Grignion showed clearly that there could be no hope of gaining absolution without reconciling oneself with others. What the preachers had said and repeated from the pulpit needed to be made directly accessible to people who were rough and in many cases illiterate. Some chose to use songs with very simple verses which imprinted themselves in the memory. Others, such as the Jesuits, thought that actions should be joined to words. Father Fulvio Fontana, in the series of missions he conducted in northern Italy, Switzerland and Upper Austria between 1689 and 1711, assigned a very important place to ceremonies of forgiveness for enmities, which he was doubtless one of the first to organise with care.[17] On Friday, he announced, there would be a sermon on loving one's enemies. At the end of it he called on his audience to make some visible sign of forgiveness, such as embracing the person whom you had offended, or, if he was not there, whoever was

---

[16] *Les Œuvres du [Bienheureux] de Montfort*, pp. 342–7, hymn entitled 'The tendernesses of charity towards one's neighbour'.
[17] Fontana, *Padre Fulvio Fontana*, pp. 347–50.

beside you. After the priests and nobles had shown the example, the people followed it – the men on their side, the women on theirs. When the sermon was over the gestures of friendship continued: each one went looking for his enemy in order to embrace him and assure him, in the presence of everybody, of his love. The procession of penitents that followed, with whips and scourges, was all the more thoughtful for what had happened, and made the crowd, thus reconciled, ready to receive the papal blessing which concluded the mission.[18]

The Fribourg Jesuit Charles Mailliardoz had doubtless learnt from his Italian colleagues the details of the reconciliation ceremony, but he practised it differently. He recorded in his diary on 2 June 1715, the fourth day of the exercises at Rue, in the canton of Fribourg, that he had introduced this innovation. As it was the day fixed for general communion by the adolescents, everyone was assembled in the church at six in the morning. First he led them in procession round the church, then, from the pulpit, he briefly explained to them the grandeur of the sacrament that they were about to receive. After that he called on them to reply in loud, clear voices to this question: 'Are you very sorry for having offended God and your parents?' When they had replied he urged them to go and ask pardon for their faults from their fathers and mothers. Amid a general chaos of chairs being overturned and benches pushed back, everyone sought out his parents in the crowd, knelt before them and asked for their forgiveness, while the parents found it hard to restrain their emotion. When all were back in their places, they recited, consciences at peace, the preparatory acts, and then presented themselves 'with great modesty' at the holy table.[19] This ceremony so impressed those who saw it that the married couples asked for it to be repeated when they took communion. On that day, at the priest's signal, it was the parents who went to embrace their sons and daughters as a sign of friendship, 'and then did the same with their enemies who came up asking to make peace with them, and who kissed the ground as a sign of their sorrow.' All of which proceeded amid cries, embracings, choking sounds and tears flowing abundantly. The climax came when the magistrate, François-Pierre de Mertenach, went up to the railing of the choir and, turning to face the people, with tears in his eyes, humbly asked pardon of them all for any wrongs he had done to them.[20] Naturally, the parishioners from nearby places who had come to follow the exercises at Rue were unwilling to be left out. On the communion

---

[18] *Ibid.*, pp. 349–50.
[19] ASJ, Zurich, MSS, *Compendium Missionum*, mission 1 in the diocese of Lausanne (Rue), 4th day, 2 June 1715.
[20] *Ibid.*, 9th day, 7 June 1715.

day for the people of Morlens, which was also the penultimate day of the mission, the Father cast, according to his own account, 'such a spell' in his sermon that the crowd could not resist their desire to humble themselves. They had to wait, however, as, having learnt from the earlier disorders, the missionaries postponed the ceremony till after Mass. Two priests then came forward to ask forgiveness, followed by those persons who had hitherto resisted joining in the movement and had surrendered only after the example given by the notables.[21]

From then onward the custom was established: the sermon and the forgiveness of trespasses immediately preceded general communion. At Châtel-Saint-Denis, near Vevey, the ceremony assumed a lustre and a special meaning because it took place on All Saints' Day. For the first time, the Father was associating reconciliation closely with communion, showing that the latter could not be received without the former. So as to ensure that the parish as a whole was effectively involved, he asked the notables to set the example, in order that refractory persons might be encouraged to take the necessary step. Communion was not distributed until two days later, when he had learnt that everyone had forgiven everyone else.[22] At Gruyères, fifteen months after this, the ceremony was given a fresh twist on the initiative of the penitents. Four great sinners appeared before the congregation to own up to their misdeeds and ask for prayers to be said for their perseverance in well-doing. There was even a priest who had caused scandal in this neighbourhood and now loudly asked pardon, ending his appeal with: '*Hugo non amplius erit Hugo*' ('Hugo will never again be Hugo.')[23]

The procedure was certainly not to everyone's liking. It was bound to astonish some people, particularly among the clergy.[24] Nevertheless, it spread widely. Father Mailliardoz introduced it in Swabia, where he served for several years.[25] In Bavaria it was mentioned at the outset, i.e., in 1718.[26] There it was sometimes made more solemn in that reconciliation between inveterate enemies took place not only in church and in the presence of the magistrate and the whole community, but also before the holy sacrament, exposed.[27] In Alsace it took place before the crucifix, held out by a priest. At the end of vespers he said: 'Let whoever

---

[21] *Ibid.*, 12th day, 10 June 1715.
[22] *Ibid.*, mission 2 in the diocese of Lausanne, thirteenth day, 1 November 1715, and fifteenth day, 3 November.
[23] *Ibid.*, mission 12 in the diocese of Lausanne, 12–25 February 1717, 'singularia'.
[24] We find an echo of this in the frequent mentions in Father Mailliardoz's diary of hostility on the part of parish priests.
[25] Duhr, *Geschichte der Jesuiten*, vol. IV, 2, p. 221.
[26] BH, Munich, *Jesuiten*, 564, p. 1 (mission to Regenstauff, diocese of Regensburg, 1718).
[27] *Ibid.*, year 1718, pp. 26–7 (mission to Miesbach, diocese of Freising).

wishes to forgive his enemies follow me.' Then he took up the crucifix, asked Christ to pardon his sins, and, turning to the assembled faithful, asked their pardon if he had offended them. Next, he kissed Christ's wounds and said: 'Jesus Christ, out of love for you, I forgive my enemies.' After that, all the participants in the ceremony, headed by the magistrates, filed past him, performing the same action and uttering the same words.[28] Inevitably, as time passed, this exercise, so impressive when it began, took on a more ritual aspect. Everyone, in order of precedence, then asked the congregation's mercy for their misdeeds, which were not detailed.[29]

That was not the case in Spain, where the act of reconciliation remained until the twentieth century one of the outstanding features of missions. Father Calatayud had made an impressive ceremony of it. In the main square of the town, in the presence of the holy sacrament set on a dais, the Father appeared without his surplice, a rope round his neck and a crown of thorns on his head, and asked forgiveness from any he might have offended. He then proceeded to denounce those who were stubborn in their vengefulness and, seizing a crucifix, held it up before the people, crying in a loud voice: 'Forgive, forgive, in the name of Jesus Christ.' All fell to their knees and, sobbing, asked pardon of each other.[30] A century and a half later a traveller was able to watch the same ceremony, barely modified, in a village of La Mancha, Don Quixote's country.

After briefly recalling the example given by Christ, the missionary addressed the faithful thus: 'People of Ucles, let us be generous, like true Christians and true Spaniards, let us forgive and forget all wrongs . . . For the love of Jesus Christ and his blessed Mother, do you forgive us, the missionary Fathers, our wrongdoings and errors and the trouble we may have caused you?' Already tears were beginning to flow. The preacher insisted, asking for a clear answer to his question. The people then said: 'Yes, Father, we forgive you.' There was more: 'Fathers and mothers, do you forgive your children?' The latter threw themselves down before their parents. 'Women, do you forgive your husbands? Men, do you forgive all those who have done you injury in your possessions, your honour or your feelings?' They replied: 'We forgive.' The priest's voice grew persistent: 'With all your hearts?' 'With all our hearts.' The bishop, who was making a pastoral visit to the village, came

---

[28] Barth, *Die Seelsorgetätigkeit*, pp. 355–6; Châtellier, *Tradition chrétienne*, pp. 433–4.
[29] BH, Munich, *Jesuiten*, 565, year 1725, p. 34.
[30] BN, Madrid, MSS, 5838, *Algunas noticias*, fos. 73vo–74 (mission to Tafalla, 1731); fo. 117–117vo (mission to Mula, 1733); fo. 120 (mission to Cartagena, 1734). BN, Madrid, MSS, 4503, *Ejercicios y misiones*, fos. 159–60 (mission to Utrera, 1758).

down the steps of the altar and knelt facing the people. The witness describes thus what happened next: 'At this sight, sobs and weeping resounded all over the church, and an indescribable scramble began. Enemies sought each other out, called to each other and embraced and the missionary was unable to finish his sermon.'[31]

This scramble, which was like those described in connection with the missions of Father Calatayud or of Father Fontana and Mailliardoz, introduced a new and surprising element into the worship of the post-Tridentine Church. The same was true of the dialogue which preceded it, even though this often took the form of a general's address to his troops, with the latter responding at his command. At least, the people were participating. There was something more important, too. By seeking each other out in order to forgive, the faithful were taking cognisance of their responsibilities as individuals not merely for their personal salvation but also for that of the community as a whole – two purposes which seemed increasingly to be indissociable one from the other.

Salvation for all

These emotional scenes of collective pardon did not do away with individual confession, as prescribed by the Council of Trent, which made this the distinguishing mark of the Catholic Christian. All the missionaries, from Vincent de Paul to Alfonso de Liguori, were emphatic about it. 'It is an acknowledged truth', the latter wrote, 'that the greatest fruit of missions is the making-good of sacrilegious confessions.'[32] On that sin the Neapolitan saint was intractable, and he did not hesitate to relate terrifying stories about it. There was the one about the pious Capuchin who, on his deathbed, tore his tongue because he had failed, during his lifetime, to confess all his sins. There was the one about the devout woman who had died in odour of sanctity but appeared afterwards to her daughter, in the shape of a stinking pig, to tell of her damnation 'for the sins I committed with your father and concealed, from shame, when I went to confession.' Then there was this other pious woman who was everywhere regarded as a saint but who once 'unfortunately cast her eyes on one of her servants and went along with a wicked thought.' As she had not charged herself with this at confession, she was damned.[33]

All the missionaries spent a substantial amount of time each day in the confessional. Philipp Jeningen, at Ellwangen, devoted an average of six to

---

[31] Gaudeau, *Fray Gerundio*, pp. 348–50.   [32] Liguori, *Instruction pratique*, p. 87.
[33] *Ibid.*, pp. 92–101.

eight hours to it.[34] In Normandy Jean Eudes and his comrades did the same, and often put off absolution of penitents, who saw with anxiety the end of the mission draw near, and with it the moment when they would no longer be able to obtain the pardon they so greatly hoped for. It even happened that some, concerned to achieve total reconciliation, went so far as to shout their misdeeds out loud in a crowded church.[35]

The old way of administering the sacraments in the form of a collective rite had not, in fact, disappeared altogether. Peter Canisius had come upon it several times during his journeying in Central Europe in the middle of the sixteenth century.[36] Bishops and theologians had combated it so strongly in the following century as thereby to reveal that it had survived.[37] The great processions of penitents which were followed, in the missions, by the ceremony of forgiveness of enemies might well bring the old practices back to life, at least in the public's mind. Furthermore, some missionaries appeared not to repudiate that way of thinking.

Examination of conscience within a family, or even by the entire parish gathered round the cross, had already introduced a new type of confession. The handbooks that were widely circulated among the faithful gave backing to this. The introduction was often provided by the contemplation of Christ's five wounds, on an image or a crucifix. 'Kiss the wounds of the right hand', one read in a little book published in Bavaria, 'and give him your thanks. Kiss the wounds of the left hand, and ask to see clearly into yourself. Kiss the wounds of the left foot, and seek out your sins. Kiss the wounds of the right foot, and repent of your sins, both present and past. Kiss the wounds of the heart, and promise to mend your ways.'[38] One then went on, all together, after reciting the preparatory acts, to what was called in the German-speaking countries the *Beichtspiegel*, 'the mirror of confession.'[39] All sins were listed, analysed and examined in all their consequences.

Abbé Bridaine proceeded in the same way in the south of France. Every evening he would assemble the parishioners in the church for an examination of conscience. After the long enumeration of sins which the penitents had to listen to in a humble posture, the Abbé exclaimed:

---

[34] Hausen, *Philipp Jeningen*, p. 37.

[35] Berthelot du Chesnay, *Les Missions de saint Jean Eudes*, p. 163.

[36] [Dorigny, Jean, SJ], *La Vie du révérend père Pierre Canisius de la Compagnie de Jésus*, Paris, 1707, p. 94.

[37] Musart, Charles, *Manuale parochorum*, Molsheim, 1669, pp. 93–5.

[38] *Geistliche Gesänger und Gebetter zum Gebrauch der heiligen Mission zusammengetragen*, Hof, 1725, pp. 52–67. 'Erforschung des Gewissens täglich und vor der h. Beichte zu gebrauchen zur Verehrung der h.5 Wunden eingerichtet.'

[39] Thus in the *Elsässisches Mission-Buch: Durch einen Priester der Gesellschaft Jesu*, Strasburg, 1765 (1st edition 1723), pp. 57–81.

'There we behold a great number of wicked crimes, deserving the harshest punishment. What means have we for appeasing God's wrath? I see but one. Bow your heads, cover your faces and your eyes. Imagine that you are in a dreadful wilderness, alone with Jesus Christ, who holds thunderbolts ready to crush you, with, beside him, Hell wide open to swallow you up. Think solely that you are a criminal before his judge, for a mere single distraction is enough for you to lose the grace of your conversion.' After which he called on his audience to lift their heads, and showed them the crucifix, in order to stimulate them to genuine contrition.[40] The preparation was completed. The faithful could then present themselves at the confessional, where they were questioned on five charges: irreligion, impurity, injustice, enmity and swearing. To these charges they had to reply with a simple yes or no. After this, the Father Confessor preceded absolution with a brief address which was also very general in character. That was all. Thus, confession as practised by Abbé Bridaine took the form of a community rite – all the more so because, according to his biographer François Le Quéré, he sometimes took confessions seated in an armchair at the top of the nave, near the choir.[41]

We can understand why the Jansenists constantly criticised the missionaries. Behind the theatricality, the new rituals and the fresh devotions introduced they sensed that a profound change was under way which would change religion itself. How, indeed, could God show himself sterner than people who had just reconciled themselves with each other in a solemn ceremony? Did not the public admission of their errors by all the participants, grouped around the missionary, imply also the forgiveness that a father always grants to his children? 'All are called', Father François-Xavier Duplessis had declared from the pulpit.[42] There was no longer any obstacle in the way of a general and total reconciliation of all men with God. At the same time, on the other side of the Channel, John Wesley was taking a path which would lead him too to proclaim, 'God willeth all men to be thus saved.'[43] The shock that Methodism was to give to the English people may help us to appreciate the profound upheaval that was beginning to appear among the masses on the Continent, underneath the inviolable semblances of a permanent Catholicism.

The missionaries' plan was thus far-reaching, since by trying to reconcile men among themselves and with God, they aimed at nothing

---

[40] Le Quéré, *J. J. Bridaine*, pp. 151–3.
[41] *Ibid.*, pp. 153–4.
[42] *Nouvelles ecclésiastiques*, *Tables*, vol. I, p. 670 (mission to Arras, 1731).
[43] Rataboul, *John Wesley*, p. 102 (Bristol, 1739).

short of reforming a world dominated by division, egoism and hatred. The task was superhuman, for when preachers came to a place that their predecessors had visited, and where they thought they had put an end to discord, they found that it had all to be done over again. Nevertheless, they applied themselves to the task, thinking that they would succeed eventually. That must certainly happen, by God's grace – but also by using a method which consisted in taking man as and where he was and persuading him gently to change the means he used to gain his ends. If they managed to convince the public that St Ignatius' water was more effective for protecting cattle than magical rites were, that the Mass was the only means to get rid of ghosts, and that processions of children could halt divine vengeance against a village where a frightful crime had been committed, then, they thought, adherence by the public to true religion would follow. Similarly, if, instead of absolving public enmities in the secrecy of the confessional, they were to have them publicly admitted by persons who forgave each other in the presence of everyone, the likelihood of a real change in the community would be strengthened. But they were unable to prevent the Church's ceremonies assuming with some people the features of rites of protection, or, with others, for confession to the priest seeming pointless as soon as they had granted forgiveness to their enemies before God and before man. Despite appearances, was this really the Catholicism of the Council of Trent that the missionaries were implanting in Europe's countryside?

9 Satan

'And lead us not into temptation, but deliver us from evil. Amen.' Man is so naturally inclined towards evil that he manages to transform the holiest things into instruments of perversion. So it was with the missions of which a priest of the diocese of Clermont observed that 'those who did not profit from it are worse than they were before'.[1] Numberless were the tricks of the demon who sometimes put on the mask of greatest devotion and sometimes brought about the collapse amid laughter of monuments which had been raised by piety. Identifying him, ousting him from wherever he crouched, pursuing him so as to crush him and stop him from doing harm, these were the tasks that the priests who were sent into the countryside took upon themselves. But did not following him into the many labyrinths of his lairs entail a risk of letting oneself be carried far, farther than was permissible, into his sinister empire and eventually getting lost in it? Perhaps it would be better not to enter those dark alleys but to lead man to choose God, to remake himself, in the hope that he would in that way break with his bad habits? Was man capable of making such a choice? Would God grant him a general pardon?

A vision of evil

In the eighteenth century, indeed, the Devil was hard to find. Father Calatayud himself did not meet him. One day, to be sure, in Medina de Riosero in Old Castile, a 'very big' wolf walked through the town from one end to the other. The people had no doubt as to the true identity of the creature. The missionary showed himself more doubtful when faced with this poor animal – thin, exhausted and with his tongue hanging out.[2] If the people were right, the infernal powers must have had a pretty poor opinion of Pedro Calatayud in sending him such a wretched devil.

[1] Randanne, *Etude historique . . . de Clermont*, p. 148, letter from the parish priest of Crozet, 1712.
[2] BN, Madrid, MSS, 5838, *Algunas noticias*, fo. 14 (1726).

In the previous century they showed much greater respect to the Society of Jesus. Julien Maunoir's first big mission, which took place at Douarnenez, was marked by an incident. Just as he was beginning his initial sermon the preacher was interrupted by an unknown individual who suddenly appeared at the church door, shouting: 'Stop thief, stop thief!' This was the signal for a general stampede, with everyone running off to check on the safety of his own property. However, no thief was found. As for Maunoir, who had in a dream seen the church deserted, 'he recognised the truth of his dream and the trick the devil had played.' Towards the end of the afternoon he had the bell rung to summon the population again to the church, and there he warned them against 'the false devices of the evil spirit.' He then showed them the absolute power wielded by the Holy Virgin over all Hell and 'persuaded them so well that the way to overcome demons was to give oneself to her that this entire town consecrated itself thenceforth to her service'.[3]

That was only a preliminary skirmish. The image of the Devil, until then seen as a mere practical joker who vanished almost as soon as he appeared, was going to be corrected. In a treatise which he wrote to help his colleagues interrogate in confession those whom they suspected of belonging to 'the Mountain', meaning witches and warlocks, Maunoir gave a precise portrait of the Evil One and also carefully described the assemblies over which he presided and the deeds he committed. 'How was he dressed', he asked his penitent: 'Like a gentleman? Or like a lackey? What colour was his coat? What shape were his feet?' If the penitent confessed that the Devil's face was black, the Father confessor said that he must be asked: 'Have you ever seen his stockings, or his shoes?' If the answer was no, the next question must be: 'You have seen his feet, then: what shape were they? Like a man's or like an animal's? Tell me the truth, you must conceal nothing from me, I know more about it than you think. Would you like to have feet like his?'[4] Then came the description of the witches' sabbath. 'In this assembly they crossed themselves and said the Lord's Prayer and the Creed backwards. They danced stark naked beside crosses and churches. They walked backwards in procession following a black banner with a goat painted on it, and sprinkled everyone as with holy water. They said Mass backwards and the priest . . . threw the host to the ground and they trampled and danced on it. They threw down the crucifix and struck and mishandled it, and did the same to the images of Our Lady and the saints. They crucified a little child. They fired at the crucifix from a crossbow. All present believed in these wretches and put their hopes in them for

[3] Boschet, *Le Parfait Missionnaire*, pp. 47–8.
[4] AJF, Vanves, Fonds Maunoir, 'Mysteria iniquitatis. La Montagne' (copy), 2° Ad/3, p. 17.

becoming rich and enjoying pleasures through their means.'[5] As regards the pact with Satan, Julien Maunoir declared: 'Similarly, when some stupid person tells you that the ink in which he wrote his name was red, and then that it was blood, there are grounds for thinking that he has seen this, for how would he have invented the fact that in the Devil's assembly they wrote in blood? And it is to be observed that it will not be just one person who will give you that answer, but many.'[6] Earlier, the Father had listed the 'signs to discern the subjects of the Mountain.' He wrote:

The first is being from a region where there is much talk of witches, where people complain of many evil spells, or where most of the crosses beside the roads have been broken. The second is to cross oneself when alone. The third is not to know the catechism, or to know it badly, though capable of learning it. The fourth is to have the cross on one's chaplet broken or not to have it at all. The fifth is to have a chaplet of many colours. The sixth is to have some agnuses or medallions in which there is something absurd or which are not like those that the Church normally uses. The seventh is to be familiar with persons whom one knows to be of the Cabbala.[7]

This precise questionnaire was what Maunoir used in the general confessions that were held at the end of the missions.[8] Its merit is not only that it shows us the picture that some missionaries, and still more their penitents, had of the Devil and his works. It also provides a commentary on the last words of the Lord's Prayer, showing what the actual nature of evil was for the men and women of the seventeenth century. Blasphemy, pride, avarice, hatred of one's neighbour, gluttony and, above all, lust in its various forms, all were found together in that central act, that crystallisation of all the world's sins, the witches' sabbath. One might even discover in this hellish hotbed a sign of all the disorders that were widespread on this earth. Disobedience by women, iconoclasm, carnival, festivals and night-time parties, even ignorance or forgetting of the catechism. There were, of course, pacts with the Devil. It even happened that well-meaning devout women who hung about the church might accuse this or that person of being responsible for them.[9] But did not the materiality of the transgression suffice to make plain that its source was an implicit pact between the sinner and the Prince of Darkness? Did not every gross habitual sin, impiety or lewdness, remind these Christians of bygone times of the whole mass of crimes committed at the witches' sabbath, like outward signs indicating immense hidden depravities? The expression attributed, in the eighteenth century, to the penitents of the *Apostoliche missioni* of the Mezzogiorno tells us a lot

[5] *Ibid.*, p. 37.   [6] *Ibid.*, p. 61.   [7] *Ibid.*, p. 51.
[8] *Ibid.*, p. 54.   [9] Hoffmann, 'Die Jesuiten in Schweidnitz', pp. 166–224.

about what they thought, fundamentally: they came, they said, 'to drive from their souls the pestiferous poison of sin.' That was what they said when they camped all night long beside the missionaries' house, or sat up like watchmen on the church roof, so as to be the first in the confessional.[10]

Similar onslaughts were made by the Norman peasants, persons not generally inclined to enthusiasm. They slept in the cemeteries, they 'traversed ladders which they used as bridges and filled the church from daybreak', and when the Eudist fathers announced that they were leaving they heard the 'poor people apparently howling rather than weeping.'[11] These men and women who, gripped by a sort of frenzy, were now howling had just become aware, after several weeks of sermons and exercises, that evil was in them, that it had entered them like a 'plague', a sort of diabolical disease, and that for rooting it out they needed God's help or that of the holy religious who had come in his name.

The latter were careful, before they left, to arouse in their listeners hatred of *all* sins. In Switzerland Father Mailliardoz devoted a day to explaining 'the seriousness of venial sins.'[12] Paolo Segneri the Elder imparted this urgent advice: 'That I may lose the taste for criminal pleasures by distancing myself from the most innocent of pleasures.'[13] All the more did they attack the disorders which seemed to them to be the most obvious manifestations of the powers of evil. First among those were the ones that appeared to challenge the Church itself.

At Toro, between Valladolid and Salamanca, Father Calatayud encountered a 'blissful person.' That expression no longer bore the exact meaning it had had in the sixteenth century, in the time of the '*Alumbrados*', but signified a 'devout person' who took part in pious conventicles which were usually held elsewhere than in the parish church.[14] In the confessional the dialogue went like this: 'Why', the Father asked, 'have you been rejected by your parish priest [who was unwilling to hear her confessions any more]?' Reply: 'Because the directors of conscience do not understand this way.' Pedro Calatayud, indignant, then told her that 'she was rejected, won by the Devil, and lost, and that everything she did was the Devil's work, including daily

---

[10] Rienzo, '*Il processo de Cristianizazione*', pp. 461–2.
[11] ACJM, Paris, *Annales*, vol. XXVIII, p. 241 (mission to Genêt, 1709), p. 334 (mission to Cérences, 1712), and p. 339 (mission to Teilleul, 1713).
[12] ASJ, Zurich, MSS, *Compendium missionum*, mission 16 in the diocese of Lausanne (Estavayer-le-Lac).
[13] Segneri, *Méditations*, vol. I, p. 91.
[14] Bennassar, Bartolomé, *Un Siècle d'or espagnol*, Paris, Robert Laffont, 1982, pp. 152–3 ('blissful persons' in the sixteenth century).

communion, prayer, recitation of the Rosary and reading a spiritual book and carrying out, to the letter, all that it recommended.' The devout woman came back at him, in a tone of 'mockery and contempt and a devilish spirit: "To the letter? To the letter? To the letter?" ' 'Yes, to the letter', he replied. And 'not wishing to hear any more from her, I rose and turned my back'.[15] What had this devout woman done to be rebuffed like that and treated as someone actually possessed by the Devil?

It is interesting to compare the accusations here recorded with those that, elsewhere, were directed at persons suspected of Jansenist sympathies. At the end of the seventeenth century the Jesuits of Holland complained to the *Propaganda* in Rome about parish priests who allowed their flocks, women included, to read the Bible in a suspect translation.[16] In the 1730s, in France, Father Duplessis attacked, according to the Jansenist periodical *Les Nouvelles ecclésiastiques*, women who followed the office by means of an ordinary of the Mass and who fancied that they 'could consecrate' simultaneously with the priest.[17] During the mission of 1742 at Pezenas, Father Jouberd, SJ, spoke contemptuously of women who, 'finding it amusing to educate themselves, took to discussing the Church's troubles, instead of sewing or spinning'.[18] What was being targeted in these antifeminist discourses was the disturbance caused by lay persons, women especially, who, through discussing questions of faith and associating themselves too closely with the celebration of Mass, ended by taking the place of the priest. According to the missionaries there was something diabolical in this inversion of the order willed by God, more especially in that it rendered void the mission itself. The mission's teaching was rejected and made fun of ('To the letter? To the letter? To the letter?') by those who claimed to know the truth for themselves. The situation was very similar to that which existed in the periphery of the Lutheran Church when the Pietist conventicles or those of the Moravian Brethren were developing.[19]

Evil could reveal itself in other ways. The mission was a holy time, but it might be profaned by games and rejoicings so that it became a period of pleasure.

---

[15] BN, Madrid, MSS, 5838, *Algunas noticias*, fo. 25vo (1729).
[16] CPF, Rome, Scritture Originali Riferite nette Congregazioni Generali, 508 (1690), fos. 244–6. The translation in question was the so-called Mons Bible, regarded as a Jansenist work.
[17] *Nouvelles ecclésiastiques*, *Tables*, vol. I, pp. 406–7 (1735) and p. 685 (1736).
[18] *Ibid.*, p. 699 (1743).
[19] For the condemnation of these assemblies by the Augsburg Confession Church at Strasburg, see Henri Strohl, *Le Protestantisme en Alsace*, Strasburg, Oberlin, 1950, pp. 236–41.

At Oberessendorf, in the diocese of Augsburg, people had business sense. When the mission was announced the village was agog. It was not a question of anyone performing penance but of innkeepers setting out benches, tables and casks, of pedlars displaying their goods, and of families inviting relatives and acquaintances to the weddings of their children, which could not be held at a better time than this, when many were gathered together. The mission became a village fair.[20] Without meaning ill, the people revived the patronal festivals of olden times. This sort of thing sometimes happened in Castile, too. In June 1728 Father Calatayud was invited to Villada, a small town situated between Valladolid and León. At the same time, however, the village community of Mayorga, not far away, decided to organise a running of young bulls (*novillos*). Here was a cruel dilemma for the population of the neighbouring villages. The male element, however, soon found the solution. After having, at Villada, loudly cried 'Hail Jesus, death to swearwords!' they slipped away to Mayorga, where other pleasures awaited them. It was there that a young man who, despite his promises, had allowed himself to utter some swearwords, received thrusts from the horns of a vigorous young bull as a recall to order. Then the platform where the men from Villada were standing collapsed, with several casualties. Punishment had not been long delayed. Father Calatayud had a ready-made theme for his sermon on 'perseverance'.[21]

Not every missionary emerged victorious from such conflicts with the Evil One. It was tempting for some of them to choose periods of great dissipation, such as carnival time (in which the post-Tridentine Church had already placed the Forty Hours' Devotion), or of long-established superstitious practices, such as Midsummer Day.[22] But it could happen that linking the traditional festival with the new pious activities resulted in the latter acquiring an unexpected flavour which was not always to the missionary's taste.

That happened to Louis-Marie Grignion de Montfort at the start of his career, in Poitiers. Invited by the nuns of the Calvary at the beginning of 1706, he gave a three-weeks' mission in their church which concluded on the eve of Lent – in other words, at Shrovetide. He had called on his penitents to abandon the instruments of their sins: licentious books or indecent pictures. He intended to make a bonfire of them and burn the lot in front of the church. The idea was not new. But Grignion de Montfort, who had a sense of theatre, wanted to make a lasting impression on his penitents. He formed the notion,

[20] BH, Munich, *Jesuiten*, 564, pp. 8–9, year 1719.
[21] BN, Madrid, MSS, 5838, *Algunas noticias*, fo. 17vo (1728).
[22] Dompnier, 'Un aspect de la dévotion eucharistique'.

derived from the example provided by a Spanish Jesuit, of representing the world in the form of a woman dressed like a fashionable lady, with all the ornaments of vanity with which they like to adorn themselves. They brought him more than 500 books and the same number of obscene pictures and he had them attached round a stake on which this straw idol was raised, so that they might burn together. His plan was to have a cross erected in place of that spectre, after it had been burnt, to show that Jesus crucified had triumphed over the world through his cross.[23]

Grignion's pious biographer does not say that the construction of this puppet must have been suggested to him by what could often be seen in carnival time. These straw images of people or large-scale dolls which were paraded through the town on Shrove Tuesday, thereafter to be burnt amid popular merriment when night fell, formed one of the principal elements in the ritual of carnival.[24] Christianising and moralising that ritual was perhaps just as much an intention of the young missionary as the pious symbolism that was attributed to him. In any case, carnival recovered its rights. 'Wanton persons, seeking to make the thing more absurd, attached black puddings and sausages to the figure's head, like ear-rings, without M. de Montfort's knowledge.' A worthy colleague of his hastened to warn the Vicar-General who, in fear 'lest that should lead to contempt of religion', came quickly, made the preacher cease preaching and put a stop to the ceremony. Meanwhile, the merry fellows carried on with the festival, as provided in the ritual, by throwing themselves on the straw image and tearing it to pieces. What had not been foreseen was the discovery that followed of the heap of naughty books and pictures which served as the image's pedestal. This was an unexpected windfall for the young men, who went off through the town brandishing their booty, with, doubtless, much laughing and joking at the expense of the involuntary supplier to Poitiers of licentious art and literature.[25]

Charles Mailliardoz, who was on his home ground in the canton of Fribourg and, moreover, the son of a notable, was not subjected to such affronts. Nevertheless, he ran into difficulties when, in 1716, he decided to conduct a Midsummer's Day mission in the south of the canton. The town of Bulle declined to receive him, insisting, with the agreement of the local clergy, on retaining for the occasion the traditional dances by young girls who formed a circle, holding each other's hands – the *coraules* which took place on the night of 21 June, by the light of resin torches.

[23] [Grandet], *Grignion de Montfort*, pp. 89–90.
[24] Van Gennep, Arnold, *Manuel du folklore français contemporain*, I, vol. iii, 1, 'Carnaval, Carême, Pâques', Paris, Picard, 1947; Duby, Georges, ed., *Les Fêtes en France*, Paris, Chêne, 1977.
[25] [Grandet], *Grignion de Montfort*, pp. 91–3.

'They danced', wrote a witness, 'singing rhythmically some old songs, to a melody that was lively in its naïve yet penetrating monotony. This was the Fribourg farandole, dear to the young people and innocent as the song of the lark frolicking in the air.'[26] Not far away, at Rue, even though the Mailliardoz family was well established there, the people also decided not to break with custom. The inhabitants sent a deputation to the Father to ask him (it was a Sunday) 'if it was permissible, on account of the bonfires that were lit on that day, to celebrate [Mass] solemnly'.[27] The Jesuit pretended not to have heard the bit about bonfires and invited his petitioners to be content with a low Mass, without a sermon and without Vespers, so that the inhabitants could be free to participate in the exercise of the mission which would take place nearby. It was being held, in fact, at Vuippens, near Lake Gruyère. The preacher saw fit to adapt the ceremony to the circumstances. Accordingly, on the opening day he led a solemn procession 'like at Corpus Christi.' On 24 June, St John the Baptist's day, he repeated the procession out of the church, this time taking it round the cemetery, 'for the cult of the angels', with an instruction during which the women were forbidden 'to sit down away from the rest.'[28] This was because some women might take the opportunity of this expedition into the country to collect 'St John's grass' (mugwort).[29] At Vuippens as at Poitiers, by seeking to substitute the Church's ceremonies for folk-customs, the missionaries revived, rather, the memory of the latter, which were thus kept up along with the ritual of the mission.

Of quite different consequence for religion itself was the way in which, in certain countries, the great Catholic festivals were celebrated. Father Calatayud was present in 1735 at the ceremonies of the Assumption at Elche, in the Levante.[30] Offices, solemn Vespers, processions followed one another during the octave, with, as for Corpus Christi, an *auto sacramental*.[31] Musicians were brought in from neighbouring towns to enhance still further the pomp of the services, which, like the hymns sung, were in the 'Valencian' language. The local character of the ritual was stressed thereby. The Father went on:

On Assumption Day there is in the morning a very solemn procession in which

---

[26] ASJ, Cologne, Hartmann MSS, vol. IV, fo. 118vo.
[27] ASJ, Zurich, MSS, *Compendium missionum*, mission 9 in the diocese of Lausanne (Vuippens).
[28] *Ibid.*
[29] Van Gennep, *Manuel du folklore*, vol. I, iv, 2, the cycle of May and Midsummer Day, pp. 1963–2002 ('St John's grass') and pp. 2002–35 (magical practices).
[30] BN, Madrid, MSS, 5838, *Algunas noticias*, fos. 172–173vo (1735).
[31] A dramatic performance in the style of a mystery play relevant to the feast-day when it took place.

all the religious communities take part, and also all office-holders. The Holy Image, laid down as though it was that of a dead woman, is borne by four priests dressed as Apostles, while six other Apostles lead the oxen who draw the 'Palio' [the carriage]. St John, a palm-branch over his shoulder, precedes the Virgin. The officiating priest, wearing a rich cope and with keys in his hand, represents St Peter. There are four stations, at each of which a hymn is sung.

The crowd was large. When they reached the church they listened quietly to a solemn Mass. That evening, solemn Vespers were sung, after which there were representations of the burial of the Virgin, her Assumption and her coronation. For the Assumption there was a stage with four musicians dressed as angels, each carrying a musical instrument. The statue of the Virgin was placed in the centre of the stage, which was hoisted up to a second platform where there were more musicians and where she was crowned. Then the whole thing was lifted up to the roof, which stood for heaven. This ceremony was motivated, according to the missionary, by the mistaken view held by some – children, he said – concerning the Mother of God. 'She did not die', they said: she went up alive to heaven.[32]

It is not quite as clear as Father Calatayud, who merely reports the opinion of his informants, seems to think, that this ceremony was constructed in such a way as to undeceive them. What did emerge was a desire to treat the Mother as the Son had been treated during Holy Week. Dead perhaps, resurrected certainly, she was enthroned in glory alongside Christ, divine, and doubtless herself somewhat a goddess. And this took place at Santa Maria d'Elche, at the very place where still lay buried, hidden from eyes but perhaps present in collective memory, the Lady of Elche.

Calatayud in Spain, like Mailliardoz in Switzerland, was not fooled. However, he preferred, for the time being at least, to shut his eyes to certain excesses and tolerate some dubious practices in the hope of reforming them when this became possible. This was what he tried to do in Vizcaya, where he criticised, with moderation, the local dances. He secured separation of the sexes. The men danced on their side, the women on theirs.[33] He was content with this achievement. What was involved, no doubt, was discreet movements, this way and that, similar to the Fribourg *coraules*, which were respected for their antiquity and did not greatly excite the senses. Quite different was the Andalusian fury. At Sanlucar de Barrameda he saw beautiful young girls, dressed like princesses, rush into the midst of a group of admiring partners and begin frenziedly stamping their feet. They 'not only shed Christian gravity and

---

[32] BN, Madrid, MSS, 5838, *Algunas noticias*, fo. 173–173vo.
[33] *Ibid.*, fo. 92vo (mission to Bilbao, 1732).

decency', observed the good Father, 'but also some of their clothing.'
Worse still, they were not ashamed about this, since the call heard at the
beginning of the dance, 'Fuera ropa' ('Take off your dress!') relieved
them of any scruples. They then became provocative. This impromptu
fandango session, of which he did not miss a detail, upset the old
missionary to such an extent that he gathered an audience together as
well as he could and preached against such frenzied dances. 'But I
cannot be sure', he wisely admits in his notebooks, 'that this disorderli-
ness is altogether abolished. I fear that in some house or other it may still
go on, as I have been told, and even that it may not be abolished at all.'[34]
It went on all the better because some, including members of the
clergy, considered that these 'entertainments [were] matters of indifference'.

That was not the view of Pedro Calatayud, who found them not only
condemned by the Sixth Commandment but also 'quite alien to
Christianity.'[35] These pagan dances bore the mark of the Devil. They,
too, resulted from that satanic 'plague' which had made its way into
man's very depth since original sin. They revealed, much better than the
popular traditions that were present in some Christian festivals, the
corruption of human nature. Evil was in oneself and it was there that the
real and most important battle had to be fought. Though Father
Hausen, SJ, was not at all a Jansenist, he wrote in his book addressed to
the rural masses and entitled 'Daily and Domestic Mission' (Tägliche
Hausmission): 'Your body is your most dangerous foe.'[36]

That conviction guided the Jesuits of Bavaria when, after the fight
against heresy in the lands of the Prince Bishop of Salzburg, they
resumed their systematic missions in the Electorate. In 1735 in the
diocese of Passau they waged a victorious campaign against lust, 'the
foulest of all vices.' The sermon which followed Mass dealt with Hell. At
noon, in an instruction specially aimed at children, they dwelt on the
perils with which they were surrounded and on occasions of sin. The
solemn sermon at the end of the day, for the adults, developed these
various points. 'We went over again our teaching according to which the
origin of many sins, and therefore of eternal damnations, was to be
found in dances, in familiar conversations between men and women, in
gross expressions and in night-time gatherings, all of them rooted habits
among the peasants.'[37]

[34] BN Madrid, MSS, 4503m, Ejercicios y misiones, leaf 9 (Sanlucar de Barrameda, 1760).
[35] Ibid.
[36] Hausen, Guilielm, Tägliche Hausmission, das ist Christliche Lebensordnung, welche bey der
apostolischen Mission vorgetragen worden: Zum allgemeinen Nutzen, und Gebrauch in
geistliche Lehrstücke zusammgezogen, Dillingen, J. Anton Schnabel, 1773, p. 43.
[37] BH, Munich, Jesuiten, 567, n.p., n.f. (account of the mission in Bavaria, 1735).

From the launching of the 'royal missions' in Lorraine in 1739 Father Jean Pichon, as usual, waged the struggle with ardour. According to the *Nouvelles ecclésiastiques*, at Nancy, after a 'strong declamation against impurity', he had called upon the women guilty of adultery to prostrate themselves. After which, so as to give them a foretaste of what awaited them in the other world, he was said to have let out from under the pulpit 'an exterminating angel' armed with a big stick, who furiously set upon the women, evoking fright and cries and inflicting bruises. This story had doubtless been a little improved, since it is hard to imagine Jesuits organising a special mission for adulterous women and still harder to imagine the latter hastening to attend it. What followed was doubtless closer to reality. When, at the moment of general communion, the girls' turn came, the boys gathered at the end of their benches so as to get a better view of them. The girls, for their part, showed by the modest slowness of their movements that this attention was not displeasing to them. Father Pichon, watching operations from the pulpit, made the boys kneel and then, pointing to the girls, cried three times in an expressive voice: 'Get thee behind me, Satan!' However, evil is so firmly grappled to human nature that the only response, apparently, in this assembly for communion, consisted of guffaws and giggles.[38]

Reducing evil

So, quite naturally, purity became the symbol of good (just as lust was the symbol of evil) and the sign of election. 'He was so unaware of everything that can contaminate purity', wrote one of Grignion de Montfort's biographers, 'that when, one day, I spoke to him of the temptations directed against that virtue, he told me that he did not know anything about that . . . It even seemed that what makes such powerful impressions on the heart of an ordinary man had no effect on his . . . He watched so carefully over all his senses that one never saw anything ill-considered in any of his gestures, looks, words or manners. His eyes were cast down nearly all the time.'[39] Such was the saint of the Catholic Reformation, kept by divine grace in a condition of 'natural insensibility', in 'holy ignorance' of everything carnal.[40] Concern to preserve this state of innocence intact led him to flee not only temptation but also everything that might awaken in him a consciousness of evil. Hence those eyes stubbornly cast down in the presence of all women, and

---

[38] *Nouvelles ecclésiastiques*, Tables, vol. I, pp. 693–4 (1740).
[39] Picot de Clorivière, *Grignion de Montfort*, pp.14–15.
[40] Expressions used by Father Claude Bernier in his report quoted in Châtellier, *L'Europe des dévots*, p. 181 (Eng. trans., p. 165).

which Aloysius Gonzaga did not dare to lift even to look at his own mother.[41] A missionary equipped with such virtues was soon preceded by a reputation for sanctity. Thus, when M. de Montfort arrived at Moncontour, between Rennes and Saint-Brieuc, on a day when a ball was in progress, he had only to snatch their instruments from the musicians and go down on his knees for silence at once to fall. 'Let all who are of God's party copy me', he said, 'and kneel so as to make up for the outrage done to divine Majesty.' Everyone followed his example. The witness who relates this event adds that 'the people were overcome with astonishment and religious fear'.[42] This missionary, so remarkable by the purity of his life, was truly sent from God.

In the absence of a living model, it was thought, examples offered by saints could wrest young people from the temptations of the flesh. Such were the holy children, venerated for their chastity, Aloysius Gonzaga and Stanislas Kostka, who were canonised in the epoch when the European missions were at their fullest extent, in 1727. Not content with presenting these two as examples to the students in its colleges, the Society of Jesus spread their cult even into the smallest villages. The iconography of retables bears witness to this, along with some more spectacular initiatives.[43] In their little residence at Wałcz, in Pomerania, the Jesuits lost no time in getting the peasants in their charge to tread in the footsteps of the pious personage whom they soon turned into a sort of 'national' hero. The feat of Stanislas Kostka was celebrated with great pomp in 1639.[44] Fifty-five years later they named their new church after him. In connection with the laying of its foundation-stone the chronicler added with pride that this would be the first church in all Poland to bear his name.[45] Thereafter feast-days, *Te Deum*s and celebrations of various kinds followed each other continually until the apotheosis of 1727. Naturally, the fifty-odd villages where the Jesuits went regularly to preach were associated with these brilliant demonstrations and kept constantly instructed in their significance. The same happened in the case of Aloysius Gonzaga. So as to enable a wide public more perfectly to learn and practise his virtues – essentially, purity of body and mind – an association called 'of the six Sundays of Saint Aloysius' was founded, with papal indulgences. Established first in Prague with the support of the Apostolic Nuncio, it spread rapidly all over Europe. Arrived in

---

[41] *Ibid.*, p. 180 (Eng. trans., p. 164).
[42] Picot de Clorivière, *Grignion de Montfort*, pp. 165–6.
[43] On the representations of St Aloysius of Gonzaga on Alsatian retables, Châtellier, *Tradition chrétienne*, pp. 442–6.
[44] *Historia Residentiae*, p. 60.
[45] *Ibid.*, pp. 140–2 (1694).

Lucerne in 1751, it already had 25,000 adherents, men and women, in that canton alone, five years later.[46]

Recourse to these recently canonised saints, who were always considered specially efficacious on account of their very newness, did not rule out more traditional cults of intercession or protection. To those persons who were tempted to return to the errors of witchcraft Father Maunoir, in Brittany, proposed that they 'go often to confession and give an exact account of their sins; pray frequently to God and the Holy Virgin, particularly in the evening and in the morning; join the Confraternity of the Rosary; have holy water by them and take it often; have an *Agnus Dei* or some other consecrated object and kiss it frequently.'[47] That last point was important for Julien Maunoir as for all the missionaries. He advised the Fathers who came to receive the confessions of persons who had had dealings with the Devil to give their penitents 'something which had been consecrated, enjoining them not to lose it and even to hang it round their neck.'[48] This was so important that the first question put to a recidivist was: 'Where is the consecrated lamb or the consecrated bead that you were advised to wear round your neck? Did the Evil One tell you to take it off? Perhaps he threatened you?'[49] In Silesia, Pomerania and Bavaria St Joan's beads (consecrated chaplet-beads) and *Agnus Dei* were also liberally distributed among persons who wore amulets and had been persuaded to get rid of them, or among those who wanted protection from an evil spell.[50] Then Father Maunoir completed his list of remedies with this:

At times when temptation is particularly strong, cross yourself, say your *Pater* and your *Ave*, and utter the names of Jesus, Mary and Joseph. Finally, and especially at times of temptation, close your eyes, think that you have God in your heart, with the crucifix, and imagine that you are kissing its feet, without ever stopping to talk to the demon or listen to him, and without fearing or fighting him otherwise than by saying 'My God, I renounce this temptation and give myself totally to you.'[51]

This therapy was prescribed not for witches only; it could be recommended also to all great sinners who were in the habit of sinking back into the same errors.

True, for those persons the Virgin was still, as in the earliest times,

---

[46] Staatsarchiv des Kantons Luzern, Cod. KK 75.
[47] AJF, Vanves, Fonds Maunoir, *Mysteria iniquitatis*, 2° Ad/3, pp. 73–4.
[48] *Ibid.*, p. 71.   [49] *Ibid.*, p. 45.
[50] *Historia Residentiae*, p. 36 (1633, St Joan's bead given to a girl under a curse); Hoffmann, 'Die Jesuiten in Hirschberg', p. 105 (St Joan's beads given to persons who had ceased to wear amulets); Behringer, 'Scheiternde Hexenprozesse', pp. 42–73 (the *Agnus Dei* and the use made of it by an accused).
[51] AJF, Vanves, Fonds Maunoir, *Mysteria iniquitatis*, 2° Ad/3, p. 74.

the best helper. In Rotterdam about 1680 the little Catholic community included a woman of far from edifying character. Living in concubinage with her brother, prostituting herself occasionally, having had two abortions and, on top of all that, being a lesbian, Miss N. nevertheless had one untouchable principle: never on Saturday. On the other days of the week, Sunday included, she gave herself up to full-time debauchery, but, on Saturday, the Virgin's day, she 'took a complete rest', as the worthy Jesuit puts it. She began by attending Mass. On returning home she lit a candle before a small image of the Virgin and prayed until the flame went out. The rest of the day 'she abstained from sinning gravely.' Her conscience at peace, and confident that Mary would reward her for the cult she devoted to her, she went back next day to her usual occupations. One night, however, she had a terrifying dream. She was brought to trial before Christ's judgment-seat. Christ was accompanied by his Mother and by St Michael, who held a pair of scales with, in one scale, her wicked deeds, and, in the other, the prayers of the Virgin and those the woman had addressed to her. Suddenly blood spurted from the Saviour's side and he said: 'Formerly it spurted forth, with greater pain, for your salvation, and, now, through your own fault, it hurls you into eternal destruction.' The ground then opened, fire and the damned appeared, and she was thrust by St Michael into that place of torment and lamentation. At which moment her foot was caught in a ring fastened above the infernal pit. As she hung there, over the flames, she appealed to her protectress, called on her to lead her into a better way of life, and obtained, through the Virgin's intercession, the pardon she sought. Having woken up with a jump, she hastened, sweating and exhausted, to a confessional. She confessed her errors 'frankly', writes the author of this account. She 'lives now, in peace, as a very pious woman, and acknowledges, with great devotion, that it is to the Virgin Mary that she owes her escape from hell.'[52]

This most uplifting story, which shows features of modification in accordance with the editor's taste, reveals nevertheless how certain traditional forms of recourse were mixed with others more recent. The Virgin, who, as we read in the Golden Legend, went down to hell to save a great sinner, is placed beside Christ, the wound in whose side gives forth the blood of salvation. The distinction between the two registers, the old and the new, is well defined by the cut separating dream from reality. In the dream the sinner, contested between the powers of Heaven and Hell is saved *in extremis* by the former, without her playing

---

[52] ARB, Brussels, Fonds jésuitique, 1422, n.p. (1683).

any part. In the waking state, the sinner gains her paradise here below, with the Virgin's help, by leading an exemplary life.

It was that late-mentioned form of behaviour that the eighteenth-century missionaries wanted to introduce among the masses: neither occasional recourse nor panic fear, but a devout life. In a country like Spain invocation of the Virgin could provide the firmest support for this. At Avila, a traditional town, Pedro Calatayud benefited from the work accomplished by the religious orders and the numerous confraternities already established there. He made use, notably, of the devotion enjoyed by Nuestra Señora del Pilar to implant among the people the practice of waking up with the words '*Ave Maria.*' Parents and children woke up like that and began their day by saying the prayer as they went about.[53] Having proceeded into Andalusia, the Father continued his efforts towards introducing this practice. At Carmona, near Seville, he noted that, every day, one heard the children greeting each other with '*Ave Maria.*'[54] At Calañas, to the north, on the estate of the Duchess of Medina Sidonia, a collective pious awakening was instituted. At three o'clock every morning the Confraternity of the Rosary paraded through the village streets singing a special hymn which began like this:

> At dawn the joyous Aves
> Salute and glorify the Creator

and which ended with:

> Most Holy Virgin
> Do not let me
> Live and die
> In a state of mortal sin.
> Ave Maria
> Conceived without sin.

(The last two lines were repeated three times.) All this was interrupted with vigorous cries of: 'Get up, quick', for the Duchess, who appreciated this initiative, insisted that her people be at work in the fields by four o'clock.[55]

Thus, the day began under the sign of the Virgin 'conceived without sin' and was put under her protection. It was to continue punctuated by prayers so that everyone might live and work sheltered from sin, or, at least, fighting against it. The best way was for one's mind to be occupied. Father Maunoir, during his Ushant mission, had taught those who came to hear him a catechism in the form of songs made up of verses in

---

[53] BN, Madrid, MSS, 4503, *Ejercicios y misiones*, fo. 84vo (1756).
[54] *Ibid.*, fo. 151vo (1758).
[55] *Ibid.*, fos. 195–204vo (1758). The complete text of the hymn is in fos. 195vo–197vo.

Breton. 'Everyone came running, attracted by the novelty, and they sing our hymns even out at sea.'[56] That was what was aimed at: it was the aim also of Louis-Marie Grignion de Montfort, Abbé Bridaine, Father Duplessis and many unknowns who circulated collections of hymns when they went on mission.[57]

The booklets of prayers were used in the same way but were not addressed to quite the same public.[58] Some, though, were very well adapted to the needs and concerns of particular categories of people. The Capuchin Martin von Cochem's 'Garden of myrrh' (*Myrrhengarten*), in widespread use in the Rhineland in the eighteenth century, was intended for countryfolk, and more especially for the women among them.[59] It included a prayer for an unhappily married woman. This began:

O merciful God, I, poor woman, am fastened to a big cross and I do not know how to complain of my wretched state. My heart is so full of bitterness that I shall never be able to empty it, and my soul so full of gloom that I shall never be able to be happy. Thou, my God, knowest this, and seest the bad husband I have, and thou knowest what sorrow and misery I have to put up with every day. I lead such a bad life with him that not only have I no earthly consolation, but I am also in danger of being damned, body and soul, on account of him.

After a supreme appeal for a change for the better in the husband, the prayer ended thus: 'But, thou who guidest all things, if it seemeth to thee that no betterment can be expected, then separate us one from the other' (*Wann dir aber vorstehest dass keine Besserung erfolgen solle, so scheide doch uns beyde von einander*).[60] This was followed by the prayer 'of a woman whose child has gone to the bad.' Here one read: 'O Lord, I pray thee to will him to improve . . . but if no betterment can be expected, then, in thy Grace, remove him from this world.'[61] The barren woman cried: 'Lord, thou hast, in a just judgment, closed up my body and made me suffer a distressing sterility. Nevertheless, I have not lost confidence in thee – console me, deliver me from my shame.'[62]

These prayers, almost wholly lacking in the ecclesiastical turn of phrase to be found in the French booklets of the same period, remained very close to the spontaneous complaint of a suffering woman.

[56] Quoted by Croix and Roudaut, *Les Bretons*, p. 228.
[57] Grignion de Montfort, Louis-Marie, *Cantiques des missions*, Poitiers, 1759; Abbé Bridaine's hymns in Le Quéré, *J. J. Bridaine*, pp. 190–207; *Avis pratiques*, part 2, Hymns (by Father Duplessis).
[58] *Le Livre religieux et ses pratiques: études sur l'histoire du livre religieux en Allemagne et en France à l'époque moderne*, ed. Hans Erich Bödeker, Gerald Chaix and Patrice Veit, Göttingen, Vandenhoeck and Ruprecht, 1991.
[59] Martin von Cochem, *Der grossen Myrrhengarten*.
[60] *Ibid.*, pp. 311–12.   [61] *Ibid.*, p. 314.   [62] *Ibid.*, p. 312.

Perceptible here, behind the Christian lamentations, were the ancient curses of which Pedro Calatayud wrote that they were so common among women. Perhaps something of them survived in these formulations wherein God was asked to take back a husband or a son whom not long before one would have sent to the Devil.

Concern for renewal

Little by little, however, the idea gained ground of effecting a more complete change. Was not mobilising all one's forces against evil showing it too much respect? Was there not a more radical way of breaking with the bad habits inherited from a long past?

Some missionaries began to think that it was indispensable to associate the faithful more with the Church's great prayers. The Council of Trent had assigned to the sacrifice of the Mass a central place in the piety of Catholics. But how to account for the fact that, as Abbé Bridaine wrote, 'so few persons attend properly to the august sacrifice offered upon our altars'?[63] The clergy themselves, perhaps, were to blame, through over-anxiety to safeguard their exclusive domain. The Mass was obligatory upon all, but mere laymen had but a single duty – to be present. The Capuchins engaged in the mission in the Engadine in the 1640s wrote to the *Propaganda* that they kept people busy when they came to Mass by teaching them the catechism.[64] What was essential, in fact, was 'hearing' Mass. 'The more Masses you hear the more you pay your debts (to God, for your sins) and so the greater glory in Paradise you gain', wrote another Capuchin, Martin von Cochem, at the end of the 17th century.[65] And he added: 'When you enter a church in which two or three Masses are being said at the same time, you have a great opportunity to hear these Masses together. When they come to the consecration, this will thus be offered several times for you, and thereby you will accumulate a large store of benefits.' It was not even necessary to be present at the sacrifice from beginning to end in order to win these favours. When you enter a church, he explained, and the priest is on the point of consecrating, 'do not leave, but stay: you are praying to Christ and offering him to his father, and in this way you are participating in that Mass.'[66] Here we have, a century and a half after Luther's severe

---

[63] Le Quéré, *J. J. Bridaine,* p. 109.
[64] *Acta S.C. de Propaganda Fide Germaniam Spectantia,* p. 443 (1638).
[65] Martin von Cochem, *Der grossen Myrrhengarten* ('the second garden of myrrh, planted with the adorable prayers of the Mass').
[66] *Ibid.*

criticism of the Mass as being perceived too often by simple folk as a magical act, a text which showed that this criticism was still relevant.

But that did not stop Martin von Cochem, a perfect representative of an epoch of transition, providing humble people with a method for following the Mass. Or, rather, he provided two, which showed his readiness to adapt himself to different publics. The first, the ideal method, already taught by the Jesuits to their pupils at the end of the sixteenth century, consisted in dividing the office into twenty-four sequences, each of which corresponded to an episode in Christ's passion and resurrection. A prayer was then provided with which to commemorate the event. Thus, when the priest was praying at the foot of the altar, the faithful were to think of Christ on the Mount of Olives and his bloody sweat (sequence 2). When the priest gave the blessing and read the final Gospel passage, this was a reminder of the ascent of God's son to Heaven and the sending forth of the Holy Spirit (sequence 24).[67] But there was another method which was doubtless better adapted to what actually went on in country places. After a few words of offering at the beginning of the office, the believer took up his chaplet and said his rosary until the moment came for the consecration. From then on, he was asked to associate himself more closely with the sacrifice by following with attention the priest's gestures and murmuring two or three words of praise which were suggested.[68]

In the eighteenth century the missionaries tried to do more than that. Father Mailliardoz recorded in his diary on 21 May 1716 that at Orsonnens, in the canton of Fribourg, 'the priests and the people, led by a missionary, began that day to utter aloud the responses to the words of the priest'.[69] This experiment appears not to have been followed up. The polemic which broke out at that time over the circulation of a Jansenist 'ordinary of the Mass' may have been the reason for its cessation.[70] The author of the initiative may also have been discouraged by the difficulty of getting the public really to participate. In the months that followed it was only a question of 'instruction about the Mass' and 'how to be present at Mass'.[71] We can form an idea of what this meant from the instruction which Abbé Bridaine developed and which consisted in a priest explaining the different parts of the office. From time to time, the audience were invited to say a prayer aloud or with a lifting of the eyes to heaven,

---

[67] *Ibid.*   [68] *Ibid.*, pp. 38–47.
[69] ASJ, Zurich, MSS, *Compendium missionum*, mission 7 in the diocese of Lausanne.
[70] Cf. this chapter, p. 166, note 16.
[71] ASJ, Zurich, MSS, *Compendium missionum*, mission 16 in the diocese of Lausanne (Estavayer-le-Lac, May 1717) and mission 18 in the same diocese (Belfaux, June 1717).

inspired by the words of the liturgy.[72] This was very far from being the ordinary of the Mass for everyone. It was to be feared that, once the mission was over, everyone would resume their old habits: the women their chaplet, the men their boredom and the children their chatter.

For bringing the masses to make a break with their past and choose with enthusiasm the party of God the missionaries counted increasingly on an act which they endowed with the maximum possible solemnity. This was the renewing of baptismal commitments. The initiative again came from Italy,[73] but it was soon taken up everywhere. Grignion de Montfort was one of the first to give it an essential place at the heart of the mission's ceremonies. 'The mission is for those who return to God as in a new baptism', he thought.[74] Father François-Xavier Duplessis, in the middle of the century, was one of those who gave it most glamour. The act took place on the Sunday following the first week of exercises, after Vespers. The sermon dealt with the promise that was to be made. There was a procession around the interior of the church, with the Holy Sacrament, the confraternities, whose dignitaries carried torches, and the entire congregation, all holding candles. During the procession the hymn *Sacris solemnis juncta sint gaudia* was sung, and after each verse the choir repeated the first one, 'which announces the renewal one is about to make.' In this way they arrived at the baptismal fonts, which were 'adorned as magnificently as possible.' A temporary altar had been prepared there, to receive the monstrance.

The deacon sings the Gospel of the Feast of the Most Holy Trinity, which tells of the power which Jesus Christ conferred on his Church, to baptise all nations in the name of the Father, the Son and the Holy Spirit. After which he places the Gospels, open, upon the baptismal fonts, below the Holy Sacrament. Then, with everyone kneeling, the preacher pronounces the acts of renewal of the commitments at baptism, and when they are finished the celebrant intones the Credo, so as to remind those present that it is by baptism that we have received the precious gift of the Faith. And during the singing the clergy and all who were in the Procession go, one after another, to the middle of the Altar to kiss the Gospel or the baptismal fonts, so as to express the gratitude and affection with which everyone is disposed to observe the promises he has made to God.

They then returned to the main altar, singing the *Te Deum*.[75]

[72] Le Quéré, *J. J. Bridaine*, pp. 109–17: Abbé Carron, *Le Modèle des prêtres, ou vie de J. Brydayne, missionnaire*, Paris, Nyon, 1803, p. 157.
[73] Recommendation by Clement XI to Grignion de Montfort, during the audience obtained by the latter, 'to cause the spirit of Christianity to be everywhere renewed through renewal of the promises made at baptism', in [Grandet], *Grignion de Montfort*, p. 101.
[74] Grignion de Montfort, *Cantiques des missions*, p. 269.
[75] *Avis et pratiques*, pp. 158–9.

This very impressive ceremony, like the forgiving of offences or the planting of crosses, was new and a feature of these eighteenth-century missions. But the ritual of the procession to the baptismal fonts, with the solemn commitment undertaken before the Holy Sacrament and the Gospel, gave the act a sacred character. It was almost a sacrament bestowed upon the whole community, a 'new baptism.' In order to receive it one had to make a promise oneself, in full awareness of what one was doing. The 'acts' mentioned in the text were probably repeated aloud, after the priest, by all the participants. The *Montfortains* required everyone in turn to speak the words that committed them. Thus, when kissing the Gospels: 'I firmly believe in all the truths of the Holy Gospel of Jesus Christ.' At the baptismal fonts: 'I renounce forever the Devil, the World, sin and myself.'[76] Father Duplessis, who preached to bigger crowds, had simplified the ritual. But the solemn and public commitment by the individual was well emphasised by the coming of each participant to the altar and his kissing of the Gospel.[77]

The ceremony was not merely impressive, as the accounts suggested.[78] It was above all intended to make a fundamental break in people's lives. The Jansenists might mock these old sinners who became, through the operations of a Jesuit, 'like children leaving the baptismal fonts'.[79] There was, though, a little of that in this completely new solemn act which arose in the Catholic Church at the time when similar professions of faith – less supervised, more spontaneous – were making their appearance in Protestant Dissenter communities. This 'second baptism' by the missionaries would not in the least obliterate the first one, the real sacrament, received at birth, but it acted upon the individual asleep in conformity, and perhaps also upon religion generally, like an 'awakening'.

In the course of the eighteenth century the idea that people had of evil underwent a capital change. From the 'diabolic plague' that one caught like a contagious illness sin became a component of human nature with which one had to learn to live. Certainly, external helps were not without their uses. The Virgin and the saints were still presented to the faithful as privileged intercessors. But they did not deliver from evil and its consequences – they were models to be imitated. Nor ought one to expect that the sacraments would bring full liberation. One started to sin again immediately, or almost, after receiving absolution. As for the

[76] Grignion de Montfort, *Cantiques des missions*, p. 270.
[77] *Avis et pratiques*, p. 159.
[78] ASJ, Zurich, MSS, *Compendium missionum*, mission 5 in the diocese of Basel, Delémont, March 1718. 'After the sermon by Father Charles [Mailliardoz] all the people renewed the baptismal promise, with great piety.'
[79] *Nouvelles ecclésiastiques*, vol. I, p. 698, mission to Roncq, near Lille (1742).

Mass, it really acted upon those alone who, through understanding it well, were led to undertake a genuine imitation of Christ. The break would, then, be made by conversion, which, although periodically called for from the pulpit, could not finally be realised otherwise than by the individual, inspired by God's grace. He it was who freely committed himself to a new life, full of hope for God's forgiveness and for salvation. In this respect the message imparted by the Catholic missionaries all across Europe was derived as much from the spirit of the Enlightenment as from the Tridentine Church.

The immense transformation of Europe's countryside between 1680 and 1750 ultimately took shape in complex form.

On the one hand, true, the missionaries were concerned to Catholicise populations that were Christian, certainly, but, on the whole, little minded to break with their ancestral traditions, their festivals and beliefs. The missionaries generally went about this task with great care for the past, seeking to correct, adapt, replace (amulets with the *Agnus Dei*, for example) and sanctify rather than suppress. A mission to a place of pilgrimage copied its rituals, its calendar of festivals and its processions. The practices which the missionaries wanted to cause to disappear died out in accordance with the ancestral rites: the carnival bonfire was set alight with bad books and playing cards as fuel, and barns or stables were freed from evil spells by means of St Francis Xavier's water and a novena instead of the mysterious prayer against witches. This gentle evolution meant, no doubt, that some people did not see any difference, and failed to change their behaviour. But crosses henceforth marked out the territory and reminded all, including the most innocent and most forgetful, that they were in Catholic country and were living under Christ's gaze.

On the other hand, the change was not confined to the laity. Through travelling about the countryside some missionaries came to wonder if Christian teaching ought not to be adapted and simplified so as to be understood by all. Others, like Father Pichon, wanted to bring ordinary believers to that daily communion which was proper to an elite close to perfection. Most missionaries called on their hearers to effect a complete renewal which should be manifested, during the period of the mission, by a complete change in way of life. Forgiving one's enemies, baptismal vows solemnly spoken, the planting of crosses, all were so many ways of expressing one's birth to a new life.

Everything happened as if a long apostleship among the rural poor had enabled the missionaries to discover the essence of Christianity. This was what a *Montfortain*, Grignion de Montfort's biographer, was saying when he wrote in the 1770s: 'Would it not be desirable that as regards devotions, everyone should be like the people?'[80] But when what was involved was sacraments like baptism or communion, not devotions alone were concerned. It was Tridentine Christianity itself that was in question.

[80] Hacquet, *Mémoire des missions*, p. 9, presentation by Louis Pérouas (quotation taken from Ch. Besnard's MS 'La vie de Messire Louis-Marie Grignion de Montfort, prêtre missionnaire apostolique').

Part 3

Towards a new religion

The second half of the eighteenth century was the decisive period for Catholicism in the rural areas. This was somewhat paradoxical. There was violent criticism of the missions, within as well as without the Church, which did not spare the great religious orders, and the Society of Jesus was eventually, in 1773, suppressed by the papacy. In the towns signs of indifference to religion were more and frequently to be observed.

And yet it was in this period that the missionary movement gained fresh impetus. This was the age of Alfonso de Liguori and the first Redemptorists. In certain regions teams of priests sought to give the peasants a more thorough education in doctrine: these were the catechetic missions. In other regions they introduced the peasants to the practice of prayer and obtained very great successes.

The contradiction was perhaps more apparent than real, since, after all, leading the countryfolk to be more reflective in their religious life was much in the spirit of the Enlightenment. What happened in the Catholic countries was happening also, in a fairly similar form, among the Protestants. Nevertheless, it was quite clear that this work to bring about deeper spirituality could not proceed, on a day-to-day basis, under the supervision of ecclesiastics. Lay persons, both men and women, as well as nuns, often played a considerable role in animating the movement. One thinks, of course, of France, left without priests during the time of the Revolution. But in South Germany and the Rhineland responsibility had been assumed, for several decades, by groups of laymen acting through the confraternities of Christian doctrine.

Thus, at the beginning of the nineteenth century the situation was totally the reverse of what it had been two centuries earlier. The rural areas were the lands of faith, even of fervour, while the towns needed to be converted. How, in the end, could the religion of the rural areas fail to affect Catholicism generally, even to the extent of becoming identical with it?

10 Changing the village

Transforming village life was on the agenda at the end of the eighteenth century. It even furnished the theme for instructive novels such as were then very popular.[1] Not only religion was involved, of course, but it did have a place in this immense process of change. However, far from asserting opposition to the past, this apostolic activity presented itself as a continuation of all that had been accomplished in the Baroque period. What was now to be undertaken, after the 'conversion' of the populations, was to effect, methodically, their religious education, by concentrating efforts upon two aspects which were seen as having priority – the catechism and learning how to pray. What had to be shown was that there could be no Christian life worthy of the name without knowledge of religion and without inner life.

From mission to pastoral work

The large-scale construction of churches in the villages at the end of the eighteenth century and, even more, the sumptuous furniture with which they were enriched in the same period do not testify merely to increase in population and affluence of communal finances. They point as well to the new position occupied by the parish church, which had truly become, after two centuries of Catholic Reformation, the centre of religious life.[2] Thenceforth, therefore, it was exclusively within the framework of the parish that the spiritual renewal of the inhabitants should take place. The Jesuits seem to have understood this in the 1730s, as is shown by the maps of their missions in Bavaria and Lorraine after that time (see Maps 9 and 10). But this was still only a tendency, a movement which had nothing systematic about it.

Alfonso de Liguori was the first to see in the mission to a village, 'however small it might be', an absolute necessity which by itself justified

---

[1] A well-known example is the *Noth- und Hülfsbüchlein für Bauersleute*, 2 vols., Dessau, 1788–9, by Rudolf Zacharias Becker.
[2] Châtellier, *Tradition chrétienne*, pp. 437–64.

the foundation of a new order.[3] He explained his idea thus in 1745: 'There are not a lot of priests in a small centre of population' and consequently many people 'are afraid to tell everything to persons who know them and encounter them continually'.[4] Regular visits by priests from outside were needed if these sacrilegious confessions were to be put right. This was 'the greatest fruit of the missions', he added a little later, in the *Instructions* he wrote for his religious.[5] Consequently there could be no further question of those 'centralised' missions in which the preacher and his assistants installed themselves in a well-situated small town and left it to the parish priests of places round about to conduct the people of the remoter villages to the chosen centre.[6] Everyone knows, wrote the Neapolitan saint, 'that, if the mission is carried out in a [central] church for several neighbouring parishes, the faithful who will come will be those who have least need of it'.[7] Sending missionaries absolutely everywhere, having them live on the spot for at least eight days in order to preach to and instruct the people, and ordering them expressly to devote all their efforts to hearing confessions – all this seemed repeating what had been said many times already. Yet it meant a real revolution, because attaining such an objective implied the existence of well-equipped teams with thorough knowledge of the places they were to live and work in. Accordingly, as the order developed, houses were set up each of which was, so to speak, the 'redemptorist' base for a whole region (see Map 13). The desire that lay behind this form of organisation was to break with what had been the intention, avowed or unavowed, of most missionaries up to that time, namely, to rally as large crowds as possible around their pulpits. Henceforth it was the individual – isolated, abandoned and forgotten in his hamlet – who mattered; he it was who had to be sought out and converted. From the masses to the individual was, perhaps, the significance of the Liguorian revolution. The novelty of St Alfonso's *Moral Theology* (1748), which broke with both rigorism and probabilism, doubtless resulted from this.[8]

If we read the instructions of the Redemptorists' founder we receive the impression that all that mattered was to convert the poor people of the countryside. One of his biographers records the saint's anger when,

---

[3] Rey-Mermet, Théodule, *Le Saint du siècle des Lumières: Alphonse de Liguori (1696–1787)*, Paris, Nouvelle Cité, 1982, p. 328.

[4] *Ibid.*, 'Réflexions utiles aux évêques' (1745).

[5] Liguori, *Instruction pratique*, p. 87.

[6] Orlandi, Giuseppe, 'La mission rédemptoriste au XVIIIe siècle', in *Alphonse Liguori pasteur et docteur*, pp. 65–92, at p. 82.

[7] Rey-Mermet, *Alphonse de Liguori*, p. 328.

[8] On the moral theology of Alfonso de Liguori, Delumeau, 'Morale et pastorale'; on the spread of Liguorian moralism among the French clergy in the nineteenth century, Boutry, Philippe, *Prêtres et paroisses au pays du curé d'Ars*, Paris, Cerf, 1986, pp. 405–20.

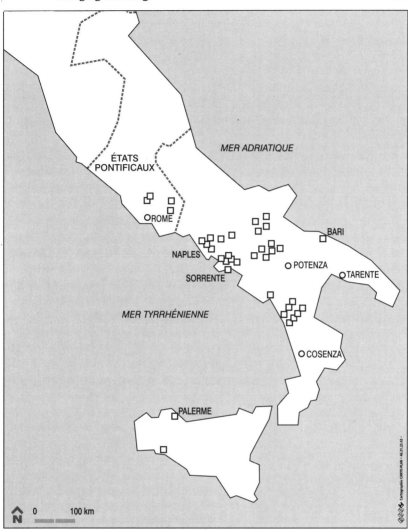

MER ADRIATIQUE

ÉTATS
PONTIFICAUX

○ROME

BARI

NAPLES

○ POTENZA

SORRENTE

○TARENTE

MER TYRRHÉNIENNE

○ COSENZA

PALERME

0   100 km

N

Map 13   The first Redemptorist establishments in southern Italy in
the time of Alfonso de Liguori (d. 1787).

one day, he heard a religious preaching without too much concern for the people listening to him. 'This', he said, 'is called betraying both the people and Jesus Christ. If you want only to preach yourself and not Jesus crucified, why did you take the trouble to leave Naples? I do not excuse you from mortal sin.'[9] The good missionary had to get rid not only of flowers of rhetoric and flashes of eloquence but also of Latin quotations and abstract teaching. The ideal was to talk like a good catechist concerned

to contribute things of practical use by teaching the correct terms that one ought to use in particular situations. Thus, when one is the object of some affront or displeasure, one should say: 'God bless you', 'May God enlighten you!' When one suffers some loss or setback: 'God be blessed!' 'May God's holy will be done!' These and similar practices should be repeated many times, so as to engrave them in the memories of the poor people who would not be able to understand Latin texts and other higher things, or would soon forget them. They will retain only these brief and easy practices which will have been taught and repeated many times over.[10]

What mattered was to be understood, and one had not really been understood until what was said had been put into practice. It was therefore necessary to keep on repeating the same thing. Alfonso de Liguori aimed at a 'return mission' to each village after four or five months had passed, which should not prevent a member of the missionary team established nearby from being called in, before or after the prescribed time, to preach through Lent, or at least to give a sermon or take a few catechism sessions.[11]

A continuous relation was thus established between the villagers and a small group of Redemptorists who, without being formally in charge of these parishes, ended by marking them deeply in all the details of their day-to-day religious life. A contemporary writer quoted by Father Rey-Mermet recalled his childhood memories in a village of southern Italy at the beginning of this century:

We set out very early, when only the cockerels felt that dawn was about to break, in silence along with Grandmother, to the church of Santa Maria. There, before Mass, by the feeble light of a candle, the Archpriest read the meditations of St Alfonso. The women, draped in their black veils, kneeling in the nave: the men on either side of the choir: the children, sometimes near one group, sometimes another, awake as one can be at night . . . A second time, in the evening, not long before the Angelus, the bell of the same church again scattered its sounds over the little region . . . And again, in little groups, mothers,

---

[9] Tannoia, R.P. Antoine-Marie, *Mémoires sur la vie et la congrégation de S. Alphonse-Marie de Liguori*, 3 vols., Gaume, 1842, vol. II, p. 144.
[10] Liguori, *Instruction pratique*, p. 85.
[11] Orlandi, 'La mission rédemptoriste', p. 85.

grandmothers, children and old men climbed up to the church. The young men stayed working in the fields until night fell. Every day of the year, without fail, the Blessed Sacrament was visited, and once more we prayed, using St Alfonso's texts, and sang his hymns.[12]

Thus, the exceptional event of the mission had merged in the routine of parish life to the point of becoming part of its substance. With the Redemptorists the distinction between mission and pastoral life ended by becoming blurred.

An example of this is given by the work of the first religious to try to implant out of Italy the order founded by Alfonso de Liguori. Clement-Maria Hofbauer failed almost completely in what was expected of him in the Holy Roman Empire. But in Warsaw between 1787 and 1808, and then in Vienna between 1808 and 1820, he succeeded in making the church or the chapel in his charge a permanent mission centre both for those who lived nearby and for the faithful who came from afar to hear him.[13] The first Redemptorist missionaries established in Northern Europe after 1820 combined the two experiences, their founder's and Hofbauer's. To the former belonged the principle of modest residences in the countryside from which it was easy to go out among the surrounding villages. To the second belonged the practice of domiciliary visits, indispensable for establishing ties with the population and giving the exercises a more pastoral character. The results were impressive: 420 missions, affecting nearly 300 parishes, were carried out in Alsace between 1836 and 1873, based on the three houses at Bischenberg, Landser and Riedesheim.[14] There were more than 460 missions in Belgium in the years 1833 to 1850 alone.[15] In the Rhineland and Bavaria the order was in full development in the middle of the nineteenth century.[16] Its role in northern France was just as consider-able, since in the diocese of Arras alone it carried out no less than fifteen

---

[12] Rey-Mermet, *Alphonse de Liguori*, p. 327.

[13] *DHGE*, vol. XII, cols.1084–6 and fasc.139–40, cols. 763–4; *LTK*, vol. V, cols. 413–14.

[14] Rall, Benoît, 'Les missions paroissiales des rédemptoristes en Alsace', in *Archives de l'Eglise d'Alsace*, 1983, pp. 65–154.

[15] Moreau, Edmond de, 'Les missions intérieures des Jésuites belges de 1833–1853', in *Archivium Historicum Societatis Jesu*, 1941–2, pp. 259–82 (statistical summary of the Redemptorist missions of 1833–50).

[16] Scholten, Bernhard, *Die Volksmission der Redemptoristen vor dem Kulturkampf im Raum der niederdeutschen Ordensprovinz: Ein Beitrag zur Geschichte der Seelsorge im 19. Jahrhundert*, Bonn, Hofbauer, 1976; Jockwig, Klemens, *Die Volksmission der Redemptoristen in Bayern von 1843 bis 1873. Dargestellt am Erzbistum München und Freising und an den Bistümern Passau und Regensburg: Ein Beitrag zur Pastoralgeschichte des 19. Jahrhunderts*, Regensburg, Verlag des Vereins für Regensburger Bistumsgeschichte, 1967.

missions a year between 1865 and 1880, often more than twice that number.[17]

This success was not due to any reputation for gentleness or laxity with sinners. In the North the Redemptorists were regarded, on the contrary, as rigorists, severe with girls who went to dances and with boys who infringed the strictest rules of sexual morality.[18] The themes for sermons included in the manual of instruction for young religious of the order were in 1930 the same as in the eighteenth century. Hell always held centre-stage. 'We think', wrote the book's author, 'that if there is one Gospel truth which, in our age of frenzied enjoyment, needs to be heard by the largest possible number of believers, it is certainly that of everlasting hell-fire.'[19] Their success thus did not result from easygoingness but simply from the fact that they lived amidst the country people, whom they knew and were able to listen to.

This was also true, in the eighteenth century already, of the *Montfortains* in Western France. They had formed the habit, since about 1740, of going in teams every year to visit a group of parishes in Lower Poitou or southern Brittany. They lived with the local people, for three to six weeks, examined their religious conduct, and tried to impart to them new habits of piety. In their accounts of visits were to be found, even as early as this, observations which, despite their rather crude formulations, resembled the appraisals made by present-day pastors who have been initiated in the sociology of religion. 'The people feel the effects of the Loire's banks', one read in one missionary's log-book: 'Much fire at first, but little firmness in devotion.'[20] At Paimbœuf, near the estuary of the Loire, 'the sea air and the concourse of strangers make the people dissolute.'[21] At Mervent, in the diocese of La Rochelle, 'the people, living in the heart of woodlands, breathe a wild air (and are themselves therefore wild), yet they are well-inclined'.[22] At Champagne-lès-Marais, on the other hand, nearer to the sea, 'if one had done one's Easter duty there before the mission, nobody, I think, would have been present: it is flat country, and that's all one can say of it'.[23] The closer one came to the saltmarshes the fewer devout persons one encountered,

[17] Hilaire, Yves-Marie, *Une Chrétienté au XIXe siècle? La vie religieuse des populations du diocèse d'Arras (1840–1914)*, Villeneuve-d'Ascq, Publications de l'Université de Lille III, 1977, vol. I, p. 383.

[18] *Ibid.*, vol. I, p. 390.

[19] Praly, Flavien, *La Mission: manuel technique et pratique de nos missions de France à l'usage des jeunes confrères*, Saint-Etienne, Duvernay, 1930, p. 329, quoted by Benoît Rall, 'La méthode missionnaire des rédemptoristes d'Alsace', in *Archives de l'Eglise d'Alsace*, 1983, pp. 155–88, at p. 178.

[20] Hacquet, *Mémoire des missions*, p. 49.

[21] *Ibid.*, p. 65.   [22] *Ibid.*, p. 59.   [23] *Ibid.*, p. 67.

'owing to their continual journeying'.[24] From time to time we find this judgment, richly evocative on the eve of the French Revolution, even though to be understood in a moral, not a political sense. The people of this place or that were 'republican', meaning undisciplined.[25] As time went by, the picture of these populations became clearer. When a missionary was responsible for one or two parishes only, to which he returned regularly, twice a year, for the 'stations' of Advent and Lent, his knowledge of the places and the people became more exact. This was the case with the 'stationaries' of Lower Poitou or Brittany, diocesan priests mostly, who, shortly before the Revolution, were sent by the bishops to preach to the villagers and prepare them for the great liturgical festivals.[26] In these regions too the mission ended by finding its place in the routine of parish life, of which it became one of the high points.

In Lorraine the initiative was taken by a secular priest, Jean Martin Moÿe. Born in 1730 in a little village near Sarrebourg, he was one of a generation of priests who, more than had been the case before, were of rural origin and therefore better aware of the country people's needs.[27] In 1754, when still at the Metz seminary, he conceived the project of 'sending girls into the country districts, and especially into the most forsaken hamlets, to teach the children and others who needed instruction'.[28] These first Sisters of Divine Providence who were sent into the villages had to operate not just as catechists. They had also to prolong and implant, in the minds of the inhabitants, the good effects of the mission. The latter, moreover, could take place only with the consent and under the direction of the parish priest. The missionary and the Sisters placed themselves at his service, becoming, as it were, his helpers. This, thought Moÿe, was the only way to ensure the lastingness of the undertaking. When he was invited to go to a village, Moÿe took his time. He heard, at length, the confessions of all the parishioners. He

---

[24] *Ibid.*, p. 71. A treatment of this information and, especially, of that contained in the reports of pastoral visits, in accordance with the method advocated by Gabriel Le Bras, will be found in Louis Pérouas, *Le Diocèse de La Rochelle de 1648 a 1724*, Paris, SEVPEN, 1964.

[25] Hacquet, *Mémoire des missions*, e.g. pp 156–7.

[26] *Ibid.*, p. 70; Roudaut Fanch, ' "Stations" et "stationnaires" de carême et d'avent en Basse Bretagne au XVIIIe siècle', in *107e Congrès national des sociétés savantes*, Brest, 1982, *Histoire moderne et contemporaine*, vol. II, pp. 437–56.

[27] On this question, Julia, Dominique, 'Le clergé paroissial dans le diocèse de Reims à la fin du XVIIIe siècle', *Revue d'Histoire moderne et contemporaine*, July–September 1966, pp. 195–216; Tackett, Timothy, *Priest and Parish in Eighteenth Century France: A Social and Political Study of the Cures in a Diocese of Dauphiné 1750–1791*, Princeton, Princeton University Press, 1977, pp. 59–65; Châtellier, *Tradition chrétienne*, pp. 373–87.

[28] Kernel, Marguerite, *De l'Insécurité selon J. M. Moÿe (1730–1793): le projet de vie des sœurs de la Providence*, Paris, Editions franciscaines, 1976, pp. 114–15.

supplemented the instruction given to all by special instructions aimed at the girls, the women, the boys and the men.[29] He was the complete opposite of the Baroque preacher dominating the crowds. As one of a team he saw himself as perfectly replaceable. When he believed that his work had been completed, he left for China in 1771. On his return, in 1783, he resumed his village missions.

It was then, in the years immediately before the Revolution, that his apostolic activity, now thoroughly matured – perhaps because of his experience in China – attained its greatest success. 'He met with approval almost everywhere', wrote a Lorraine churchman.[30]

The priest of Réchicourt-le-Château, near Sarrebourg, mentioned with enthusiasm, in his parish register, all that the missionary had accomplished in his parish during the winter of 1788.[31] What, however, was most remarkable was perhaps the choice of locations for his missions, which showed concern to continue the work done by his predecessors, devoting themselves to the ordinary villages of a neglected region (see Map 10b). He also operated in another way, by training disciples who trained others in their turn. Abbé Rohrbacher, the organiser of the missions in eastern France in the Restoration period, aimed in this way to push on with the work begun by Abbé Moyë.[32]

When Catholicism becomes the religion of the book

An important moment came in the history of Catholicism when books, hitherto confined in country places to only a few, entered into current use. This event, contemporary with the extension of primary education, took place in the second half of the eighteenth century. Thereafter, teaching the Christian doctrine had as its necessary basis the printed catechism to which all were referred.[33] 'We have sought', wrote the author of a Bavarian manual used by the Jesuits in their missions, 'to include in this book the principal points of Catholic teaching, so that you may every Sunday or feast-day question your children and do some reading yourself, thinking over at leisure whatever, when you were a

[29] Sevrin, Ernest, *Les Missions religieuses en France sous la Restauration (1815–1830)*, 2 vols., Paris, Vrin, 1948 and 1959, vol. I, pp. 168–9.

[30] Quoted in F. A. Weyland, *Une Âme d'apôtre. Le vénérable Jean-Martin Moyë, prêtre du diocèse de Metz. Missionnaire en Chine. Fondateur des Sœurs de la Providence en Lorraine. Organisateur des vierges chrétiennes au Su-Tchen*, Metz, Beha, 1901, pp. 260–1.

[31] *Ibid.*, pp. 259–60.

[32] Sevrin, *Les Missions*, vol. I, pp. 168–9, vol. II, p. 336: Richard, Gabriel, 'Le sentiment religieux en Lorraine sous la Restauration et les missions', *Annales de l'Est*, 1959/1, pp. 39–71.

[33] On this question see my article 'Livres et missions rurales au XVIIIe siècle. L'exemple des missions jésuites dans les pays germaniques', in *Le Livre religieux*, pp. 183–93.

child, you did not fully grasp in Christian teaching.'[34] The book should be read and reread ceaselessly until one reached extreme old age. Above all, the book's presence thenceforth in every household meant that there was no further excuse for the ignorance which the Council of Trent had rightly wished to correct.

The first effective instrument to this end had been introduced into town and country alike by Charles Borromeo, Archbishop of Milan between 1564 and 1584. The aim of the institution he developed, the Confraternities of Christian Doctrine, was to spread to even the smallest parishes the teachings of the Council of Trent. The method used was original. The parish priest was aided by a team of men and women, and even children, who undertook to collaborate, through their exemplary lives, their presence and their support, in the instruction which the priest directed. Already well implanted in the Milanese when St Charles died (1584), these confraternities continued to spread thereafter.[35] They enjoyed a new upsurge in the eighteenth century and were able to take root systematically in the rural parishes when use of the printed catechism had become current there. In Bavaria and Austria the associations multiplied in the 1730s through the efforts of some Jesuits.[36]

But the renewal gained strength above all thanks to Father Ignaz Parhamer, SJ (1715–86), who was not content to found confraternities but wanted, so that they might be established firmly, to precede them with 'catechetic missions'. At the head of a team, he undertook these missions with zeal, from 1754 onward, in the lands of the House of Austria, giving special attention to the frontier regions where there were non-Catholic communities, such as Styria, Carniola and Carinthia, and Tyrol.[37] The Salzburg mission of September 1758 was famous. The cortège of small children who, 'in perfect order' and preceded by their banners, processed singing through the town had a great emotional effect on the crowd who watched them. The Prince-Archbishop and all the members of his court wore publicly the insignia of the Confraternity of Christian Doctrine and had themselves registered as members, followed by burgesses of the town and their wives to the number of more

---

[34] *Tägliche Missions-Erneuerung, oder auserlesene geistliche Uebungen eines recht Christlichen Lebens-Wandel nach Anleitung der apostolischen Mission in Bayern; einem jedem fromen Christen leicht, und sehr nützlich zu gebrauchen. Zusammen getragen durch einen Missionarium der Gesellschaft Jesu*, Munich, 1763, p. 129.

[35] Dhotel, *Les Origines du catéchisme*, pp. 120–6.

[36] Baumgartner, *Die Seelsorge*, pp. 300–3. Role of Father Ignaz Querck in the diocese of Passau from 1717 in favour of the confraternities of Christian Doctrine. A confraternity with the same title was formed in Vienna in 1732.

[37] Duhr, *Geschichte der Jesuiten*, vol. IV, 2, pp. 238–9.

than 6,000 in nine days.[38] Parhamer saw in this an official recognition of his institution.

The catechetic mission had specific aims which Parhamer developed in a booklet which was first published in 1750.[39] 'There is nothing more to be feared', he wrote in the preface, 'than teaching children what is beyond their capacity to understand'. But it would be equally bad to remain satisfied, all one's life, with such elementary instruction. One had to realise, in fact, that 'young children learn only words. Later, they begin to become aware of the mystery, but it is only when one is grown up that one applies oneself to the truth, and mere capacity to know develops into continual thinking about holy matters.' It was therefore necessary to keep that book by all one's life long, to read and reread it and to go deeper into it.[40]

These justifications offered a remarkable defence and illustration of the catechism in the age of Enlightenment. The Council of Trent had already emphasised the need to know in order to be saved. In the eighteenth century, however, this requirement was considerably strengthened. 'So that you may not find death where you are looking for life', we read in an Alsatian manual of the same period, 'try to know well what it is that is demanded of you in order to make a good confession.'[41] Finally, this apologia for knowledge was related to the progress of human reason, which, fully enlightened and instructed, could not but lead to the highest good. In this way Faith and Reason, Tridentine Catholicism and the spirit of the Enlightenment were united.

The instructions that followed drew their inspiration from these two sources. The first sermon on the first day bore the title 'On ignorance in general'; the second dealt with 'The effects of ignorance'; and the third explained 'The source or origin of ignorance'. Then only was the subject 'The necessity of penitence' tackled. It was the same during the following days, when the ignorance of adults and children and the attention they should give to the Christian doctrine led to 'The danger of putting off penitence' (second day), or 'The means of uprooting ignorance' to 'Shame before holy confession' (third day) and to 'The education of children' (fourth day). Study of the rules of the

---

[38] ARSI, Austria, 229, fos. 165–7.
[39] *Allgemeines Mission-Fragebüchlein, in drey Schulen ordentlich eingetheilet mit beygesetzten Gesängen, nebst nutzbaren Bericht von der Christenlehrbruderschaft vermehret: und mit den fünf hauptstücken Petri Canisii versehen: zum Gebrauch aller Seelsorger, Schulmeister, Aelteren, Kinder und Mitglieder der Christenlehrbrüderschaft in der wienerischen erzbischö-flichen Diöcese herausgegeben, von P. Ignatio Parhamer der Gesellschaft Jesu,* Augsburg, Matth. Rieger und Söhne, 1771.
[40] *Ibid.,* preface, n.p.
[41] *Elsässisches Mission-Buch,* p. 57.

confraternity (from the fifth to the tenth day) was accompanied by consideration of the evils it was intended to root out (lust, superstitions) or to avoid (Hell).[42] The plan was quite different from that of the penitential missions, which aimed to produce a shock-effect on individuals. From now on there was to be insistence on the absolute need for everyone to behave as a sensible and rational person if he was to be saved. The entire method was based on sharing of responsibilities, which would be all the better assumed in that each person received instruction adapted to his age and capacity. The young people of a village were divided into three 'schools'. The first was concerned with 'little children completely ignorant'. The second was aimed at those who were preparing for confession and first communion. In the third the pupils were taken over everything that had been studied, going into the greatest detail.[43] All this was done without any claim to erudition – the basic book was still Canisius' small catechism in five parts.[44] So as to make sure that his organisation was fully effective, Parhamer had provided for each 'school' to be divided into small groups of ten children, every one of which had its supervisors and persons assigned to question the children or hear them recite what they had learnt.[45] The latter might be older children, though in most cases they were grown-up men and women.

Thus, the laity were very closely associated with the work of the Austrian Jesuit. It was a way for them to keep from forgetting what they had learnt. The missionary's passage gave an opportunity to put questions on points of doctrine or to bring up doubts.[46] The lay persons drawn into those confraternities were thus not mere assistants to the clergy, confined to subordinate tasks. A share of initiative was allowed them, and this became substantial when fathers and mothers were involved. They alone were responsible for the first religious education to be given to small children. They 'are to talk to them of the Holy Name of Jesus and that of Mary with much respect and they are to teach them to know our most beloved Father and our Mother of Heaven, full of love'. Later, when they can understand it, the children are to be made 'to cross themselves and to say, every day, the Lord's Prayer, the Angelic Salutation and the Credo, slowly and distinctly, without anything else,

---

[42] ARSI, Austria, 119, fos.169–73.
[43] *Allgemeines Mission-Fragebüchlein*, pp. 21–86.
[44] Duhr, *Geschichte der Jesuiten*, vol. IV, 2, p. 241; Baumgartner, *Die Seelsorge*, p. 307.
[45] Baumgartner, *Die Seelsorge*, p. 310.
[46] BZAR, O.A-Gen.97, 'Stiftung einer Katechetischen Mission (Christenlehren) für das Bistum Regensburg . . . mit den Berichten des Diözesan Christenlehrers P. Joseph Gruber SJ' – account of the first mission entitled *Relatio missionis Catecheticae per Dioecesin Ratisbonensem primo habitae anno Domini 1767*, 3 fols., n.p.

and they are to learn the principal articles of faith.'[47] The parents' role did not stop there. When they observe 'that the children are beginning to recognise what is sinful and what is not, they will gradually instruct them in holy confession and will not allow them to go to confession before they have properly understood what it is and how to perform it.'[48] However, Father Parhamer's intentions certainly did not include the emancipation of the Catholic masses. That was shown plainly enough by the quite military ritual for the setting-up of confraternities at the end of missions. On the appointed day the different congregations established in a region converged on the chosen centre. They marched 'to the sound of military trumpets, as laid down by our predecessors for Austria, Styria, Hungary and Croatia when, at Laxenburg, [a service] was solemnly celebrated in the presence of His Imperial Majesty and all his court.'[49] Each group marched behind its standard. When they reached their destination the flags were collected and placed in the middle while the confraternities with their directors, themselves divided into groups, each with their examiners, formed a circle. The missionary then advanced to the mid-point in order to bless the standards, after which he addressed the immense assembly surrounding him: 'Do you abjure the Devil and his acolytes? Do you believe in God the Father, Son and Holy Spirit? Do you believe all that the Holy Catholic Church requires you to believe? Do you promise to live in its holy faith, to fight manfully in its ranks (*in ea viriliter certare*), and to die in it?' After the customary prayers had been said, the proceedings ended with a vibrant *Te Deum*. The ceremony could be described like this: thousands of children and young people, divided into 'sections' and 'companies', came, at the missionary's command, to swear an oath on the flag to accept and defend the Tridentine confession of faith.[50] This impressive demonstration already had more about it of the Scout jamboree than of a traditional end-of-mission. But the very military character of the ritual, the terms used, the trumpet-calls, the flags, and the presence, on one occasion at least, of Emperor Francis I in person, lead us to suppose that political considerations were perhaps not absent. During the Seven Years War (1756–63), when Austria felt threatened by Prussia, such gatherings, especially when they took place on the border of Hungary and brought together delegations from the different parts of the Empire, amounted to oath-takings of loyalty to the Emperor. The catechetic mission culminated in proclamation of the unity of the lands of the House of Austria around a principle recognised by all – the Catholic religion.

This way of conceiving catechetics was not approved by all. Parhamer

[47] *Allgemeines Mission-Fragebüchlein*, pp. 21–3.   [48] *Ibid.*, p. 46.
[49] ARSI, Austria, 229, fols. 169–73.   [50] Duhr, vol. IV, 2, p. 239.

had to justify himself in Rome, and the Prince-Bishop of Passau loftily declared that he regarded all that ritual with the flags as 'superstition'.[51] The same prelate, however, encouraged catechetic missions, while wishing them to be less spectacular and to be under his direct control. Father Karl Helbling, who was responsible from 1751 for the 180 parishes of the Bavarian part of the diocese of Passau, gave this description of his work.[52] He had, in four years, visited the ten deanships and all their parishes, together with their chapels of ease and annexes.

This is done within a deanship in accordance with the location of the parishes. One goes from one to the other in the order of their proximity and after notifying the respective priests concerned. The period of stay is eight, ten or fourteen days depending on the size and population of the place. Each day, two catechetic instructions are given, one at about eight in the morning, after Mass, and the other at about two or three in the afternoon, the first being for the adults and the second for the children.

When 'all the parishes of a deanship have been visited', the missionary added, 'one passes to the next deanship and proceeds in the same way. In this manner one can cover two or three deanships in the course of a year.'[53]

In 1765 the Bishop of Regensburg adopted the method which had shown its effectiveness in the neighbouring diocese. A Jesuit missionary was sent into each parish, equipped with an order calling upon the priests to give him all the help he might need and to take example from his zeal, 'so that this holy work may succeed'.[54] That was not all. In 1768 the Elector of Bavaria sent a similar order to his magistrates to provide every necessary help to the Jesuit Fathers, 'with all the zeal and readiness required in order that this holy work' might go forward successfully.[55] The visitors thus bore something of an official character, which enabled them to take action against recalcitrant or negligent persons, who were sentenced to pay fines.[56] Active participation in the mission had become an obligatory civic act. When the missionary's

---

[51] *Ibid.*, p. 240.
[52] Baumgartner, *Die Seelsorge*, pp. 314–23.
[53] BZAR, O.A.-Gen.97, 'Stiftung einer Katechetischen Mission', item entitled *Modus et Ordo Missionis Catecheticae ab eminentissimo Card. de Lamberg Episcopo Passaviensi pro sua Diocesi in Bavaria prescriptus*, 2 fos.
[54] BZAR, Kl.85/9, *Jesuiten Allgemein*, order by the Prince-Bishop's suffragan, 4 February 1771.
[55] *Ibid.*, printed order by Maximilian Josef, Elector of Bavaria, 18 January 1768.
[56] This was the case in the first years, at least. Schrems, Karl, *Die religiöse Volks- und Jugendunterweisung in der Diözese Regensburg vom Ausgang des 15. Jahrhunderts bis gegen Ende des 18. Jahrhunderts*, Munich, Druck der Salesianischen Offizin, 1929 (Veröffentlichung des Vereins zur Erforschung der Regensburger Diözesangeschichte, 1), pp. 259–65.

approach to the parish was reported, parents and children threw themselves on their catechism, testing each other as they sat up of an evening.[57] The more enterprising tried to get into the presbytery, where the Jesuits were lodged, in hope of finding out in advance what questions would be asked of them next day. It had been noticed that the priest's servants were always the first to answer, and to give the right answers.[58] A strange time, when for several weeks a whole village lived in tune with the lessons of Peter Canisius' small catechism.

In this well-ordered world the suppression of the Society of Jesus in 1773 produced the effect of an earthquake. In his report for 1774 the missionary of Regensburg diocese recalled those distressful moments and trembled again from the memory. What 'welcome would he receive now that he was only an ordinary diocesan priest', which amounted to saying: nothing or almost nothing?[59] Thanks to the duke and the bishop, nothing changed. Father Josef Gruber continued for over ten years more his ministry in the diocese of Regensburg, methodically covering two or three deaneries each year, while his former colleagues did the same in the dioceses of Chiemsee and Freising, and the archdiocese of Salzburg.[60]

Above all, prayer

One of the first concerns of the missionaries in the time of the Counter-Reformation had been to teach the Christian populations their prayers. The *Pater*, the *Ave Maria* and the *Credo* had been rehearsed with children from their earliest years, constituting, as a rule, their first apprenticeship to religion.[61] Then there had been talk of 'meditations', exercises carefully directed from the pulpit and usually reserved for Lent. Finally had come personal prayers, logically organised in successive 'points', for which the booklets of spirituality furnished the model. Despite the efforts of certain missionaries, such as the Breton canon Jean Leuduger, few had managed to bring the rural faithful to that stage.[62]

---

[57] Baumgartner, *Die Seelsorge*, pp. 314–15.
[58] Schrems, *Die religiöse Volks- und Jugendunterweisung*, p. 359.
[59] BZAR, O.A.-Gen.97, 'Stiftung einer Katechetischen Mission', report on the mission of 1774.
[60] OP, Munich, *germ. supp.*, II, 11. Powers given by the Bishop of Freising to Andreas Unger, superior of the mission in Bavaria (1777); authorisation given him by the Bishop of Chiemsee in 1782; permission given to the missionaries by the Archbishop of Salzburg in 1782: Schrems, *Die religiöse Volks- und Jugendunterweisung*, pp. 264–88 (Father Gruber).
[61] *Allgemeines Mission-Fragebüchlein*, pp. 21–2 ('primary school for small children who are completely ignorant').
[62] *Bouquet*, p. 212.

Accordingly, it is not surprising that Alfonso de Liguori's attempt to train up the humble folk of Naples to this high state of inward life seemed to many to be far-fetched. For those night-time gatherings called *cappelle serotine* were, when they began in 1727, 'chapels' only in name. They met in a barber's shop or an inn. There it was that men engaged in 'the thousand trades of the poor people of Naples' assembled of an evening to learn to pray under the guidance of a labourer or a craftsman.[63] They began by reciting the rosary, this being followed by acts of faith, hope and charity. Then came a homely lecture by the man in charge, on a lesson of the catechism, a Gospel text, the cult of the Blessed Sacrament or the devotion to the Holy Virgin. An initiation to prayer ended the evening's proceedings, and lasted no more than a quarter of an hour. The leader proposed to the gathering a short meditation on death and judgment, or on Christ's passion.[64] This was still very modest. Nevertheless, the public flocked to these gatherings. In 1788 there were seventy-five 'chapels', with a regular attendance of one thousand persons. In 1834 there were 30,000 in Naples and its neighbourhood.[65] This large-scale movement was beginning to interest wide circles of the Catholic people.

In the intervening period, in fact, initiation to prayer had become widespread. In France the growth in the number of retreats, which, in some regions, replaced the former missions, and the establishment by the missionaries of associations for prayer such as that of the Perpetual Adoration were so many signs of deepening spirituality.[66] In Spain Father Calatayud devoted his last missions in the villages of Andalusia in 1759–60 to giving instruction about prayer. At Carmona, a large village near Seville, he introduced 'the practice of morning prayer at home for persons who could not get to church'.[67] At Almonte, between Huelva and Seville, the 'exercise of prayer' was intended for the whole population, who were instructed 'for four hours in the practical, mild and easy way' to pray. They were read the points for meditation and then, in the next half-hour, the missionary started them off by uttering some maxim or by letting his heart overflow in 'effusions' (*affectos*), depending on what the subject required.[68] These instructions often

[63] Rey-Mermet, *Alphonse de Liguori*, pp. 171–81; Orlandi, 'S. Alfonso Maria de Liguori e i Laici', pp. 393–414.
[64] *Histoire de Saint Alphonse de Liguori*, pp. 49–50; Rey-Mermet, *Alphonse de Liguori*, p. 177.
[65] Rey-Mermet, *Alphonse de Liguori*, p. 180.
[66] Hacquet, *Mémoire des missions* (importance in the west of France of the retreats given by the Montfortains from 1767); Bergier, *Histoire de Beaupré*, p. 154 (the missionaries of Beaupré in Franche-Comté and the spread of the Perpetual Adoration).
[67] BN, Madrid, MSS, 4503, *Ejercicios y misiones*, fo. 151vo (1758).
[68] *Ibid.*, fos. 233 and 233–234vo (1759).

accompanied the introduction into the villages of the devotion to the Sacred Heart, which, through the establishment of a confraternity, was the best way to ensure the continuation of those exercises.[69] In connection with the last mission of his career, carried out at Campillos on 30 December 1760, Father Calatayud mentioned two facts which seemed to him to be important, namely, the foundation of a confraternity of the Sacred Heart and the initiation to 'mental prayer' of the 800 inhabitants of the village.[70] By ending his career amid the peasantry, busy with teaching them to pray, was Spain's greatest preacher obeying a personal need or was he sensing, like many of his contemporaries, the need to get down to essentials?

At the time when Pedro Calatayud was entering these new paths a new institution made its appearance in Italy, with the approval of Pope Benedict XIV (1741). The Passionist order founded by Paul of the Cross (1694–1775) set its aim as promoting the remembrance and cult of Christ's passion, by teaching the faithful to meditate on the mystery of salvation.[71] The new order soon met with success, and not only in Italy but even in parts of north-western Europe, where it was particularly active in the nineteenth century.[72] In the middle of the eighteenth century the mission was tending to become a school of meditation.

This characteristic was especially marked in a remote part of the Jura. The young curate of Les Fontenelles, near Morteau, Antoine-Sylvestre Receveur, had noted that, despite the fervent missions of which they had enjoyed the benefit, his parishioners kept falling back into their bad ways. He aimed to convert them by means of retreats.[73] The idea was not new, but the method was. He began his enterprise in 1783, to celebrate the completion of his new church. A downstairs room in the presbytery was specially prepared for the purpose. Inspired by what he had seen once in Besançon, when he was at the seminary, he draped the room all over in black. A large crucifix stood out, together with skulls and crossbones set here and there on palls spotted with silver tears. In the middle of the room was a catafalque surrounded by torches. Inscriptions were designed to guide the retreatants' meditations. 'O death, how wise are your warnings!' one read. 'At my death, what would I wish to have done?' 'God's judgments are terrible.' 'What would one of the damned do in my place?' And, to conclude: 'O Paradise, how desirable you are!' When they entered a room with such a gloomy decor,

[69] *Ibid.*, fos. 88–9 (1756).   [70] *Ibid.*, leaf 13, n.p.
[71] *Dict.spir.*, vol. XII, cols. 540–60.
[72] Hilaire, *Chrétienté au XIXe siècle?*, vol. I, pp. 385–92.
[73] Bonnard, Mgr Fourier, *Le Vénérable Père Antoine-Sylvestre Receveur, fondateur de la Retraite Chrétienne (1750–1804)*, Lyons and Paris, E. Vitte, 1936.

not well ventilated moreover (which resulted in one group nearly suffocating), the penitents were carried away and did not find it hard to obey when Abbé Receveur implored them, saying: 'Ah, my children, my dear children, why do you not weep?' And, when he let them go, he added: 'Ah, please, in a year's time come to me with the hollow of your hand filled with tears.'[74]

Some men and women were soon won over by the enthusiasm of the retreat's director. 'When you heard this man of fire speak of the eternal verities you were quite carried away', wrote one of the first female participants, 'you felt as though out of this world and already living in eternity. He drew such lively, tangible pictures of the things of the other life that it seemed they were there before us. Your heart was so touched, your mind so penetrated that you forgot to eat and failed to notice bodily fatigue.'[75] It must be said that when the curate spoke about eternity, his theme was rarely Paradise. 'I see you', wrote one lady retreatant, 'holding a handkerchief streaked with red and soaked with your tears, and you were still saying: "Ah, if I am so unfortunate as to go to Hell, don't follow me, for they burn there, they burn!" And when you added that there would perhaps be no more than four of us who would escape that experience, that took me aback. But now I already see a little more clearly, when I perceive what I am becoming.'[76] After having wept a great deal, retreatants sometimes asked the Father the favour of remaining all night alone before the catafalque, in order to pray and meditate on what had been said.[77]

In this already intensely romantic setting of quivering flames, a barely lit tomb and abundant tears, all these souls (except for the four fortunate ones) who had been doomed to the eternal fire constituted an extra sombre touch to complete the picture rather than providing a proof of Jansenism. For Receveur's supreme purpose was to bring all these highland peasants to the practice of prayer. 'Whoever can pray can save himself' was a saying of his, or: 'Promise me to spend a quarter of an hour each day in meditation and I promise you Paradise.'[78] All of which was not very Jansenist, and it led those who heard it to practise very carefully the exercise he prized so highly. During his retreats the meditation, begun at six in the morning, lasted one hour. Its subject had been decided the previous evening, so that everyone could think about it overnight. The meditation was performed aloud either by the director or by some person in the assembly. There followed another hour wholly devoted to prayer, after the way to pray had been explained.[79] This was

[74] *Ibid.*, p. 88.   [75] *Ibid.*, p. 58.   [76] *Ibid.*, p. 87.
[77] *Ibid.*, p. 59.   [78] *Ibid.*, p. 79.   [79] *Ibid.*, p. 61.

the basis of his teaching. 'Our sovereign devotional practice for succeeding in every way is meditation on the eternal verities',[80] he said. Soon he was no longer satisfied with the parishes round Les Fontenelles, and he caused to be built, in an isolated spot (Froide-Combe), a huge retreat-centre where the most fervent of his disciples lived like hermits, working with their hands, bringing up orphans and welcoming persons who were desirous of spending a few days in silence and prayer. The new community took up residence within its walls in November 1789. In 1791 the centre received more than 1,200 retreatants who arrived by groups, in procession, intending to submit themselves to a new experience.[81]

This work, which kept going during and after the Revolution, owed its success to the fact that Antoine-Sylvestre Receveur, like Alfonso de Liguori much earlier, with his *cappelle serotine*, insisted that the laity must feel themselves responsible. In 1785 he began to compile a list of the participants in his retreats, and, later, he brought them together in an association, the Association against Mortal Sin, or Association for Thinking about Eternity, which at the beginning of the Revolution had over 4,000 members. It was present in every parish, with its leaders, its pious exercises, its meetings conducted by one of the Association's members. The latter had been led to read works of spirituality and to find texts in Holy Scripture suitable for guiding the little groups in their charge. Abbé Receveur, like Alfonso de Liguori before him, certainly kept himself informed of what was happening there, but this was much more so as to get the Association's members to forge ahead than to supervise them. 'Stay faithful, then, dear Associates, to our old resolutions for mutual loyalty', he wrote. 'Woe to whoever breaks the chain! Go on, march without fear behind the cross!'[82]

'Chains' of devotion were numerous at the end of the eighteenth century, from those of St Aloysius Gonzaga and the Christian Doctrine to the 'evening chapels' and Receveur's association for Christian retreats. But these were only the most obvious manifestations of a wider phenomenon. All the missionaries were accustomed to establishing confraternities in the villages that they visited.[83] Many of these were created in the eighteenth century.[84] They were destined, as in Spain in

---

[80] *Ibid.*, p. 167.   [81] *Ibid.*, pp. 157–83.   [82] *Ibid.*, pp. 81–4.

[83] Dompnier, Bernard, 'Les missionnaires, les pénitents et la vie religieuse au XVIIe et XVIII siècles', in *Les Confréries de pénitents (Dauphiné-Provence)*, Valence, Histoire et Archives drômoises, 1988, pp. 138–59.

[84] According to research in progress, one-third of the confraternities that existed in the former diocese of Toul in 1789 had been founded between 1730 and 1780; nearly 40 per cent of those that existed in the former diocese of Strasburg at the time of the Revolution had been founded between 1750 and 1789. Châtellier, *Tradition chrétienne*, p. 438.

Father Calatayud's time, to become so many schools of prayer, under the leadership of the parish priest but with participation, often very active participation, by the faithful.

An evolution was under way in the Europe of the 1770s. The missionary was yielding the first place to the parish priest, and the mission was standing back in favour of networks of associations, schools of doctrine, confraternities, congregations, retreats and links. A map showing these networks as they were at the end of the eighteenth century and the beginning of the nineteenth would undoubtedly be a useful aid to study of the evolution of contemporary Catholicism. By itself, the fact already reveals a change. The 'new' village missions aimed no longer at crowds but, within the often very narrow framework of the parish, at the religious education of the individual.

11   The missions challenged

A time came when the missions themselves came under challenge. It was not merely the question of pastoral work that was at issue. The essence of doctrine itself was involved. Without this being said in so many words, the Council of Trent was central to the debate. In its name bishops and parish priests forbade missionaries to concern themselves with parish life, which, they said, was none of their business. For diametrically opposite reasons, theologians blamed the religious who came to preach in the rural areas for fostering among the inhabitants a state of mind which mistook the accessory for the fundamental – a charge often levelled, in the age of the Enlightenment, against the Council of Trent. This argument was used in the struggle against the missionaries, starting with the most famous of them, those, who, from the middle of the sixteenth century, had devoted themselves to spreading Catholic doctrine in town and country, namely the Jesuits. In 1773 Pope Clement XIV, urged by the upholders of both views, and by laymen who acted in the name of a new conception of the state, suppressed the Society of Jesus. It was possible to wonder if this action put an end to a form of apostleship which had outlived its time.

A movement of rejection

The 'enlightened' Italian prelates who assembled at Pistoia in 1786 set themselves categorically against the missions, which they condemned with the utmost severity. 'This new practice, irregular and noisy, to which the name of "exercises" or "missions" is given', they wrote in their decree on penitence, 'rarely succeeds in producing a genuine conversion, for its outward manifestations only bring about [in those who participate] shocks, mere short-lived and natural flashes.'[1] In this condemnation we find again the criticisms of the Jesuits that had been formulated before the Brief of Suppression in 1773. Already at the

---

[1] Orlandi, 'L. A. Muratori e le Missioni', p. 191, n. 138.

beginning of the century the great historian Muratori had indicated to Father Paoli Segneri Junior that, although he greatly admired him, he found excessive the role he assigned to the senses. What need was there to display those instruments of mortification and to make so much of those public demonstrations of penitence which had about them something ridiculous and morbid?[2] He was not far from sharing the view of an opponent of the missions for whom the flagellations of themselves by men which were intended, in principle, to chasten the flesh actually seem to 'arouse concupiscence' in women.[3] That was what was thought, in Spain, by Father de Isla, and described with humour in his novel *Fray Gerundio*.[4] Muratori made another criticism, too. This related to what was ambiguous in the cult of images propagated by the Jesuits. Missionaries sometimes gave the impression of allowing the faithful to direct their veneration 'to the tangible matter' and not, as required by the Council of Trent, to the holy personages who were represented.[5] This reproach was expressed even more sharply in the reports of missions that appeared in the Jansenist periodical *Nouvelles ecclésiastiques*. 'Father Serrurier', wrote the chronicler, concerning the mission to Stenay in 1759, 'a tragi-comic actor with . . . the gestures of a regular farce-player, lining girls up to sing Jesuit hymns . . . A special altar erected in the choir to support a statue of the Virgin, decorated with the jewels of fashionable women and brightly lit, as the unique object for the people's devotion.'[6] In this account one sees clearly the possible slippage from sensitive piety into pure and simple superstition.

The religion preached by the missionaries was thus suspect and their orthodoxy considered questionable – that was the idea which it was sought to implant in people's minds and get widely accepted. In Spain several missionaries had their sermons or their writings referred to the Inquisition.[7] Though Father Calatayud was famous, he was obliged to preach in the presence of a commissioner of that tribunal who had been sent to inquire into the purity of his doctrine.[8] In France Abbé Antoine-

---

[2] *Ibid.*, p. 183.   [3] Orlandi, 'Missioni parrocchiali', p. 330.
[4] Cf. above, chapter 4.
[5] Orlandi, 'L. A. Muratori et le Missioni', p. 184.
[6] *Nouvelles ecclésiastiques, Tables,* vol. I, p. 766.
[7] *Diccionario de Historia ecclesiastica de España*, Madrid, 1972, vol. I, pp. 301–2 (the Capuchin missionary Diego-José of Cadiz and his trial before the Inquisition at the time of his death, 1801); Callahan, William J., *Church, Politics and Society in Spain, 1750–1874*, Harvard University Press, 1984, pp. 65 and 285 (trials of Father Calatayud, SJ, and Diego-José of Cadiz).
[8] BN, Madrid, MSS, 5838, *Algunas noticias*, fos. 117–117vo, 119–22, 'Rumours' concerning the orthodoxy of Father Calatayud in the year when his work on devotion to the Sacred Heart was published; *Incendios de Amor sagrado*, 1733, a commissioner from the Inquisition is present at the missions to Mula and Cartagena.

Sylvestre Receveur was severely penalised by his archbishop when he undertook the work of Christian Retreat in 1787. He had to wait until 1791 before the same prelate (now in exile) gave him back his powers, in particular the right to say Mass.[9]

In his case, however, it was not so much the content of his exhortations that was indicted as the liberties he took with clerical discipline. His gatherings of laymen seemed suspect in themselves, and all the more so because they were outside of control by the natural pastors, meaning the bishops and parish priests. This was the criticism that was constantly aimed at missionaries in the eighteenth century and which appeared in the text of the Pistoia censors, where they spoke of a 'new and irregular practice'. The French Jansenists had already shown how this charge was to be understood. Describing the closing ceremony of the mission to La Charité-sur-Loire in 1758, the journalist wrote: 'Planting of the cross, with all the usual mummery and with an exercise as well drilled as with the Indians in Paraguay.'[10] France was no more a 'missionary land', in the juridical sense of the term, than the other countries of Europe, but part of Christendom, with an established church, dioceses and bishops. They it was who possessed the right to teach doctrine and guide the faithful. That had been decided by the Council of Trent and reaffirmed, individually or collectively, by a large number of bishops who, in the eighteenth century, wished to assert their rights in relation both to the Pope and to their subordinates (episcopalism). As they saw it, the Jesuits were usurping their functions.

The Society of Jesus, it was held, utilised this usurpation to spread a doctrine of its own which was often completely contrary to what the bishop was teaching and causing to be taught to children in his diocesan catechism. The Bishop of Tarragona, in Spain, spoke of 'Jesuitical subversion', referring to the populations whom the members of the Society were separating from their pastors.[11] Village people certainly lacked any taste for joining in the theological debates between the Jesuits and their opponents. But they were well aware of the different ways in which their behaviour was judged when, after confessing to their natural pastor, they confessed to some Jesuit who was passing through. As the counsel given them was not always the same in both cases, and the parishioners would then reproach their priest, who, they considered, had shown excessive strictness, the bishops were led to think, like the Archbishop of Toledo at the end of the eighteenth century, that the doctrine of the Society of Jesus was an 'invitation to dispute'.[12]

[9] Bonnard, *Le Vénérable Père Antoine-Sylvestre Receveur*, p. 177.
[10] *Nouvelles ecclésiastiques, Tables*, vol. I, 1, p. 755.
[11] Saugnieux, *Les Jansénistes*, p. 286.   [12] *Ibid.*, p. 255.

Jean-Marie Vianney, as a young parish priest at Ars, near Lyons, often encountered this sort of situation in the 1820s. During the proceedings for his canonisation one of his former parishioners told how the Curé d'Ars regularly refused her absolution for going every year to dance 'at the patronal festival at Mizérieux', adding: 'If you don't stop going to the dance you are damned!' 'My mother', the witness went on, 'asked if I might make my confession elsewhere. "As you wish", he replied, "but I would rather that she should fail to do her Easter duty than that she make her confession elsewhere."' Of those who went, secretly, to obtain absolution from a priest who was passing through, or in a neighbouring village, M. Vianney simply said that they were going 'in search of a passport to Hell'.[13] We can understand that parish priests of the late eighteenth and early nineteenth centuries, who were not all saints like the Curé d'Ars, must often have felt irritation at the outsiders who sought to take their place. Where they were able, as in the Empire in Joseph II's time, they caused the outsiders' activities to be banned, as 'insulting to parish priests perfectly capable of instructing the people.'[14] As for the bishops, they no longer tolerated any missionaries but those whom they authorised to carry out a particular task.

This was the case in Bavaria, where the Jesuits who, in the middle of the eighteenth century, undertook catechetic missions, did this in fulfilment of very precise instructions from the diocesan authorities and under their strict control. The same applied in Spain, at the end of Father Pedro Calatayud's career, and in southern Italy in the time of Alfonso de Liguori. Many in those days were the bishops who thought of the diocesan priests trained in their seminaries, and wholly subject to them, as the ones who should carry out the task formerly left to the religious. One might suppose that this arrangement was such as to satisfy everyone. However, in practice, the missionaries' freedom of action was annulled. Their itinerary, the time to be devoted to each village, the nature and content of the teaching they were to impart, all were carefully defined in an instruction which was given them by the Vicar-General before they set out, and their conformity to which was checked on their return, against the report which they had to render to the bishop's chancellery.[15] This was very different from the three, four or six weeks that Vincent de Paul and Jean Eudes had freely allowed themselves in accordance with what they knew of a place's requirements, and the specific orientation they gave to their teaching on the basis of the needs they had identified.

[13] Boutry, Philippe, 'Le curé d'Ars confesseur', *La Maison-Dieu*, 167, 1986, pp. 70–1.
[14] Moreau, 'Les missions intérieures', p. 259.
[15] Cf. above, chapter 10.

Henceforth, a mission might be perceived by the population more as a tour of inspection carried out on the bishop's behalf than as an apostolic function. As for the catechism lessons, during the few days that the emissary of higher authority was present these became mere series of questions on doctrine which sometimes had a smell of the Inquisition about them. When he was sent to Almonte, Father Calatayud was shocked at what he found. 'The ignorance [is] lamentable', he wrote.[16] In those parts of Andalusia 'the ordinary people, especially the shepherds, day-labourers and share-croppers, live in the greatest ignorance of doctrine'. The parish priests were to blame, for they were just as ignorant as their flocks, incapable of preaching, and 'reduced to reading the catechism to their parishioners on holy days'.[17] The solution lay in firm warnings to be given to the clergy to make them finish their training and bring them to a proper performance of their task. The priests must then examine all the faithful 'on their doctrine, before they do their Easter duty . . . for he is penitent in name only who is examined merely on his knowledge of the Creed, the Commandments and the mystery of the Trinity.'[18] Without further delay Father Calatayud got down to work with his team. 'It was a great consolation', he added, 'to see how, in their houses, at all hours, and even in the fields, people were questioning each other on points of Christian doctrine, with many families coming together for that purpose.'[19] In Bavaria, the well-controlled practice of the catechetic missions ensured that these excesses were avoided, especially as, through the protracted activity of the Jesuits, in the towns and villages, the faithful were, of course, no longer ignorant of Catholic doctrine. Eventually, however, the peasants became irritated at being treated as yokels incapable of thought. In the 1780s it was increasingly difficult to secure the presence of children at the lessons, let alone that of their parents. When a missionary complained about this to the authorities, the latter fobbed him off with sympathetic words without having any intention of taking action against the offenders.[20] One of Father Gruber's last reports, in 1782, bears all the marks of an admission of defeat. At Cham, near the border with Bohemia, this Jesuit had to hold out in the pulpit against a turbulent crowd that showed its discontent by shouts and gestures. From some villages he had to withdraw for lack of an audience, while in others he found only a few women ready to hear him. 'I thought', he wrote, 'that, given the sixteen years I have been travelling about the diocese [of Regensburg], I was

---

[16] BN, Madrid, MSS, 4503, fo. 233vo (Almonte, between Huelva and Seville), 1759.
[17] *Ibid.*, fo. 121–121vo (Ecija, north-east of Seville), 1758.
[18] *Ibid.*, fo. 121vo.   [19] *Ibid.*, fo. 233vo – 234.
[20] Schrems, *Die religiöse Volks- und Jugendunterweisung*, pp. 265–6.

known to all, and I had visited this sector twice already, but on my third visit, despite the letters I sent ahead to announce my coming, I received only one reply.'[21] Discouragement shows through those lines.

It happened that missionaries found themselves up against actual expressions of hostility. In one place in Franche-Comté, a region with the reputation of loyalty to Catholicism, some parishioners ambushed the priests who were coming to instruct them, and gave them a thrashing, while in another they organised a counter-mission in the form of a play. The chronicler who reports the incident does not say whether, perchance, the play in question was *Le Mariage de Figaro*, which at the date when this occurred, 1788, would endow the incident with even greater significance . . .[22] Thirty years earlier, at Neufchâtel, in Normandy, Jesuits had been received with jeers and repeated shouts of 'Portugal oranges!' at the time when, in fact, they had just been expelled from that country.[23]

Ecclesiastics' distrust of missionaries was thus accompanied by a comparable movement on the part of the laity which could sometimes take the form of brutal rejection. One must not, however, misunderstand what this meant. During one of his last catechetic missions in Bavaria, in 1784, Father Gruber recognised in his audience a group of young villagers who had been present at his explanations on an earlier occasion. He asked them why they had come. 'Ah!' they said, 'it's because that was a long time ago and we can't remember anything at all.' The Father led them into the house where he was staying and, as he writes, 'taught them to perform the devotions of a confraternity.'[24] The catechetic mission was losing its effectiveness, and was being replaced by the Confraternity of Christian Doctrine, run by a group of youngsters. Basically, the main criticism addressed to the missions concerned the constraint which some missionaries imposed on the minds of the faithful. In the age of Enlightenment everyone wanted to go to God in his own way.

The Christianity of the Enlightenment at Everyman's level

At the end of his long career as historian of the Church, theologian and priest of an important parish in Modena, Lodovico Antonio Muratori (1672–1750) wrote a devotional work aimed at all the faithful, the most

---

[21] BZAR, O.A-Gen.97, 'Stiftung einer Katechetischen Mission', item 34, 2 fos. (report for 1782).

[22] Bergier, *Histoire de Beaupré*, pp. 184–5.

[23] *Nouvelles ecclésiastiques, Tables*, vol. I, 1, p. 768.

[24] BZAR. O.A-Gen.97, 'Stiftung einer Katechetischen Mission', item 63 (report for 1784).

learned and the most humble alike. *Della regolata divozione dei Cristiani*, published posthumously in Venice in 1766, was, in its way, a spiritual testament, and revealed what constituted the heart of religion for the man who was perhaps the most eminent Enlightenment figure in Catholic Europe.

Does God want us to resist the promptings of unbridled lust, of anger, of gluttony, of vengefulness? . . . Is this not for our benefit? . . . It all comes down to ordaining what the laws of nature themselves require for our well-being, and non-observance of which leads to our detriment or to a diminution of man's temporal happiness. We are foolish, therefore, if we do not acknowledge that God, in obliging us to obey His commandments, wills only our good, and we are unjust and ungrateful if, instead of thanking Him, we complain of the strictness of His laws. They conduce solely to rendering us happy in this life and blissful for all eternity in the next.[25]

In these words, understandable by everyone, was not only the language of the Enlightenment – 'well-being', 'nature', 'happiness' – but, even more, its spirit. The idea that this world below, far from being a 'vale of tears', might be already, for the Christian who follows God's commandments, the antechamber to Paradise was a new thought, full of hope, and which, at the same time, called for effort. Hope, moreover, was at the heart of old Muratori's discourse. It was there, doubtless, that his thinking reached its culmination in clarity and strength. 'By the word "hope"', he wrote, 'I mean the confidence possessed by the Christian that he will come to enjoy the highest good, which is God, through God's supreme kindness and through the merits of Jesus Christ our Lord, and also that he will obtain from the same God the means to reach that end.'[26] He adds:

We ought to hold it as an article of faith that God's mercy will be forever greater beyond comparison than anything that the wickedness of all men can possibly amount to. For which reason, while great sinners who repent may very properly go about with bowed heads as they remember their so great offences committed against God and the lamentable irregularity of their past lives, they must not doubt the immense goodness of Him who has called them back to His fold. Can we doubt the power of Him to whom nothing is impossible? Or the will of Him who likes to be named the Father of Mercies?[27]

He demonstrates this in a sudden flash, in a Vision of Judgment that is the exact opposite of Michelangelo's:

It is indeed true that remembrance of our sins ought not to be banished from our hearts . . . But this should not be at all allowed to give rise in us to bad moods of

---

[25] Muratori, Lodovico Antonio, *Della regolata divozione dei Cristiani* (*Opere Tutte*, vol. VI, Arezzo, 1768), p. 64.
[26] *Ibid.*, p. 96.   [27] *Ibid.*, p. 103.

melancholy and anxious scruples . . . That could only tend to cool the faithful in their love and service of God . . . In fact, the Lord wishes to be served with gladness of heart, as He has told us in many places in His divine Scriptures . . . We shall see, yes, we shall see, if one day, through God's mercy, we arrive in Paradise, a far greater number of penitent sinners that of innocent persons admitted to that glory.[28]

This message of hope he deduced from his faith, which he summed up thus: 'Above all we should frequently remind ourselves that we believe in life everlasting. This is the ultimate end of man.'[29] What does this religion which is so pure and bright require from man? One thing only: love.

In the love of God and of our neighbour and in our veneration of and confidence in the Mediator between God and mankind, Jesus Christ, consists the primary, the essential and, I would almost say, all the solid devotion and piety of Christians. This is what is prescribed to us in the sacred books of the New Law, what was taught by the Saints and what also is recommended today by all our wise spiritual directors. With this the Christian can be saved, and without it no other devotion can take its place. Consequently, if anyone should be found to advise the faithful to spend the greater part of their devotion on what are only matters of counsel, while neglecting that which is more important, and a matter of precept, necessary for salvation, such a person would be disturbing the beautiful harmony of Christ's religion.[30]

This is indeed 'the true devotion' which has for its chief enemy that exaggerated piety, almost idolatry, directed towards the Virgin and the Saints which distracts the faithful from what is essential, namely, Christ. It is not an ideal accessible only to educated persons, it is for everyone. He writes:

As for the ignorant people, they ought at least to know the Apostles' Creed, and this not in Latin but taught to them in the vernacular, so that the mind understands what the tongue is saying. The rough folk should learn that there is a God, one in essence and in three persons, and that this God . . . will reward the good . . . and punish the wicked and impenitent . . . and that the Son of God, having become man, and called by us Jesus Christ, died to save us all and by His merits to obtain from His heavenly Father forgiveness of our sins if we truly repent. And that this same Lord, out of admirable graciousness and love, comes to be really and personally present in the Sacrament of the Altar. The Christian ought also to know the other sacraments of the Church. As regards the speculative dogmas of religion, the aim of the ignorant must be to believe firmly all that the Catholic Church believes and detest whatever she condemns. As for the moral dogmas, however, that is to say, knowledge of what we call sin and what causes us to lose the grace of God . . . every Christian ought to learn God's Ten Commandments, the mortal sins and the five Precepts of the Church . . . *With the help of these first principles, by the light of reason,* and by hearkening to the

[28] *Ibid.*, p. 102.   [29] *Ibid.*, p. 94.   [30] *Ibid.*, p. 102.

Christian catechism and the preachers of God's words, even they who cannot read can acquire light sufficient for them to discern what is sinful, though in doubtful cases they ought honestly to seek the advice of their respective pastors or other wise directors of conscience.[31]

Thus the humble men and women of the fields were also invited to practise a reason-guided Christianity.

Muratori had fully shown his esteem for the great missionary Paolo Segneri Junior. In the work already quoted, he writes: 'Because they are adapted to the capacity of any listener, the sermons of the Apostolic Missionaries bring forth more fruit than all the over-subtle discourses of the most famous orators.'[32] But in Paolo Segneri's own time he warned the missionary against exaggerated devotions which risked diverting the faithful from what was essential.[33] All the more would he have opposed those missionaries of the end of the eighteenth century whose sole concern was to get people to recite the catechism word for word. Similarly, his work was a real antidote to the sermons of those who were convinced that fear of Hell alone opened the way to conversion. As for Jansenism, he was poles apart from thought exacerbated by fear of 'the excessive sternness of our God'. Muratori drew his readers into a different path, that of reconciliation of religion with the world, or rather of union between the development of the individual, morality and Christianity. These three objectives become but one in this spiritual guide wherein the Christianity of the Enlightenment finds expression in completest form. Nevertheless, one should make no mistake here. What is meant by this expression has nothing to do with the disgust with religion felt by persons who do not want to be held in check by dogmas that are perplexing to common sense or by a restrictive morality. Muratori's religion is wholly founded upon Christ. 'If the Christian be asked', he writes, 'what is the reason for his hope, he should boldly answer, like the Apostle: '*Christus Jesus spes nostra*, Jesus Christ is our hope.'[34]

At the very end of the eighteenth century and the beginning of the next the Bavarian theologian Johann-Michael Sailer developed, for the benefit of priests and of the ordinary faithful, this idea of the centrality of Christ in the doctrine of salvation. 'Through Christ God had become reconciled with the world', he wrote. 'But this is not just what Christianity teaches, it is fundamental to Christianity and not merely that, it is its very basis. It is the basis that contains or holds up all the rest.'[35] Proceeding from this principle, Sailer developed his idea by

---

[31] *Ibid.*, p. 92.   [32] *Ibid.*, pp. 124–5.   [33] Cf. above, p. 207.
[34] Muratori, *Della divozione regolata*, p. 97.
[35] Sailer, Johann-Michael, *Geistliche Texte*, ed. by Konrad Baumgartner, Munich and Zurich, Verlag Schnell und Steiner, 1981, p. 15.

freely using compact, sometimes elliptic formulations, so as, like his friends the Bavarian *Illuminati*, to make it better realised that, in everything which was with difficulty laid open, there remained an element of mystery. 'God is in Christ, the Salvation of the world', was one of his aphorisms.[36] This could be understood as a message of hope addressed to all men, similar to the universal salvation preached by John Wesley in great popular gatherings, even if the commentary offered by Sailer remained within the limits of Roman orthodoxy.[37] This elating vision of man's destiny on earth and beyond it fitted in well with the thinking of the Enlightenment and, like that, took account of the realities of life on earth. Just as Voltaire ended his *Candide* with the precept: 'let us cultivate our garden', so Johann-Michael Sailer devoted many homilies, chapters in his treatise on pastoral work, and, above all, his famous *Complete Prayer-Book for Catholic Christians* (Munich, 1803), to guiding ordinary believers in the various stages of their existence. The days of the week, Sundays, the annual festivals, marriage, family life, illnesses, old age and the approach of death were all so many circumstances serving to recall to readers their duties to their neighbour and the fact that their life, present and to come, was 'in God's hands.'[38]

It is hard to define precisely the extent to which this Enlightenment Christianity reached the faithful in town and country. Did it enjoy, in the Catholic countries, a means of transmission comparable to the *Popular-philosophie* of the German Protestant countries? Did a work like the *Noth- und Hülfsbüchlein* have an equivalent – even if only in the form of pious almanachs – in the regions which were still loyal to the Roman Church?[39] Some current research may enable us to answer this question. All the same, it is right to mention that, even if they had not themselves read Muratori's *Della regolata divozione* or Sailer's *Gebetbuch*, the countryfolk might be aware of their content through the sermons of their parish priest, or of preachers passing through, who did not fail to seek inspiration, in their homilies, from some passage in a well-known prayer-book. Now, the teaching which emerged from these works showed some discordances with that of the Council of Trent. The title that Muratori gave to his work clearly showed that he was criticising a certain conception of piety. On reading it one soon realised that this conception, commonly called 'baroque', was the most widespread form in the post-Tridentine period. The grand definition of the Church given by Sailer ('an assembly of all the living, scattered throughout the world,

---

[36] *Ibid.*   [37] *Ibid.*, pp. 20, 34.   [38] *Ibid.*, p. 132.
[39] Siegert, Reinhart, *Aufklärung und Volkslektüre, Exemplarisch dargestellt an Rudolph Zacharias Becker und seinem 'Noth- und Hülfsbüchlein'*, Frankfurt-am-Main, Archiv für Geschichte des Buchwesens, 19, 1978.

who have been anointed in Christ's name and fight for the Kingdom of God, together with all the crowned victors who are already there') was close to Luther's.[40] Muratori's profession of faith: 'Jesus Christ is my hope', sounds like the opening words of a Lutheran chorale. The 'works' of the Christian, seen as essential in the process of salvation by the Council of Trent, were here ignored as also were the role of the saints as intercessors and the place of the Church as an institution. Neither Muratori nor Sailer, who became Bishop of Regensburg, could be suspected of Protestant sympathies or even of acting in favour of reconciliation between all Christians. For them it was, as in general for the Catholicism of the Enlightenment, a matter of concern to free themselves and all the faithful from the constraints imposed by the Council of Trent, of a will to transcend so as, in their view, to make possible a deepening of religious life. It is important to note that they did not suppose that they could promote this change without acting upon the Christian people in ways which must include questioning the instructions and habits of piety inherited from the missionaries of the baroque period.

The ways of the Spirit

In a period when the poet Novalis was speaking of the 'regeneration' of religion through a 'second Reformation' or even through the 'profound conception of a new Messiah', the break with the past could take much sharper forms both without and within the Church.[41] The historian Marina Caffiero has analysed this prophetic and millenarist trend in Mediterranean Europe at the very end of the eighteenth century. The first signs of it appeared in the 1770s and 1780s. They were considerably amplified, however, through the real traumatism caused by the French Revolution in such profoundly Catholic countries as Spain and Italy.[42] The woes of the papacy and of Rome were sometimes interpreted as signs of a curse laid upon the new 'Babylon' (Rome) which had betrayed its mission. At other times, however, and much more often, these events appeared as Heaven's punishment for the impiety of the eighteenth century, which had surpassed anything previously seen. This was the view of the ex-Jesuit Alfonso Muzzarelli, expressed in his work *On the causes of the present evils and of the future evils to be dreaded* (1792). He saw

---

[40] Sailer, *Geistliche Texte*, p. 30.
[41] Novalis, *Fragments*, ed. Paul Gorceix, Paris, José Corti, 1992, pp. 253–6.
[42] Caffiero, Marina, 'La fine del mondo. Profezia, Apocalisse e Millennio nell' Italia rivoluzionaria', *La Chiesa italiana e la rivoluzione francese*, ed. Daniele Menozzi, Bologna, Ed. Dehoniane, 1990, pp. 287–357.

salvation only in the reconstructing of traditional Christian society.[43] These ideas circulated, especially in the Rome of 1796, in a city which seemed to be living its last days, with realisation of the most frightful prophecies of the Book of Revelation. Processions of penitents, public supplications and preachings followed one another, while news was passed around of appearances by the Virgin or of extraordinary miracles.[44] In these circumstances missions had their place, but their aim was no longer the same. It was not now a question of teaching but rather of expiating collective offences, or of exorcising evil through a demonstration of piety on as large a scale as possible. These missions could also, in this climate of exaltation and fear, take the form they had had in the heroic age of St Vincent Ferrer – that of crowds of people thronging together to listen avidly to the words of a man of God, and sometimes just to see and touch him. The almost prophetic aspect of the original mission reappeared in a time when everything seemed to be collapsing.

The Spanish Capuchin Diego-José of Cadiz (1743–1801) was not brilliant intellectually. While still young he had been given in the convent the nickname (a bad omen for someone who wanted to preach) of *el borrico mudo* (the dumb ass).[45] But wonders multiplied around him. One day, the crowd accompanying him saw a heavenly triangle appear above his head. An excellent illustration of the Trinity, this sign began the revival of the confraternities bearing that name.[46] The miracle produced by the Gospels placed on a sick man and read aloud proved the divine origin of the book.[47] The custom he had of preaching the forgiveness of insults while holding the monstrance was a way of showing that it was Jesus Christ who asked us to forgive.[48] But what above all contributed to his extraordinary success throughout southern Spain was the 'inspired' character of his preaching. His 'natural' ignorance – which was perhaps exaggerated by those who extolled him – signified that each of his sermons seemed to be altogether the work of the Holy Spirit. This began in Malaga in 1773. Ignorant as he was, he took it into his head to combat both the English Protestants and the French *philosophes*. A hard task. After having striven greatly, he found himself, when before the lectern of the cathedral pulpit, quite tongue-tied. A text from St Paul suddenly appeared before his eyes and, 'driven by the Spirit', he commented upon this for two whole hours. 'What confusion was mine!' he wrote later to his director of conscience, 'How cruel the torture of my mind while I was speaking, not aware either of

[43] *Ibid.*, pp. 310–14.   [44] *Ibid.*, pp. 302–6.
[45] Damase de Loisey, *Le Bienheureux Diego-Joseph de Cadix*, p. 16.
[46] *Ibid.*, pp. 130–1.   [47] *Ibid.*, pp. 74–7.   [48] *Ibid.*, p. 231.

where I was or of whither I was going.'[49] This was indeed the miracle which soon made Diego-José famous all over Southern Spain. When he opened his mouth it was not he who spoke but the Spirit of God. 'You see', he said to a religious of his own order, after a sermon, 'there is nothing of me in all this. God has brought about this great wonder in me, poor ignorant creature that I am, so as the better to shine forth his power.'[50]

In the midst of the Enlightenment and the triumph of Reason, even in the Church, Diego-José of Cadiz looked like a sign of contradiction. He was the saint of 'inborn knowledge'. Thereafter, miracles, prophecies and wonders of various kinds were almost to be expected. The Spirit of God was in him and ruled him totally. The very places to which he went on mission were pointed out to him supernaturally. If he did not expect to achieve great results as a missionary, this was doubtless because God's intentions were different. When he set out for Galicia in 1794 he said to his companion: 'Let us go then, as pilgrims, to Santiago-de-Compostela. We shall have the joy of venerating the relics of the great Apostle and we shall win the indulgences that Holy Church offers to the faithful in that blessed place.'[51] This walk to Santiago decided on, in the year of the Terror in France, by the greatest missionary of the eighteenth century's final decade, surprises us. It shows that the mission was changing in these new conditions. The people had greater need of witness than of preaching and the catechism. Benedict Joseph Labre (1748–83) was not a preacher nor even a religious. He was content to remain 'constantly under the direction of Grace, so as to let himself be led by the lights and movements of the Holy Spirit.'[52] The Holy Spirit took him along the roads of Europe to the most famous shrines, especially to Our Lady of Loretto and to Rome, whither he went as a model pilgrim, carrying nothing, begging his bread and praying continually, in the most profound meditation. Sometimes he would emerge from his meditative state, and then could be heard announcing, like a new Jeremiah, the impending end of a world that was to be wholly given up to the flames by God's wrath.[53] In so doing Labre acted in conformity with his mission, which was, according to a contemporary, 'to denounce the ostentation and pomp of Rome, to preach Christian humility, to censure the slackness of the clergy and the Church's luxury, and to teach evangelical poverty and mortification.'[54]

[49] *Ibid.*, pp. 67–9.   [50] *Ibid.*, p. 159.   [51] *Ibid.*, pp. 142–4.
[52] Plongeron, Bernard, 'Benoît-Joseph Labre au miroir de l'hagiographie janséniste en France (1783–1789)', in *Benoît-Joseph Labre: errance et sainteté. Histoire d'un culte 1783–1983*, ed. Yves-Marie Hilaire, Paris, Cerf, pp. 25–54, at p. 39.
[53] Caffiero, *'La fine del mondo'*, p. 300.
[54] *Ibid.*, p. 349.

This sort of old-time missionary, ceaselessly covering great distances and preaching by his mere example, was more common in the great plains of Russia. There were still a lot of them in the nineteenth century, such as that pilgrim, a simple peasant, who was transformed by reading the little collection of texts from the Fathers of the Greek Church, published in 1794 under the title *Philokalia*. Walking with downcast eyes, he repeated continually 'the prayer of Jesus', which he had learnt one day from a blind man he met in an almshouse. The man told him:

Begin to put the prayer of Jesus into your heart and to bring it out whenever you breathe, that is, when you breathe in, say or think: "Lord Jesus Christ", and when you breathe out, say: "Have pity on me". If you do that often enough and long enough you will soon feel a slight discomfort in your heart, but gradually a salutary warmth will appear there. With God's aid you will in this way achieve a constant state of prayer within your heart. Above all, though, beware of any representations, any images that may enter your mind while you are praying. Drive away all imaginings, for the Fathers command us, so that we may not fall into illusion, to keep our minds free of all forms during prayer.

What was essential was that prayer must be as continual as heartbeats, that it must set the heart 'wholly afire with the memory of Lord Jesus.'[55] Such was this simple and fundamental prayer, 'inspired' in the physiological sense of the word, which was the sole object of the Russian pilgrim's mission.

The many attacks to which missions were subjected at the end of the eighteenth century were concerned much more with a certain procedure practised since the Counter-Reformation of the sixteenth century than with apostolic activity in itself. That activity was in full swing, taking a variety of forms, from the Confraternities of Christian Doctrine to the prophesyings of men like Benedict Joseph Labre, with an increasingly important role played by books of piety. Two facts stand out, however. On the one hand, lay persons were becoming more and more important either as initiators of particular enterprises or groups or as indispensable supporters of such activity. On the other, the flagging observable in traditional missions in no way signified a decline in the religious life of the faithful. Much more were they being invited to deepen it, sometimes in critical fashion, by reading works by great spiritual writers and profound theologians of the age like Lodovico Antonio Muratori and, later, Johann-Michael Sailer.

---

[55] *Récits d'un pèlerin russe*, translated and presented by Jean Laloy, new edition, Boudry (Switzerland) and Paris, La Baconnière/Seuil, 1978, pp. 145–6, 181.

12 From the religion of the poor to the religion of modern times

In the 1780s a bishop contrasted the disaffection of the urban elites who no longer even went to church with the fidelity of the humble people of small towns and villages. 'Our countrysides, above all, are inhabited by true believers', he wrote, 'who serve you [Lord] in the uprightness of their hearts.' And he added: 'It is by them and for them that your holy religion will maintain itself.'[1]

The constancy and fervour of the humble people implied official recognition by the church authorities of the religion which had been practised and lived in the rural areas ever since the missionaries arrived to teach it. But was it very reasonable, after the attacks of which the missionaries had been the target at the end of the eighteenth century, to expect support from particular churches? Rome alone could decide, under pressure from the faithful. A new image of the Church thus began to emerge.

A God close at hand

The decision taken by the Holy See in 1765 to authorise the celebration of a feast-day of the Sacred Heart was, in a sense, the first sign of official recognition given to the religion of feeling which had been spread so widely in the country districts, all through the eighteenth century, by the missionaries.[2] It showed plainly that this devotion which the Jansenists and many 'enlightened' Christians were prone to regard as a manifestation of the quasi-heretical religion that they attributed to the Jesuits was henceforth endorsed by the Pope and the entire Church – 'their feast of the Sacred Heart of Jesus', the compiler of the *Nouvelles ecclésiastiques*

[1] Order by Mgr Toussaint Duvernin, Suffragan Bishop of Strasburg, Lent 1782, quoted in Châtellier, *Tradition chrétienne*, p. 409.
[2] Taveneaux, René, *Le Jansénisme en Lorraine*, pp. 683–6. *Dict.spir.*, vol. II, cols. 1035–7. It was only in 1856 that a decree of the Congregation of Rites prescribed celebration throughout Christendom of the Feast of the Sacred Heart, on the Friday following the octave of the Blessed Sacrament.

had once written, which the Jesuit fathers exalt 'above that of the Blessed Sacrament, assuring salvation for those who communicate or sacrifice, on that day, to *this* Sacred Heart, in their Church'.[3]

The consecration thus conferred by Pope Clement XIII strengthened still more the current of affection and piety directed towards a Christ suffering through love of mankind. The Passionist order made themselves the special propagators of this devotion. They repeated the prayers – in the form of a heart's effusions – of their founder, Paul of the Cross:

> Thy sufferings, beloved God, are proofs of thy love,
> Thy crosses are my heart's delight.[4]

Love of Christ became a message of hope. It was the herald of salvation for whoever answered love with love. A God who had so loved mankind could not wish for their destruction, their damnation. What was already perceptible in Marguerite-Marie Alacoque found more precise expression in the middle of the eighteenth century. At the beginning of the nineteenth century Gaspare del Bufalo went still further by forming a congregation of missionaries, under the title of the Precious Blood, whose purpose was to spread everywhere unlimited confidence in the power to save possessed by the Redeemer's blood (1815).[5] In the constitution of the women's order which was formed with the same title these words appear: 'The nuns will have a profound devotion for the inestimable price of our redemption, the precious blood of Jesus Christ, and will strive to arouse in others love, tenderness, affection and gratitude for so inestimable a treasure' (1857).[6] Meditation and prayer then acquired their full significance.

It was not a matter of indifference that the theologian who broke most sharply with rigorism, Alfonso de Liguori, had begun his career as a missionary by founding those schools of prayer, the 'evening chapels'.[7] The two things went together: the greater the love of Christ among the penitents, the greater the mildness of the priest who heard their confessions. But what was characteristic only of certain priests in the eighteenth century became conduct adopted by the majority of them when Pope Leo XII, in his encyclical *Caritate Christi* (1825), called on the clergy to be less stern in their administration of the Sacrament of Penitence and not to abuse delay in granting absolution.[8] What had been the general practice of the missionaries, finding its finished form in

---

[3] *Nouvelles ecclésiastiques, Tables*, vol. I, p. 670 (1731).
[4] *Dict.spir.*, vol. XII, col. 546.
[5] *Catho*, vol. IV, col. 1765 (Gaspare del Bufalo, 1786–1836).
[6] *Dict.spir.*, vol. XIV, col. 332 (Institute of the Precious Blood).
[7] Cf. above, chapter 4.
[8] Boutry, *Prêtres et paroisses*, p. 414.

Alfonso de Liguori's *Moral Theology*, became almost the rule for the whole Church. The Curé d'Ars, who had been so strict at the beginning of his career, took account, as the years passed and pilgrims flocked to his confessional, of how impossible it was to keep to the requirements, laid down by the old writers, which he had learnt from his teachers.[9] When this was mentioned to him, he sighed: 'Can I really be strict with people who come from so far away, who undertake so much expense and sacrifice and who are obliged to hide in order to come here?'[10] Though shut up from morning till evening in his confessional at Ars, M. Vianney was experiencing a situation such as had often been familiar to the Capuchins and Jesuits of the seventeenth and eighteenth centuries, namely, that one could not be both a missionary – which he was, even though his mission was 'stationary' – and rigorous in one's examination of consciences.[11] Above all, perhaps, the evolution of the forms of piety in the eighteenth century – revealed in its very title, *Caritate Christi*, by the encyclical of 1825 – led him more and more to feel that he represented Christ the compassionate. Moreover, it was because they realised this that the faithful flocked to him.

When we read the notes or letters received by M. Vianney we perceive that it was not only the Sacrament in the forms prescribed by the Council of Trent that pilgrims came for but also in order to find a listener, an adviser, a refuge. '*Monsieur*', wrote one woman, 'please allow me to write to you to ask in God's name that you talk to me, it is in the order of God that you give me this consolation, I have been here several days, I am greatly at fault. Where we live I have need of consolation, I have lost everything, belongings and child, I have had many other great misfortunes, my sorrow worsens all the time, I can no longer put up with my suffering, death would be better than such a life. Please, *Monsieur*, do not refuse to talk to someone so afflicted as I am' (1845).[12] A mother wrote: '*Monsieur le curé*, pray for Charles, he is almost cured. One more effort with God, I beg you, all his letters urge me to pester you to pester God. He beseeches you, he has every confidence in you and will come to thank you as soon as he is well. Pray, then, to God, pray for him also to the Holy Virgin and to St Philomena . . . One more effort with God, pray, do it again, the sick man is getting better' (1847).[13] The father confessor thus became the preferred intercessor, in accordance, more-

[9] Fourrey, Mgr René, *Jean-Marie Vianney, Curé d'Ars. Vie authentique*, Paris, Desclée de Brouwer, 1981, pp. 51–73.
[10] Quoted by Boutry, 'Le curé d'Ars confesseur', p. 77.
[11] The expression 'stationary mission' (*mission immobile*) is from Boutry, *ibid.*, p. 73.
[12] Quoted in Boutry, Philippe, 'Le mal, le malin, le malheur. Le curé d'Ars face à la souffrance', *Le Monde alpin et rhodanien*, 14/2–4, 1986, pp. 59–81, at pp. 68–9.
[13] *Ibid.*, p. 69.

over, with an impeccable logic which showed that the applicant knew her catechism well: since the priest forgives in Christ's name, why should he not also heal in his name?

Another letter deserves attention because it bears witness to both continuities and differences in relation to earlier periods. A farmer wrote in 1858:

'*M. le curé*, Divine Providence has been pleased, during the last four years, to afflict me through my cattle. Over a period of twelve years I bought nine cows, of which the first four brought me some benefit, but in the last four years all of them that have entered our byre have brought us ruin . . . Dear sir, I have examined my conscience to see if I owed something to the good souls in Purgatory. I have done more than double what my late parents ordered, but I still feel that there is some good soul in Purgatory who has the right to expect something from me, since our household is under this calamity. Dear pastor, if it has pleased God to give you some light on our situation, please, dear pastor of afflicted souls, tell me of it.[14]

The priest-missionary was 'the pastor of afflicted souls'. Placed between Heaven and Earth, he was able to cast an eye upon the great book wherein are recorded entries into and departures from Purgatory. He alone, doubtless, possessed the means to find his way through this very difficult book-keeping, celestial and familiar ('our situation') which poor human beings, bent over the soil, were unable to interpret. They were, at least, no longer reduced to the makeshift diagnoses and chance therapies of some Jesuit or Capuchin who happened to be passing through. Henceforth, thanks to the Curé d'Ars, the solution was in sight. A rational confidence is apparent in what was written by this solid peasant who knows that God is, after all, not so far away.

He is even less remote for the authors of the thousands of prayers hastily scribbled in the books placed at the disposal of present-day visitors to shrines of pilgrimage.[15] These appeals for help in all the woes of life, both immense and laughable, are akin, if less poetic, to the song of the black slave in America who trudges along beside Jesus, in the negro spiritual *Jesus on the waterside*:

> Heaven bell a-ring, I know de road,
> Heaven bell a-ring, I know de road,
> Heaven bell a-ring, I know de road,
> Jesus sittin' on de waterside.
>
> Do come along, do let us go,
> Do come along, do let us go,

[14] *Ibid.*, p. 72.
[15] Bonnet, Serge, *Prières secrètes des Français d'aujourd'hui*, Paris, Cerf, 1976.

> Do come along, do let us go,
> Jesus sittin' on de waterside.[16]

Since Jesus is there, it is from him that we must ask, before we follow him, forgiveness for our trespasses. Hence this song, in the form of a story of conversion:

> One day when I was walkin' along, Oh yes, Lord,
> De element opened an' de Love come down, Oh yes, Lord,
> I never shall forget dat day, Oh yes, Lord,
> When Jesus washed my sins away, Oh yes, Lord.[17]

While this hymn was being sung on the banks of the Mississippi, a missionary priest working in the outskirts of Turin was calling on the young people with whom he concerned himself to follow a God who was close to them. To be sure, John Bosco derived his message from sources other than those of America's blacks in the time of the War between the States. To the poor adolescents who surrounded him, however, he spoke a language that they, too, could understand. 'If Jesus is my friend and companion, I have nothing more to fear', he said in 1864.[18] The conclusion he drew from this was exactly the same as that of Father Jean Pichon, who, over a century earlier, had caused such a scandal.[19] 'If you now want to know what I wish', said John Bosco in 'a word at evening' in 1864, 'this is it: communicate every day. Spiritually? The Council of Trent says: *Sacramentaliter!* Accordingly . . . '[20] This time no blame followed. Bishops were beginning to say the same things. Through the missions, daily communion, with all that it implied in relations between man and God, had entered into the habits of the most zealous Catholics. Hitherto practically forbidden, it was now enjoined.[21]

From earth to heaven

Thereafter, everything that might bring man closer to God was strongly encouraged by Rome. This applied to the cults of intercession which had been so firmly rejected by the Protestant Reformation of the sixteenth century and, more recently, by the Jansenists and many theologians of the Enlightenment. One of the latter, an expert at the Pistoia synod of 1786, had said that 'enlightened and pious persons view with displeasure these silly tablets, called *toties quoties*, which are sometimes hung at the entrances to churches and which serve as lures to

---

[16] Chenu, Bruno, *Le Christ noir américain*, Paris, Desclée, 1984, p. 76.
[17] *Ibid.*, p. 74.
[18] Quoted by Francis Desramaut, *Don Bosco et la vie spirituelle*, Paris, Beauchesne, 1967, p. 94.
[19] Cf. above, chapter 7.   [20] Desramaut, *Don Bosco*, p. 142.   [21] *Ibid.*, pp. 142–3.

ignorant believers. According to the ridiculous sellers of these foolish things, we can obtain indulgence from them as many times as we wish.'[22] This meant disagreeing on an essential point with the Council of Trent, which had affirmed the existence of a treasury of merits of the saints into which the Church would dip for the benefit of sinners, whether living or dead (souls in Purgatory). This doctrine was the source of devotions that were widespread among the Christian people and which, in fact, had not ceased developing in the course of the eighteenth century, through the confraternities of All Souls, of the Good Death or of Souls in Purgatory.[23] The Popes solemnly confirmed the legitimacy of such pious practices by stating: 'The Communion of Saints is one of the articles of the Apostles' Creed, and from this communion we cannot without temerity exclude those pious souls, now deceased, who are not thereby separated from the mystical body of the Church but are also members thereof' (commentary on the bull *Auctorem fidei*, 1794, condemning the decisions of the Pistoia synod).[24]

The devotions to saints with powers of healing or intercession which had often been viewed askance by bishops in the eighteenth century were now held in honour with Rome's encouragement. In Naples in 1794, when Vesuvius erupted, the *Apostoliche missioni* organised a great mission of expiation, starting from the cathedral, with the statue of St Januarius (San Gennaro).[25] During the cholera epidemic of 1830 it was St Roch who, in Naples as in Montpellier, was the object of an extraordinarily fervent cult.[26] More bodies of martyrs were discovered in the catacombs.[27] The Curé d'Ars had a particular veneration for one of these 'new' saints, Philomena, whose relics he had succeeded in obtaining.[28] In Alsace the pilgrimage to St Odile, not much thought of by the Church authorities in the middle of the eighteenth century, was in great favour a century later.[29]

[22] Boutry, Philippe, 'Le bel automne de l'indulgence. 50,000 suppliques à l'âge de la Restauration (1814–1846)', *Provence historique*, 156, 1989, pp. 337–53, quoted pp. 340–1.

[23] Châtellier, *L'Europe des dévots*, pp. 220–6 (Eng.trans., pp. 204–10); Vovelle, *Vision de la mort*.

[24] Boutry, 'Le bel automne', p. 343.

[25] Rienzo, 'Il processo de Cristianizazione', p. 465.

[26] Cholvy, Gérard, and Hilaire, Yves-Marie, *Histoire religieuse de la France contemporaine*, 2 vols., Toulouse, Privat, vol. I, pp. 161–2.

[27] *Histoire de la France religieuse*, ed. Jacques Le Goff and René Rémond, vol. III, pp. 435–7.

[28] Fourrey, Jean-Marie Vianney, *Curé d'Ars*, pp. 166–9.

[29] Châtellier, *Tradition chrétienne*, p. 395; Epp, René, *Le Mouvement ultramontain dans l'église catholique en Alsace du XIXe siècle (1802–1870)*, 2 vols., Lille and Paris, Atelier de reproduction des thèses université Lille III and Librarie H. Champion, 1975, vol. II, p. 661a.

The Marian devotion had, thanks to the missionaries, developed steadily all through the eighteenth century. From Grignion de Montfort, who consecrated to her a famous collection of hymns, to Alfonso de Liguori, who wrote one of his best-known works in her honour (*Le glorie de Maria*), all were ardent devotees of Mary.[30] Redemptorist historians record that Alfonso's reputation of sanctity in the country districts of southern Italy began with the miracle at Foggia. When, in March 1731, he was invited to visit this little town in Apulia, to preach a novena in honour of the Virgin, she appeared to him, in the presence of the crowd. There was a miraculous picture in the church where Alfonso was preaching. It had been placed near the pulpit when he began his sermon. As the preacher spoke of the protection given by Mary, her portrait lit up and a spurt of light, like a ray of sunshine, shot from the picture to shine on Alfonso's face, which caused a veritable 'electrical commotion' in the assembly. Some people prayed aloud, others wept copiously and everyone cried out that a miracle had taken place.[31] Thanksgivings to the Virgin were more resonant than ever.

Villagers went to the mission reciting the litanies of the Virgin, especially of Our Lady of Loretto, which accompanied them as they marched behind the parish banner. When they reached the church where the exercises were to take place, the faithful began reciting their chaplet while awaiting the arrival of the other parishes. In order to make fast the piety of these people who were often exhausted by their long journey, Grignion de Montfort inserted, between the decades, some strophes from one of his hymns. They sang:

> Chrétiens, voulez-vous être heureux?
> Servez fidèlement Marie,
> Car elle est la porte des cieux
> Et le chemin de l'autre vie.
> C'est une mère de bonté,
> Personne n'en est rebuté.

> Christians, do you want to be happy?
> Serve Mary faithfully,
> For she is the gateway to heaven
> And the way to the other life.
> She is a kind mother
> No-one is rebuffed by her.[32]

---

[30] *Les Œuvres du [Bienheureux] de Montfort*, p. 133–83 (hymns to the Virgin); *Studia et subsidia de vita et operibus S. Alfonsi Mariae de Ligorio (1696–1787)*, Rome, Collegium S. Alfonso de Urbe, 1990, p. 509 (1750).

[31] *Histoire de saint Alphonse de Liguori*, pp. 57–61.

[32] *Les Œuvres du [Bienheureux] de Montfort*, p. 165 (hymn entitled 'The zealous devotee of Mary').

The doctrine according to which Mary is the only human being spared the consequences of original sin (hence the name 'the new Eve' which was often given her in the Baroque period) had long been widespread. In the eighteenth century, however, it had really taken off, thanks mainly to the Jesuits. In every town where they had a residence or a college there was a Marian congregation bearing the title 'of the Immaculate Conception'. Through their zeal, images of the Virgin crushing the serpent of evil were placed on church altars, over the doors of houses and even in public squares.[33] This cult, spread in this way, sometimes ended up being seen by the Jansenists as characteristic of 'the Jesuits' religion'. 'As directors of conscience to the Daughters of the Holy Sacrament in the Rue Cassette', we read in the *Nouvelles ecclésiastiques*, '[they] gave them the Immaculate Conception as the object of their worship. Maxims concerning this devotion were distributed by the nuns like passports to the other world and preservatives against all dangers and perils' (1737).[34] Comic details followed, aimed at mocking still further this new cult.

Sermon by Father Pepe in Naples on devotion to the Immaculate Conception of the Holy Virgin. Distribution by the Jesuit of little papers containing a Prayer of the Conception, which he gets sick people to eat in order to be cured; sermon every Saturday in the church in their college of the New Jesus, to announce two or three miracles worked during the week by these little papers, which are given to their chickens by the humble folk, entranced by the idea of getting lots of eggs. (1758)[35]

An unnecessary devotion with a tendency to superstition, spread by the Jesuits among the simple people of town and country – that was how many Catholics saw the Immaculate Conception at the end of the eighteenth century and at the beginning of the nineteenth.

The appearance of Mary Immaculate to Catherine Labouré in 1830, followed by the representation of this vision in the form of a miraculous medal which was circulated widely across Europe, helped to spread the cult further. It began to enjoy quasi-official recognition when, in Rome, the 'miracle' of the conversion of Marie-Alphonse Ratisbonne (1842) was ascribed to the Virgin whom Catherine had seen. Four years later came the appearances to some little illiterate shepherds at La Salette.[36] Pius IX's proclamation of the Immaculate Conception in 1854 was to some extent a victory of the humble folk. It conferred the status of a

---

[33] Châtellier, *L'Europe des dévots*, pp. 33, 177, 182–3 (Eng. trans., pp. 19, 161, 167).
[34] *Nouvelles ecclésiastiques, Tables*, vol. I, p. 683.
[35] *Ibid.*, pp. 752–3.
[36] *Histoire de la France religieuse*, vol. III, pp. 495–505.

dogma for the whole Church upon something they had already believed long since, upon a well-rooted devotion.[37]

The new dogma had another consequence. By encouraging the faithful to put their trust in intercession by the Virgin it confirmed the teaching of the missionaries of the second half of the eighteenth century on the importance of prayer.

It was in the patois of Lourdes, probably, that the rosary was recited by the Soubirous family in 1858, the year of the appearances.[38] The first fifteen appearances succeeded one another, in the manner of the Mysteries of the Virgin, like a wondrous introduction to the recitation of the chaplet. On 11 February (date of the first appearance), when Bernadette saw the white form in the grotto, she grasped her chaplet, but with her stiff arm she was unable to make the first movement of prayer. The apparition showed her how to begin, with a sweeping sign of the cross. It repeated this on the occasion of the fifteenth appearance (4 March), as though to demonstrate, this time before the huge crowd that had gathered, the essential place of this sign in the life of a Christian.[39] About the *Paternoster* and the *Ave Maria* the apparition said nothing. What point would there have been in an *explication de texte*? When the Russian pilgrim encountered a monk, he received this lesson from him: 'There is a beneficent power in the very words of the Gospel, for those words printed there were spoken by God Himself. It does not matter if you do not understand, just read with attention.'[40] It happened once however (on 1 March, the day of the fourth appearance) that the 'Lady' made Bernadette do something more. Suddenly, before everyone, she lifted up her chaplet 'to the level of her eyes.'[41] Was this to show the gathering how one ought to carry it, proudly, with raised arms, not shamefacedly, with lowered arms? The apparition said no more about the recitation of the rosary. When, however, during the sixteenth appearance, it announced who it was: 'I am the Immaculate Conception', this gave a supernatural value to everything it had previously taught.[42] The Virgin did not merely teach Bernadette the right way to say her chaplet. During the eighth appearance (24 February), she cried: 'Penitence!' and asked the young girl to 'climb up on your knees and kiss the ground, in penitence for sinners'.[43] Next day Bernadette

---

[37] Aubert, R., *Le Pontificat de Pie IX (1846–1878)*, Paris, Bloud et Gay, 1952 (Histoire de l'Eglise depuis les origines jusqu'à nos jours par Augustin Fliche et Victor Martin, 21), pp. 278–80.

[38] Laurentin, René, *Lourdes, récit authentique des apparitions*, Paris, Lethellieux, 1987, p. 38.

[39] *Ibid.*, p. 196.   [40] *Récits d'un pèlerin russe*, pp. 50–1.

[41] Laurentin, *Lourdes*, pp. 50–1.   [42] *Ibid.*, p. 225.

[43] *Ibid.*, pp. 118–19.

repeated her actions, obeyed the Lady's order to scrape away the mud in the grotto, and discovered a spring there.[44]

What is most astonishing to the historian is, perhaps, not what occurred in the grotto but what went on round about it. The strange thing was not the crowd – crowds often gather for no great reason. But these hundreds of people – a thousand, eventually – prayed along with Bernadette, each bringing out his or her chaplet and reciting it aloud. In some aspects, the gatherings at Massabielle continued a tradition. As we follow Bernadette climbing towards the grotto on her knees, kissing the ground again and again, and repeating after the Lady the word 'Penitence', a memory comes to mind of the Baroque missionaries, from Segneri to Calatayud. Here, though, there was no missionary, nor any priest either. The parish priest of Lourdes was mistrustful and even hostile. How could he not be? Did this backward girl who, at fourteen, had not yet been considered ready for her first communion, and who was ignorant even of the mystery of the Trinity, claim to communicate the wishes of the Holy Virgin?[45] This was the absolute contrary of what had been required of Christians since the Council of Trent. An ignorant girl was acting as guide. No preacher there, either, of course. But a supernatural presence was there – she revealed her name only at the sixteenth appearance – and directed the gathering through an intermediary. And this gathering, regardless of what may have been the original intentions of those present, became an assembly for prayer which felt that it had been invaded by the Holy Spirit. Carried forward by a rhythm, an increasing tension, reaching a paroxysm and then stopping short in expectation of the appearance, prayer resumed thereafter more calmly, as the crowd was either appeased or disappointed. The first miracle at Lourdes was there: the miracle of a 'reawakening', the expression of a religion which had doubtless been formed and ripened in the setting of the great popular missions, and which now suddenly revealed itself to the Catholic world as a whole.

The situation in the west of Ireland in the years before and after the great famine of 1846 was certainly very different from that in south-western France. The prevailing poverty, the oppression of the tenant farmers by their English landlords, and, above all, the close union which had existed there, since Daniel O'Connell's time, between political activity and the Catholic religion, endowed the latter with a specific character.[46] Nevertheless, the appearances of the Virgin in the village of

---

[44] *Ibid.*, pp. 123–5.   [45] *Ibid.*, p. 163.
[46] Hoppen, K. Theodore, *Ireland since 1800: Conflict and Conformity*, London, Longman, 1989; Keenan, Desmond J., *The Catholic Church in nineteenth Century Ireland*, Dublin, Gill and Macmillan, 1983.

Knock, in Co. Mayo, during 1879 and 1880, fit perfectly into the setting of the vast movement of 'reawakening' which can be perceived, from the end of the eighteenth century, from the Mezzogiorno to Europe's far West, and also in the United States.[47] At Knock the Virgin did not appear to anyone unusual, like Alfonso de Liguori, Catherine Labouré or Bernadette Soubirous, nor to shepherd boys who were given a message, as at La Salette. In that little Irish village there was no message given, and the 'vision' was witnessed by quite large groups of people who mostly remained unidentified thereafter. What was essential was, as at Massabielle, the initiation to prayer that was given by the Virgin herself. Her eyes and hands were raised to heaven as a sign of adoration. That was the picture which appeared, for two hours, on the wall of the parish church, in the heart of the village, on 21 August 1879. Miracles followed – 637 of them in less than a year. These, in turn, brought to Knock immense crowds of people, whom we see, in a photograph of 1880, on their knees before a wall covered with crutches and various prostheses. These pilgrims were doubtless reciting the Virgin's prayer *par excellence*, the rosary. As at Lourdes, at the beginning, there were no priests directing the faithful. The clergy here were no less cautious and divided regarding the attitude to be adopted towards a phenomenon that was not only strange but even suspect, in the eyes of some, on account of the controversial personality of the local priest, Archpriest Bartholomew Cavanagh. A big landowner, he was under attack by the poor peasants organised in the Land League, and there were mutterings to the effect that the Virgin's appearances, even if he had not actually produced them with a magic lantern, had turned up in good time to distract attention from his problem.

When left to themselves, the faithful practised the rites and devotions they were used to. First, recitation of the rosary. Then a Way of the Cross, marked out by stations, or 'beds', standing stones which recalled the visit of the seven Irish saints to Lough Derg, the famous pilgrimage to St Patrick's cave. Then Knock's devotees of the Virgin entered the church and, kneeling before the Blessed Sacrament, recited the *Credo*. As at Lourdes, this was not a spontaneous creation by the Christian people but an amplification, with maximum intensity and fervour, of what was called in Ireland the devotional revolution of the mid-nineteenth century. This renewal of religious life, marked especially by great missions to the most deprived villages, culminated at Knock, while the preachers were divided and the local clergy looked on without daring

---

[47] I use here the results of the investigation made by Anne Herberich, 'Histoire du pèlerinage de Knock 1879–1979, Comté de Mayo (Irlande)', Institut d'Histoire des Religions de l'Université de Strasbourg II, typescript, 1991.

yet to comment. Recognition of the step taken by the p..., henceforth presented as an ideal for all Catholics, came from Pope J... Paul II. When he visited Knock in 1979, the centenary of the appearances, he said, 'I wish at this time to recall to you an important truth affirmed by the Second Vatican Council, namely, "The spiritual life . . . is not confined to participation in the liturgy" (*Sacrosanctum Concilium*, 12). And so I also encourage you in the other exercises of devotion that you have lovingly preserved for centuries . . . ' He went on to speak of the exercises practised in the great Marian sanctuary of Ireland: 'Benediction of the Blessed Sacrament, Holy Hours and Eucharistic processions'. All these works of piety that were in use at Knock constituted, he said, 'a great treasure of the Catholic faith'.[48]

Rome blesses and corrects

One should not, however, conclude from this that Rome was willing to welcome everything that was being taught in town and country, and, in particular, to acknowledge a new role for the laity in the evangelising of communities.

The ecclesiastical authorities were all the less inclined in that direction because, since about the 1780s, certain bold ideas were circulating, due, especially, to missions' preaching. It may seem obvious that every Christian should regard Jesus Christ as 'the *redemptor mundi* in the full force of the term'. But to draw from this the conclusion that was drawn, at the end of the eighteenth century, by Abbé Bergier that 'God wishes all men to be saved' may seem to some to be questionable.[49] This proposition cannot, moreover, but recall the doctrine of universal salvation by faith which was preached by John Wesley around England's great cities[50] – or even 'the religion of Voltaire' and the Deists. This optimistic vision of salvation found additional support, furthermore, in the new dogma of the Immaculate Conception. Over and above the support she had always given to sinners *in extremis*, the Virgin now, by her very nature, showed that man was not doomed to evil by inexorable decree, through original sin. So man was, perhaps, not so remote from God as had been said. Appearances and miracles occurred precisely in order to confirm this presence on earth of the supernatural. Perhaps prayer was all that was needed. The catechism and knowledge of the

---

[48] Extracts from Pope John Paul II's homily in Phoenix Park, Dublin, 29 September 1979, quoted by Herberich, 'Histoire du pèlerinage'.

[49] *Un Théologien au siècle des Lumières: Bergier. Correspondance avec l'abbé Trouillet 1770–1790*, presented by Ambroise Jobert, Lyons, Centre André-Latreille, 1987, p. 221, 35.

[50] Rataboul, *John Wesley*, p. 101.

did not even know of the dogma of the Trinity!)
the priests, people had done quite well without them
on . . .
:r the works of Alfonso de Liguori nor the sermons of
:ontained such heresies. But persons who heard a
,eyed by priests with diverse opinions, while they them-
.re unable to leave out of account what they learnt and read
ou side of the church, were perhaps led to engage in such unwonted
reflections. That seemed all the less unlikely when, at the moment when
the Christianity of the countryfolk received official recognition, the
clergy took firmly in hand what had seemed for a moment to escape
from their authority or to have been put under it only to a limited extent.
In this category were the confraternities, those pious associations of
laymen which traditionally enjoyed broad autonomy. Already before the
Revolution, and still more after it, all of them passed under direct
supervision by their parish priest, to whom they were thereafter to be
'wholly subject'. The bishops, backed by the civil power, had decided
so.[51] Some eighteenth-century pious associations founded by missionaries and run by laymen were later suspected of having been, during the
Revolution, centres of Jacobinism. That happened to several Marian
congregations of craftsmen and to Abbé Receveur's work of Retreat. As
for the *cappelle serotine* of Alfonso de Liguori, they were accused, owing
to their recruitment among the common people, of being responsible for
the revolution in Naples.[52] It was as though any association which was
not directed by priests was bound to be seditious.

Behind this accusation there lay, perhaps, a real fear: by letting laymen
act alone in the field of religion one risked compromising orthodoxy.
This risk of heresy came, no doubt, from the religion of the poor, which,
though Catholic and formed on the basis of the teaching of the
missionaries of the post-Tridentine period, was sometimes not clearly
separated from the philosophy of the age and the profession of faith of
certain Protestants. In it, along with prophetism, there were to be found
the quest for the sacred and the search for recourse against the ills of life,
a collection of beliefs and rites which did not coincide with Catholicism
in the strict sense, but belonged rather to the phenomenon of religion in
its most fundamental and most primitive form. As this became apparent,

---

[51] *Pratiques religieuses dans l'Europe révolutionnaire (1770–1820)*, Proceedings of colloquium at Chantilly, 27–9 November 1986, Paris, Brepols, 1988, pp. 519–20.

[52] Châtellier, *L'Europe des dévots*, pp. 256–60 (Eng. trans., pp. 244–6), on the Marian congregations; Bonnard, *Le Vénérable Père Antoine-Sylvestre Receveur*, p. 64 (Abbé Receveur's Christian Retreat). Orlandi, 'S. Alfonso Maria de Liguori e i Laici', pp. 409–10, reproduces the analysis of this question made by R. de Maio in his work *Società e vita religiosa a Napoli nell'età moderna (1656–1799)*, Naples, 1971, pp. 277–8.

the religion of the countryfolk seemed both powerful and disquieting. The welcome accorded to this religion in the Eternal City had something in it both of triumph and of exorcism.

However, in the period when the First Vatican Council was held in Rome (1870), some priests were discovering a different category of poor people in the big cities. John Bosco in the Turin area and Antoine Chevrier in the parish of La Guillotière, in Lyons, found themselves surrounded by a nameless crowd of uprooted persons who were being gradually alienated from religion, while no-one tried to prevent this happening. With them there could be no question of teaching and preaching in the way that was practised among the countryfolk. Entering these poverty-stricken suburbs or quarters of the big cities one entered, as a twentieth-century missionary put it, 'missionary lands', even if, at the time, they were not yet regarded as 'heathen lands'. Here one could not base oneself on Christian habits or ancestral practices. Christianity had to be presented 'as Saint Paul had presented it to the proletarians of his time.'[53]

Nevertheless, despite these considerable changes, missions were still missions. One of the first moves made by Antoine Chevrier after his 'conversion' was to visit the Curé d'Ars (1856). A man who was going to go as an apostle to the poor of a big city sought counsel from a man who had shut himself away in a tiny village.[54] Continuity asserted itself between what was to become, later, the endeavour of the worker-priests and the rural missionaries of former times. This went beyond appearances. Between the desire of a militant priest of the 20th century to make the inhabitants of the manufacturing centres perceive 'in the doctrine of Christ a truly working-class ideal'[55] and the concern of the eighteenth-century missionaries to persuade the peasant masses of the existence of a near and loving God we can observe some continuity. The religion of the Catholics of Europe in the age of Vatican II had doubtless begun to be preached in the country districts of Germany, Italy or France in the eighteenth century.

[53] Godin and Daniel, *La France*, p. 101.
[54] Six, Jean-François, *Un Prêtre, Antoine Chevrier, fondateur du Prado (1826–1879)*, Paris, Seuil, 1965, pp. 126–33.
[55] The expression is taken from Godin and Daniel, *La France*, p. 100.

Conclusion

Though it was old Christian territory, Europe was ceaselessly crossed and re-crossed by missionaries from the beginning of the Middle Ages onward. It had its bishops, parish priests and churches, but the danger of heresy, appearing in a village in the form of a strange preacher with seductive ideas and attractive speech, the risk that these little Christian communities, isolated from each other, might sink into ossification and routine, made necessary the giving of other forms of help to them. At first the missionaries were men who aroused the Christians by teaching them, or reminding them of, the rudiments of their faith. They were also soldiers of orthodoxy, present on all fronts, for the fight against Protestantism, and often, during the seventeenth century, for instructing in their new faith those who had been converted by force (from Bohemia to France after the Revocation of the Edict of Nantes).

A major change took place in the eighteenth century. Thereafter it was no longer, with rare exceptions, a matter of effecting conversions, but of intensified teaching and deepening of people's knowledge of Christianity. Following the example of Alfonso de Liguori, the missionaries made it their business to penetrate the remotest villages and hamlets. They aimed to transform completely the populations whom they took in hand. Not a single village, not a single individual, must escape their efforts. All the old-established religious orders were mobilised. New orders (Redemptorists, Passionists) were created to realise this ideal. That was connected also with the nature of the change that they wanted to bring about. This did not consist merely in initiation into Christianity and a brief catechism: it amounted to a complete transformation of the individual and his everyday conduct. They also wanted to turn the simple folk of the countryside into Christians who were instructed in their religion and capable of arguing for it – 'inward' men and women who could raise themselves to the highest states of prayer. This aim was inspired both by the great spiritual authors of the seventeenth century who had educated an elite in devotion and by the new and generous spirit of the Enlightenment, which aimed to raise the people up and

234

enable them to profit from what, in previous centuries, had been given only to a few. It was, to some extent, with the adaptation needed for Catholic countries, what in Protestant Germany was called *Popularphilosophie*.

In the villages, however, the missionaries discovered a world which, behind familiar appearances, was really quite alien to them, and sometimes hostile. They very soon perceived that they would not succeed in bringing God into the lives of these peasants unless they presented Him first as a God of flesh, a man among men, and suffering among men. The cross, the Passion and the Sacred Heart were indispensable mediations and became obligatory aids to all teaching. They also took account of the fact that in the 'lands without bread' of the South and in those, richer but subject to climatic hazards, of the North, preaching pure evangelical disinterestedness when famine threatened and poverty was really present must incur the risk of ineffectuality. Whereas teaching Christian justice and starting to put this into practice by promoting restitutions of property, undertaking arbitrations and leading people to become reconciled with each other was likely to be better understood and to leave more traces. Should one go on talking about the damned to people who were suffering so much in their daily lives and who came forward so big-heartedly to forgive each other? It was more natural to dwell upon God's generous forgiveness, offered to all.

Without wishing in any way to break with the past, and in particular with the Church's rules as laid down by the Council of Trent, the rural missionaries, who were in daily contact with the immense mass of the poor, were led to emphasise whatever might help and console them best, while leaving in shadow, and eventually in oblivion, that which worried, troubled or conduced to despair. It was an inflection of Christianity that was under way, heralding a religion in which the world and human problems would occupy a bigger place. The fact that this movement, starting from the countryside, should have succeeded, despite much opposition, in gradually dominating the entire Church, ultimately triumphing in the nineteenth century under Pius IX and Leo XIII, explains, perhaps, some of the features of present-day religion.

We are, however, still left wondering if this evolution, which inspired apprehension, already in the eighteenth century, among some, especially the Jansenists and the men of the Enlightenment, did not contribute to their detachment from Christianity. And, on the other hand, it may be that the aggressive and sometimes indiscreet zeal of the missionaries caused, in some cases, a section of the people whom it was desired to convert in depth to reject Christianity out of hand in order to escape from this pressure.

What is true is that the distribution still observable today of regions which have remained faithful to Catholicism reproduces, more or less, the map of the most intense and most numerous missions of the age of the Enlightenment, and this shows how greatly these missions contributed to the shaping of modern Catholicism.

Index